MARIE LAURENCIN

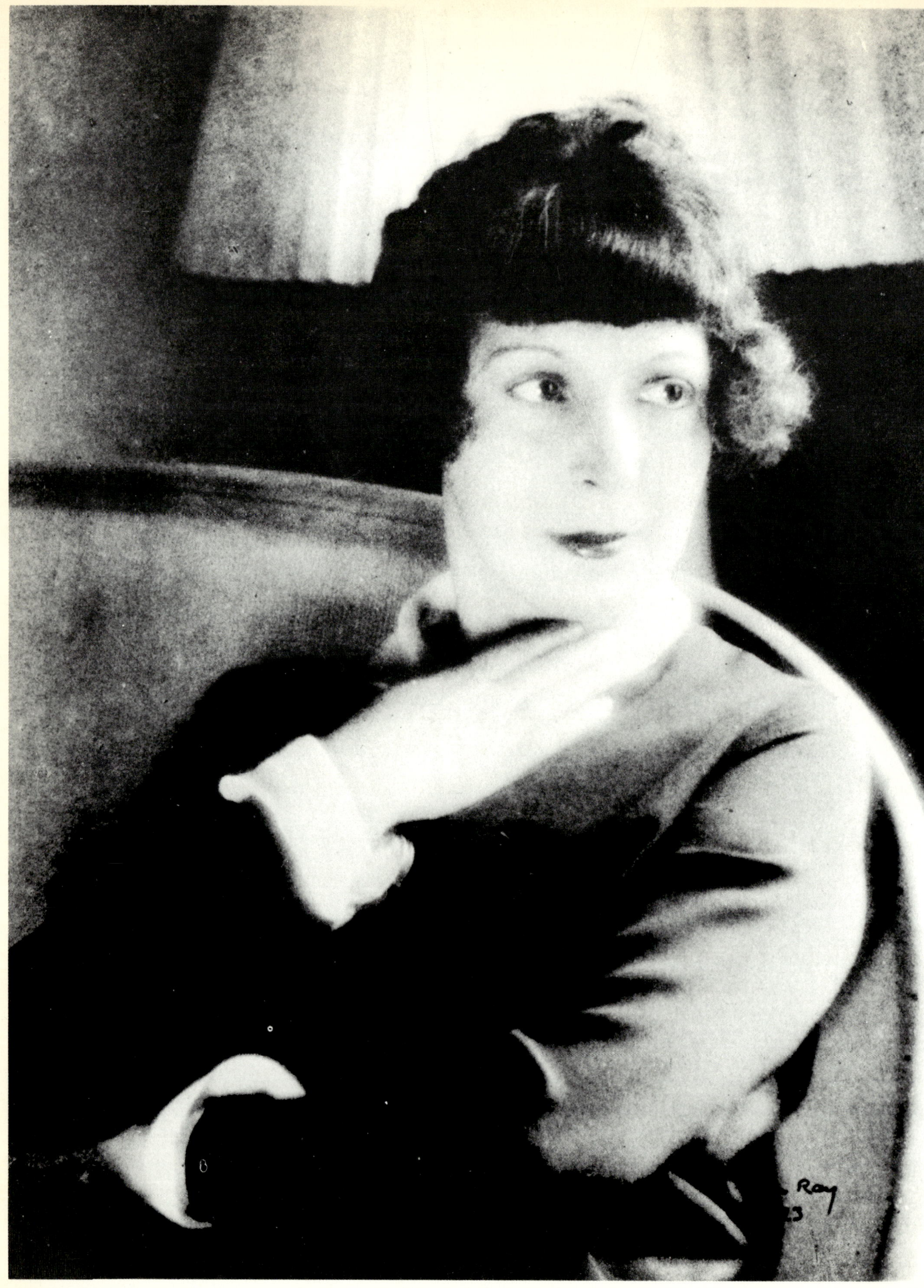

MARIE LAURENCIN

CHARLOTTE GERE

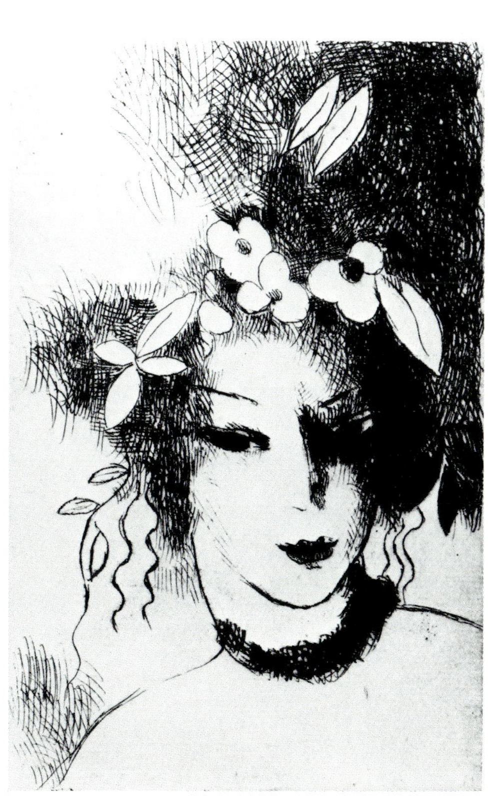

RIZZOLI

ACKNOWLEDGEMENTS

I would like to thank all the galleries, institutions and private collectors for allowing works from their collections to be reproduced, and Sotheby's Belgravia for supplying photographs.

In particular I am grateful to the following people who have helped in a number of ways, both in tracing works by Marie Laurencin, and in retailing details of her life, few of which are supplied in the published studies of her art:

Sir Geoffrey Agnew, Lady Ashton, Mlle. Roseline Bacou of the Cabinet des Dessins, Musée du Louvre, Miss Carole Berman of Sotheby's, Miss Mary Clarke of *The Dancing Times,* James D. Draper of the Metropolitan Museum, New York, Rudolph S. Joseph, William S. Liberman of the Museum of Modern Art, New York, Mrs Oldham and Mrs Houston Rogers.

Frontispiece
Man Ray
Photograph of Marie Laurencin, 1923
© A.D.A.G.P. Paris 1977

Title page illustration
Marie Laurencin
Tête de femme couronnée de fleurs/Head of a woman wreathed in flowers, *c.* 1930
Drypoint 15.2 × 8.8 cm.

Illustrations on pages 8 and 13 © S.P.A.D.E.M. Paris 1977

Published in the United States of America in 1977 by
RIZZOLI INTERNATIONAL PUBLICATIONS, INC.
712 Fifth Avenue/New York 10019

Library of Congress Catalog Card Number: 77-74340
ISBN: Hardcover 0-8478-0105-5 Paper 0-8478-0104-7

Printed and bound in Great Britain

CONTENTS

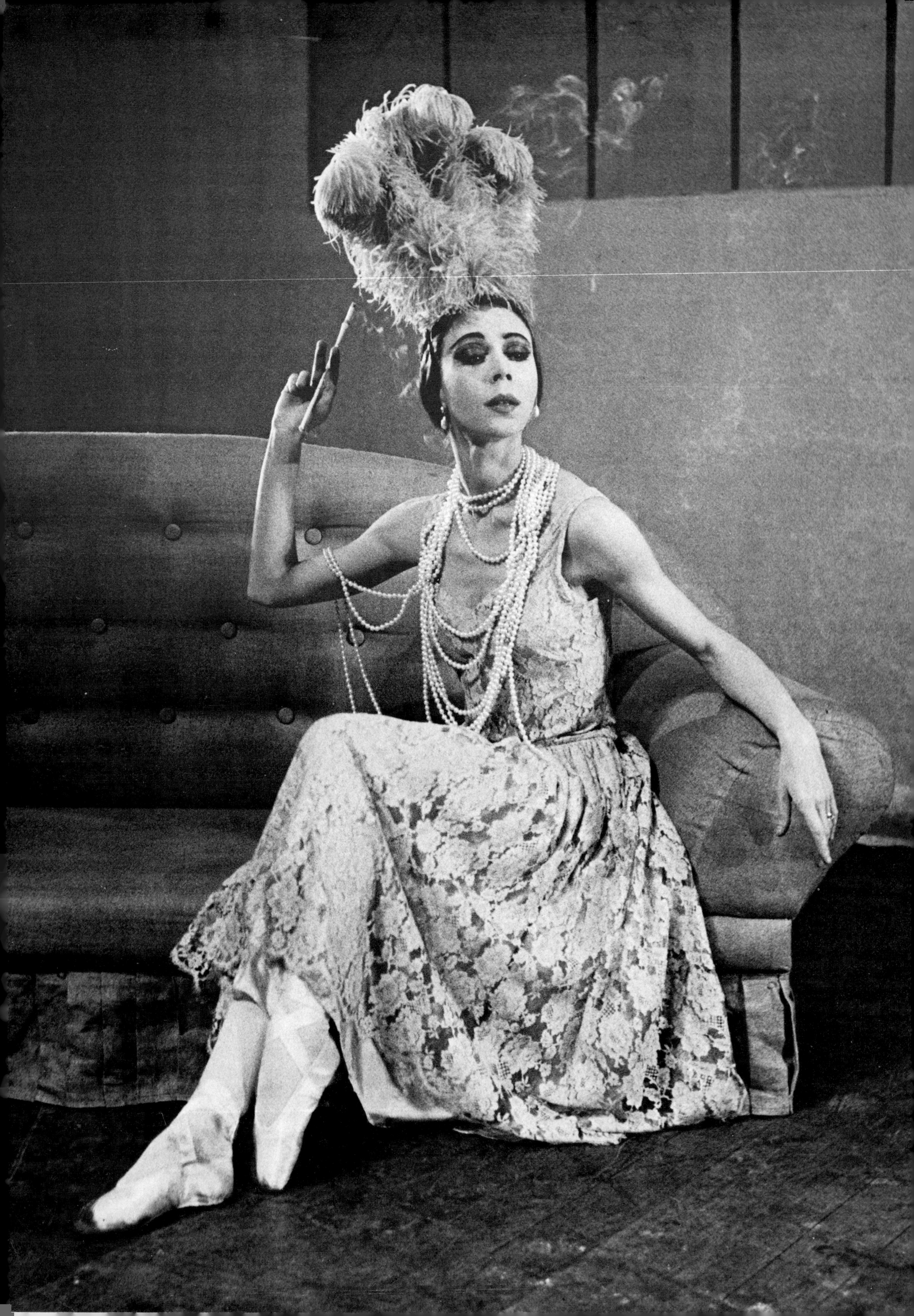

Qu'elle rie	(How she laughs
Et Marie	And Marie
Laurencin	Laurencin
L'or enceint	The gold circles
Dans ses belles	In her beautiful
Prunelles	Irises)

Jean Moréas (*L'Eventail de Marie Laurencin, 1922*)

MARIE LAURENCIN'S career began most auspiciously, as an intimate of the circle surrounding Picasso and Juan Gris, as an *habituée* of the studio in the rue Ravignan where Cubism was born, and as the fortunate recipient of critical notices of her work containing the most fulsome praise from no less a figure than Guillaume Apollinaire, the prophet of the Modern Movement. She was blessed with advantages that fall to the lot of few young artists. Her name was synonymous with the *avant-garde* for more than two decades, and she was always included in the roll-call of artists admired for their originality, with Picasso, Braque, Matisse, Juan Gris, Othon Friesz, Delaunay and Marcoussis, with whom she shared the endless sessions of discussion and artistic speculation which took place in the rue Ravignan. Her first sale was to one of the first and most fervent admirers of the Fauves and the Cubists, Gertrude Stein, who bought the earlier of the two large group portraits of Apollinaire with his friends which were painted soon after the first contact with Picasso.

It is thus with some astonishment that one reads the somewhat obituarial judgment of Somerset Maugham – 'She was not a great artist, far from it, but a pleasing one' – written in 1962 in the book which describes Maugham's picture collection, at that time about to be dispersed. Although the text was written in 1962 the implication in the account of Marie Laurencin seems to be that this judgment of her position as an artist was arrived at in the late 'thirties, still a period of great activity and popularity for her. Maugham, like many English collectors in the 'twenties, admired Marie Laurencin more than the more 'difficult' Cubists, and as he owned four of her pictures, painted between 1923 and 1927 (she later gave him a fifth, a rather unsuccessful portrait of himself), it must be assumed that this was no ignorant or hastily formed estimate of the relative importance of her work. The truth probably lies somewhere between the eulogies of Apollinaire and the patronising dismissal of Maugham. Apollinaire's adulatory notices of her early *Salon* pictures were certainly prompted by his private feelings, and her identification with Cubism and Dadaism was largely the result of proximity rather than of intellectual rationalisation or artistic conviction. Marie Laurencin herself vigorously repudiated the notion of an intellectual basis for her work, for she was an entirely instinctive painter who repeatedly defended her curious vision of a world peopled entirely by beautiful young girls and boneless animals on the grounds that they appeared in her pictures as she saw them. No compromise with reality was apparently possible, and when Lady Cunard was so incautious as to object to the horse upon which she appears in her portrait, the artist threatened to change it into a camel unless the objection was withdrawn. Marie Laurencin's greatest strength lay in her ability to resist the pressures of her surroundings which, in the case of one of weaker vision or a less instinctive approach, would have led her into becoming a Cubist or Dadaist camp-follower, executing feeble travesties of the work of her companions.

It is impossible to tell how successful she would have been without this advantageous début. With the wisdom of hindsight she can now be seen as a perfect embodiment of the artistic mood of the 'twenties, since her work is decorative and light-hearted, a perfect complement to the prevailing fashions in décor and clothes, but with some more

Opposite
The hostess in *Les Biches*
Royal Ballet, Covent Garden 1964. (Photo Houston Rogers)

profound quality which has enabled her work to survive without becoming hopelessly anachronistic, the inescapable fate of the more ephemeral arts of fashion and interior decoration. Her work is sufficiently of the same *genre* as that of her friends and fellow artists, Moïse Kisling, Pascin, Foujita and van Dongen, as to be regarded as belonging to a 'school' of decorative painting which existed independently from the increasingly complex abstraction and intellectualism of the Cubists and later the Dadaists, which was enjoyed on a different level. Gertrude Stein did not continue her patronage of Marie Laurencin. She may have recognised early on that this artist did not have in her the same seeds of innovatory genius which drew the Steins to the work of Picasso and Matisse, but other discerning patrons were not lacking. Despite the over-enthusiastic praise lavished on her work by Apollinaire, which distorted the true picture of her abilities, Marie Laurencin happily achieved the reputation which she deserved during her lifetime when it could be of some benefit to her. She was admired first and foremost for her seductive and charming sense of colour. The 'incomparable' pink, the pale blue and the viridian, used with white, white and still more white, which characterise her work from the time of the formation of her mature style, make her pictures immediately recognisable. The whole style is not hard to distinguish, and her work remained remarkably consistent through a career which spanned nearly half a century – the earliest works illustrated here date from *c.* 1905, self-portraits survive from 1904, and the latest work in this book was executed in 1953 – but there are three distinct phases of work which culminate in a distinguishable alteration of approach.

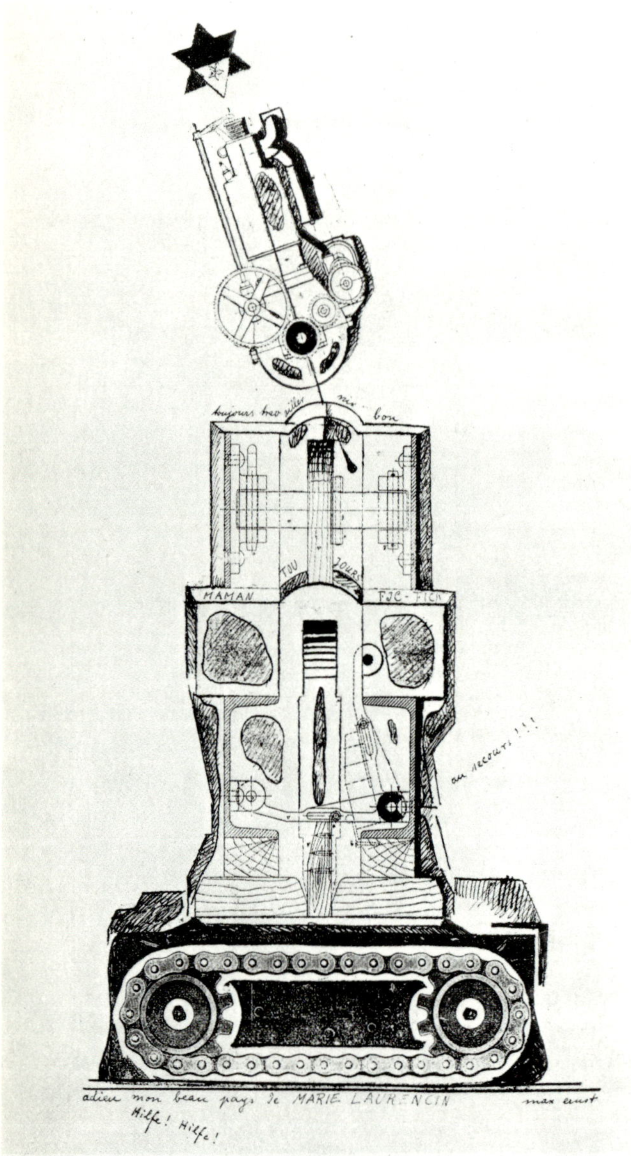

Max Ernst
'Adieu mon beau pays de Marie Laurencin'/'Farewell my beautiful land of Marie Laurencin', *c.* 1919
Altered technical engraving (Museum of Modern Art, New York)

The first phase, lasting from her introduction into the *bateau-lavoir* until the end of the First World War, saw the realisation of some of the most complex and ambitious group compositions. This began with the two versions of *Apollinaire et ses amis,* and included the carefully structured *Maison meublée* of 1912 and *Les Deux Sœurs* of 1913, which has been described as her personal interpretation of Cubism.

The next phase, dating from 1920 until about 1937, saw the production of her most typical work. By this date she had formulated her mature style and evolved the colour scheme for which she is remembered first and foremost. It is perhaps no coincidence that 1920 was the date at which she began her long and successful business relationship with Paul Rosenberg. He must have seen the direction in which her greatest chance of making her reputation lay, and encouraged her to pursue the aspects of her talent which would be most to her benefit. He certainly tried to discourage artistic activities which he believed would damage her image in the eyes of her admirers. He once tried to stop her from presenting her milliner, who had become a great friend, with an elegant sketch designed to be used as an advertisement. Marie Laurencin's generous temperament must have been the despair of Rosenberg. So many works were given away, so much done for no financial reward – including the murals for Boulestin's restaurant; but she was unbusinesslike in a very businesslike way, on one occasion telling a friend who was deploring the enormous commission which Rosenberg exacted from her that he paid

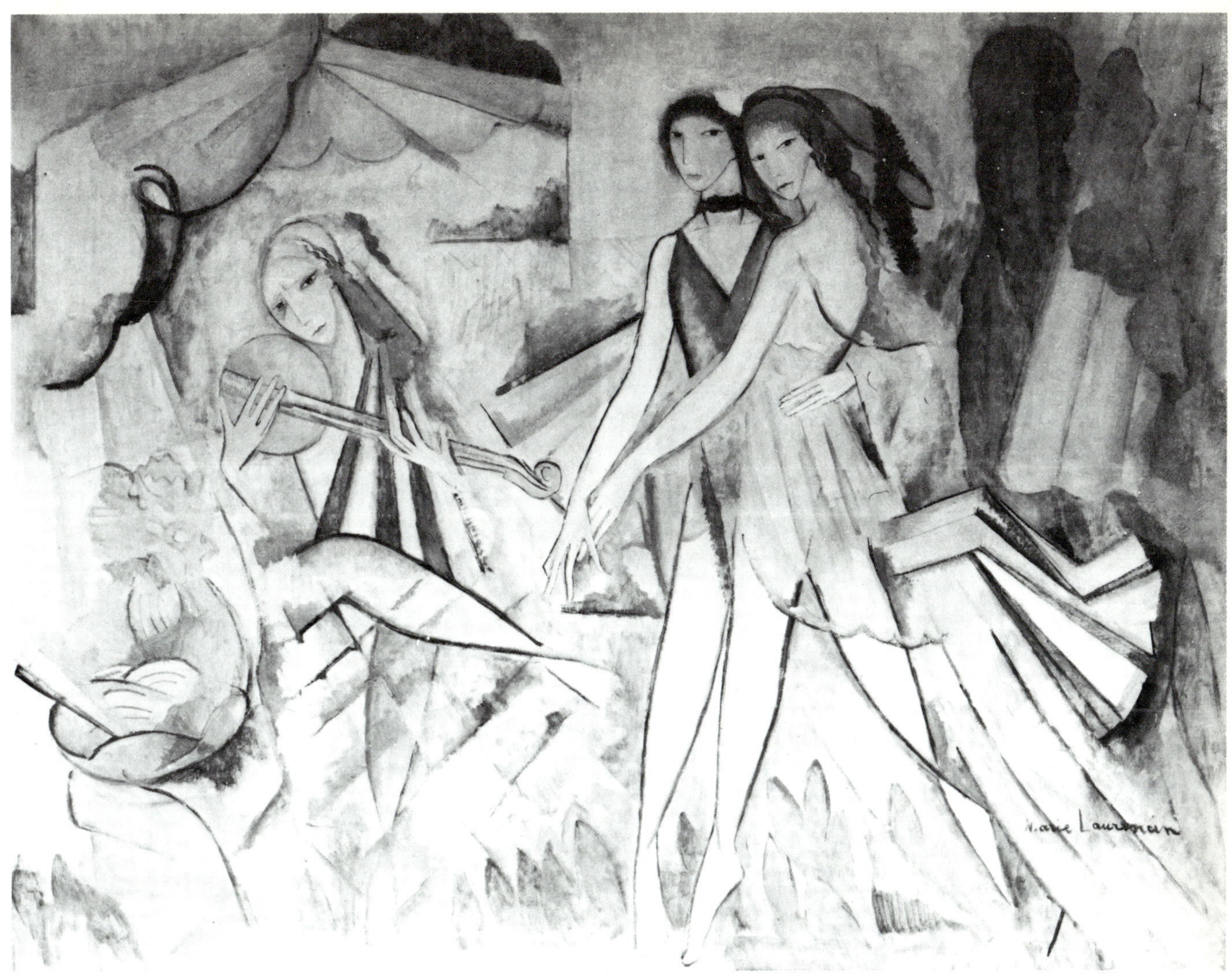

Marie Laurencin
La Danse à la campagne/The Country Dance, 1913
Oil on canvas, 112 × 144 cm.

her rent and her grocery bills, clearly believing, with some justification, that to be relieved of pettifogging financial worries is worth a great deal. On the other hand she protected herself from unwelcome commissions with unexpected hard-headedness by charging more for work which bored her, double in the case of men (with the exception of Somerset Maugham who was presented with the portrait which she did of him), and something extra in the case of brunettes, whom she found less inspiring than pale blonde women. She had the reputation for painting only children whom she liked, and was known to succeed best with portraits of sitters with whom she felt in sympathy spiritually. From this phase of her career comes some of the most personal and successful of all her work, the *Femmes dans la forêt,* bought by the American collector John Quinn in 1920, and the elegant designs for the set and costumes of Diaghilev's ballet *Les Biches* as well as a large number of portraits. Roger Allard states in his brief biographical account of her published in 1921, *Marie Laurencin,* that she had already completed seven hundred pictures – excluding lithographs and etchings and other decorative work – by 1921. Both the successive phases were to be immensely prolific and the standard of quality both in imagination and execution remains a constant source of amazement. Bearing this in mind it is perhaps not too ungenerous to record that the final phase of her work, from 1937 to 1953, is widely considered to be the 'bad' period, when the delicate work of the 'twenties gave way to a much coarser use of form and colour.

When Marie Laurencin said that she painted the world as it appeared to her, this was no subtle discussion of the psychology of visual perception but a statement of the literal truth. She was extremely short-sighted all her life, and René Gimpel records in his *Journal* that her sight was so bad in the 'twenties that she could only negotiate a staircase with difficulty. This condition was

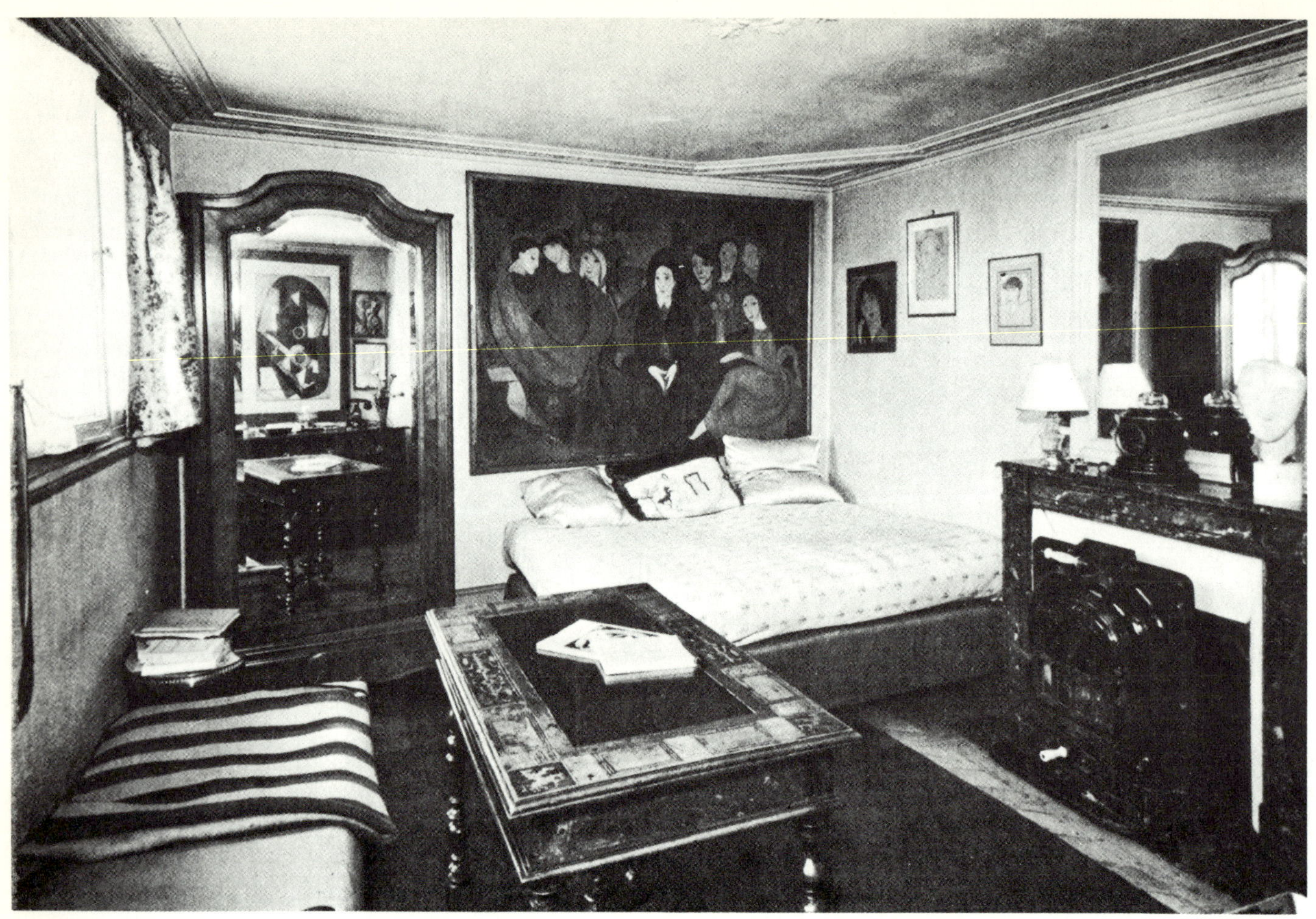

The Bedroom of Apollinaire's appartment at 202 boulevard St-Germain where he lived from 1913.
(M. Boudard)

exacerbated with time. By the mid-thirties it was apparent that she would have to resort to the use of spectacles, and these were duly acquired in about 1937, and were known as 'mes lunettes d'Académie'. As can be seen from Marie Laurencin's work of this period, 'mes lunettes' transformed the world for her, but they did not affect either the vigour of her imagination or the painterly quality of her work, which remained as seductive as ever even through the last years.

Marie Laurencin was born in Paris in October 1885. She was an illegitimate child and knew nothing about her father – she once told Colette who questioned her about her origins that she had not dared to ask her mother about him. Her mother came of a Creole family, and was a woman with elegant taste and a strong character. Her daughter frequently spoke of her childhood and her early surroundings with respect for her mother's management and aesthetic discernment. Marie Laurencin drew from an early age, an activity not much encouraged by her mother who had little faith in her daughter's artistic talents, and the painstaking efforts were regularly burned. In spite of this she was allowed to go to the Académie Humbert when her education at the Lycée Lamartine was completed. Her modest ambition at this stage was to be a porcelain painter and to this end she spent some time studying at the Ecole de Sèvres, but a fellow pupil at the Académie Humbert, Georges Braque, discerned in her a talent which could be extended beyond the restricted demands of this somewhat pedestrian *métier* .

Through Braque's intervention she was introduced to Picasso and his circle, at this time based on the studio at number 13 rue Ravignan in the curious six-storey wooden building at the top of the Butte Montmartre nick-named the *'bateau-lavoir'* on account of its resemblance to the boats moored by the banks of the Seine from which clothes-washing was done. Marie Laurencin's acceptance into this enclosed and jealously guarded world was confirmed by her inclusion in the list of guests who attended the banquet given for Henri Rousseau in 1908. The circle included, as well as Juan Gris and Max Jacob with whom Picasso shared the studio, Metzinger, Apollinaire, André Salmon, Maurice Raynal, Daniel Kahnweiler and Leo and Gertrude Stein. The strongly literary bias of the group is explained by the fact

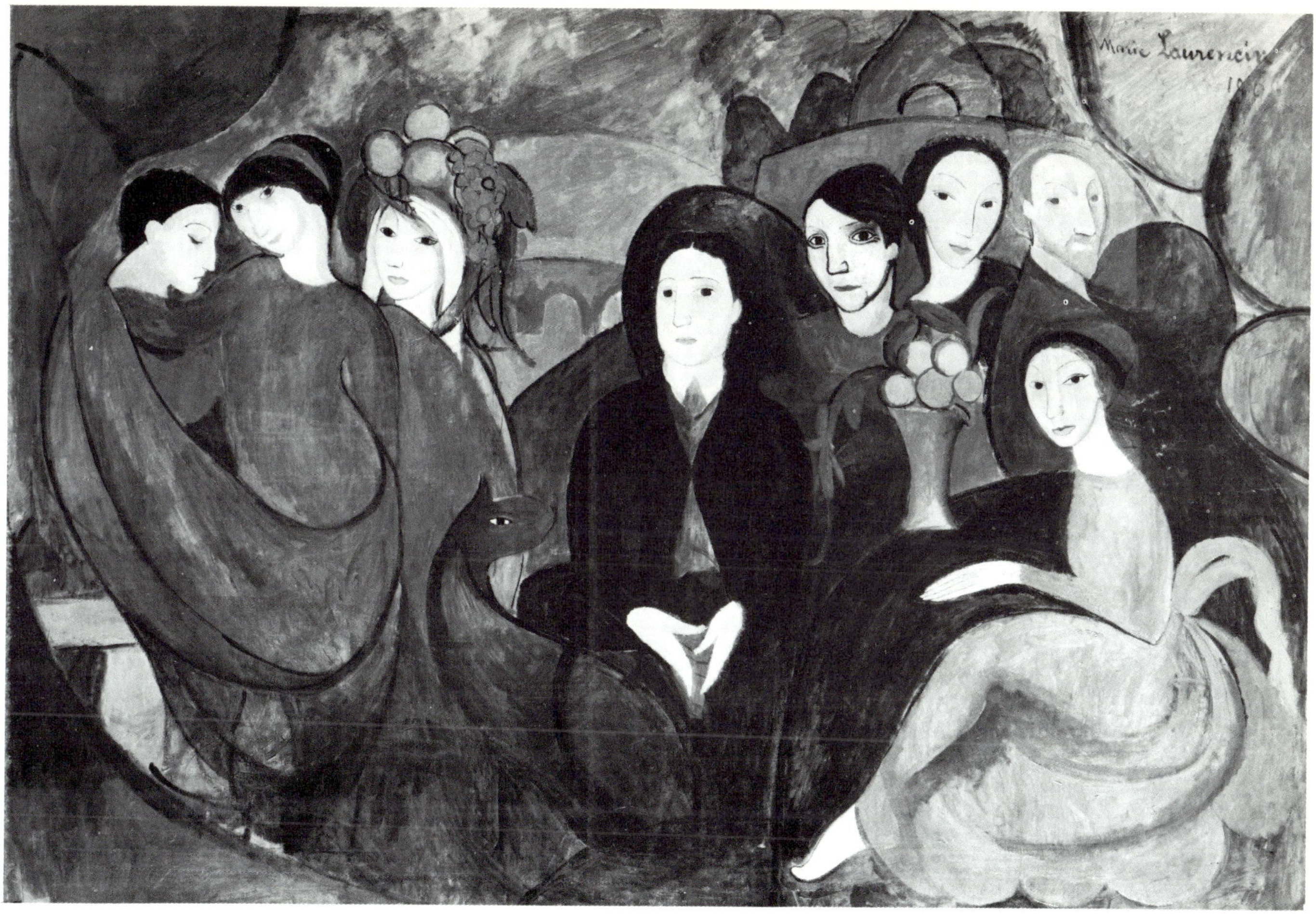

Marie Laurencin
Apollinaire et ses amis/Apollinaire and his friends, 1908
Oil on canvas (Musée National d'Art Moderne, Paris)

that they believed, like the Symbolists, that art and literature are interdependent, and much of the inspiration of the painting of this period is literary or in some way intellectual. *Avant-garde* magazines dedicated to publicising the work of new artists were always being started and nursed through a number of issues in spite of daunting financial problems, and of these Apollinaire's *Festin d'Esope* and the *Section d'or* were among the most influential. André Salmon was for some years the editor of *Vers et Prose.*

Although Marie Laurencin had met Georges Braque at Académie Humbert in 1905 she only began to frequent Picasso's studio sometime in 1907, and it was in this same year that she was to meet Guillaume Apollinaire, by that time an established friend of Picasso, whom he first encountered at the Critérion bar in the rue d'Amsterdam in 1904. Even so the meeting did not take place at the rue Ravignan, but on the premises of the dealer Clovis Sagot, a former chemist's shop in the rue Laffitte. Sagot was one of the first to buy from Picasso, and was a good friend and advocate of the young generation of artists. This momentous meeting, which was achieved through Picasso's intervention – he told Apollinaire that he had found him a 'fiancée' at Sagot's – was a tribute to Picasso's prescience as the *rapprochement* between the two of them was immediate and they were to become inseparable companions for the next six years.

At this date Apollinaire was twenty-seven years old, already an established literary figure, prominent amongst the rising generation of poets and *littérateurs* who at this time still saw themselves as the new Symbolists. His most influential writings on art were to to appear in the next few years, and he had the inestimable advantage of being present at the birth of both Fauvism and Cubism. His eloquent defence of the latter removed the taint of mockery from the term which was invented by Louis Vauxcelles. Apollinaire died a few days after the end of the First World War aged only thirty-eight. Thus his affair with Marie Laurencin occupied the greater part of the remainder of his life; his late marriage, which took place in May 1918 lasted, by contrast, for only six months. Inevitably Marie was to be the inspiration for much of the poetical work completed by Apollinaire during the period of their liaison, and some of the

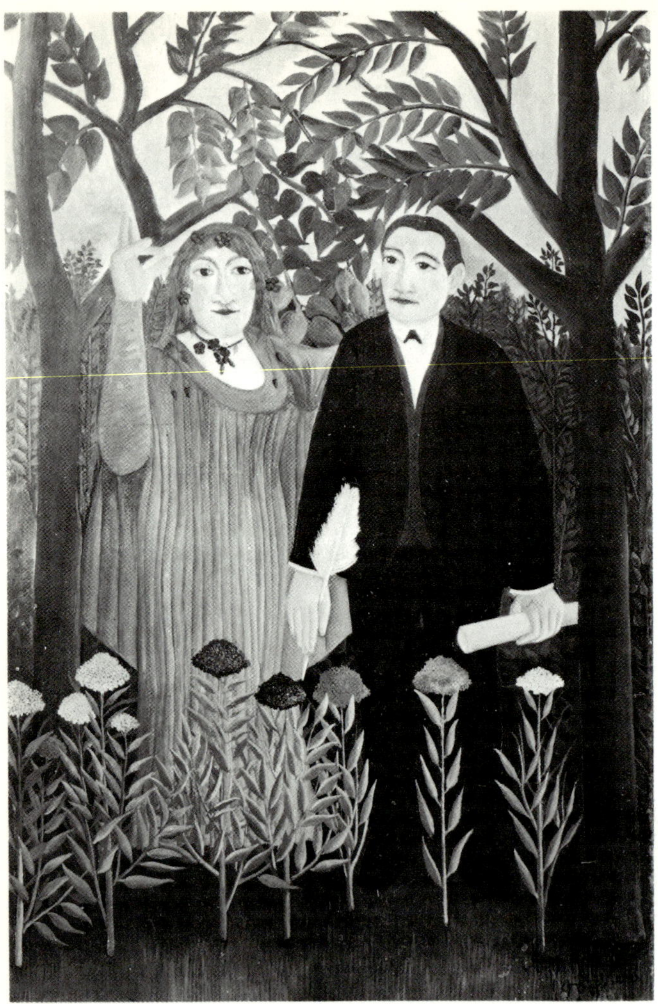

Henri Rousseau
La Muse inspirant le poète/The Muse inspiring the Poet, 1909
Oil on canvas, 146 × 97 cm. (Kunstmuseum, Basle)

poems are addressed directly to her, the original version of *Mon destin* beginning with the *cri du cœur* of the rejected lover:

> 'Mon destin, ô Marie est de vivre à vos pieds
> En redisant sans cesse: 'ô combien je vous aime'
>
> My destiny, oh Marie, is to live at your feet
> In repeating unceasingly, 'Oh how I love you'

She is recognisable as the painter Tristouze Ballerinette of *Le Poète assassiné*, which appeared in 1916 some time after their liaison had ended, and the booklet entitled *Vitam Impendere Amori,* published in 1917, was a tribute to the memory of their relationship. Early in their association Apollinaire described Marie as gay, good, witty, as a little sun, a feminine counterpart of himself. Her appearance at this date can be judged from the many self-portraits which have survived, if not from the other work of this date in which she appears. The two versions of Rousseau's *La Muse inspirant le poète,* showing her with Apollinaire, give little idea of her unusual oval face and her elegant figure. She claimed that Picasso used her as a model for one of the formidably unseductive nude figures in his great Cubist work *Les Demoiselles d'Avignon,* which was begun in 1906 and abandoned, and was still unfinished in the autumn of 1907. It was almost inevitable that, having been thus precipitated into the maelstrom attending the birth of Cubism, Marie Laurencin should have been identified with the movement in the following years.

Apollinaire unquestionably influenced Marie Laurencin's work profoundly during the period up to the outbreak of the war. These years are sometimes referred to as her 'best' period, and it is certainly true that the work of this date is in the mainstream of European artistic development in a way in which her post-war work is not. The only pictures which have any claim to being Cubist (a claim understandably rejected without hesitation by Douglas Cooper in *The Cubist Epoch* (1971), who states that her position as Apollinaire's mistress was the only reason for her inclusion in his earlier book on Cubism) were painted in 1912 and 1913. They were only remotely connected with the very first of the Cubist experiments like *Les Demoiselles* and the *Three Women* by Picasso, or by Marcel Duchamp's later *Portrait* (1911), but not at all to the fragmented forms of analytical Cubism. Marie Laurencin was never able to subordinate her natural inclination towards curvilinear forms, and the jagged lines of Cubist composition remained outside her imaginative range.

Soon after her introduction into the *bateau-lavoir* circle Marie Laurencin embarked on the group portrait entitled *Apollinaire et ses amis,* showing the poet in the centre of a group including herself, Picasso, Fernande Olivier and Picasso's dog Fricka. This picture was bought by Gertrude Stein, and was soon followed by a second version which again shows Apollinaire surrounded by his friends, a much enlarged group now including Miss Stein, presumably as a tribute to her perceptive patronage. This second version belonged to Apollinaire himself, and was eventually hung above his bed in the apartment in the boulevard Saint-Germain where he had settled early in 1913. He was to occupy this apartment when in Paris for the rest of his life, and after his death it was preserved unaltered by his widow, as it still remains today even though she too is dead. The building is decorated with a plaque commemorating Apollinaire's occupation of the premises, and it is therefore with a curious frisson that one reads the name 'Apollinaire' amongst the list of tenants

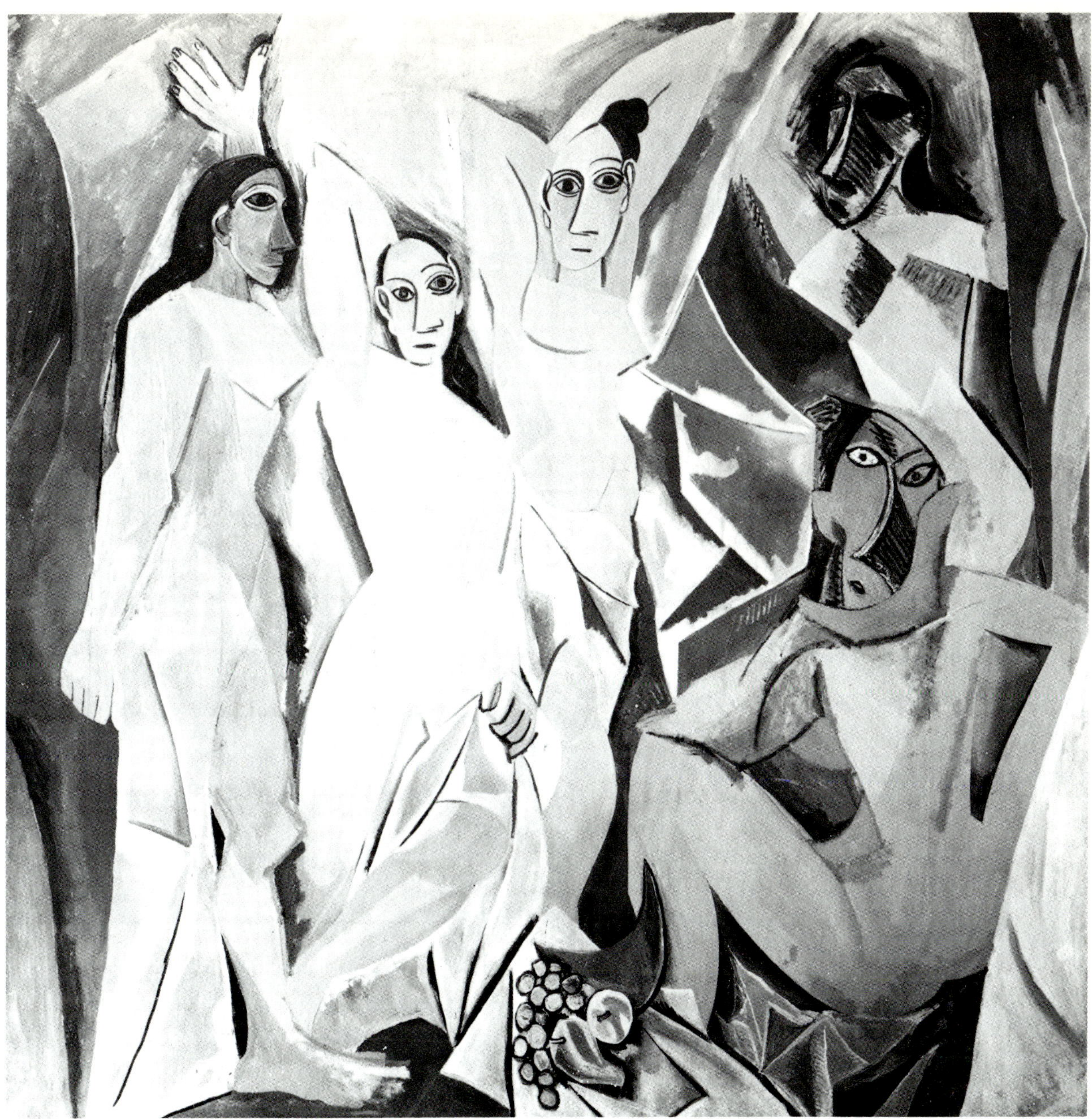

Pablo Picasso
Les Demoiselles d'Avignon, 1907
Oil on canvas, 24 m. 38.5 cm. × 23 m. 36.7 cm. (The Museum of Modern Art, New York)

posted up in the courtyard. It seems to suggest that a ring on the bell may summon his ghost from the fifth floor where the now uninhabited rooms are situated. By the time that Apollinaire was installed in the boulevard Saint-Germain his long liaison with Marie Laurencin was almost at an end and he saw her only rarely, their encounters being fraught with recriminations and unhappiness.

Throughout their relationship Apollinaire, who was of a formidably jealous temperament himself, had assumed a tolerance in his companion of inhuman dimensions and had in no way moderated his philandering behaviour in recognition of her unwritten rights. Picasso had referred to Marie as a 'fiancée' for Apollinaire and Henri Rousseau called her 'your little wife', but the question of their marrying does not seem to have arisen, perhaps because they themselves were both illegitimate as well as the fact that in the Bohemian atmosphere of the world which they frequented, marriage was by no means the inevitable outcome of even long liaisons. At the end of 1912 she at last carried out the threat she had so often used in the past in an attempt to make him more considerate in his behaviour, and refused to see him any more.

Marie Laurencin's artistic *début* took place at the *Salon des Indépendants* in the autumn of 1907. Apollinaire first mentioned her work in one of his reviews in the following year and thereafter he repeatedly described her work in the most adulat-

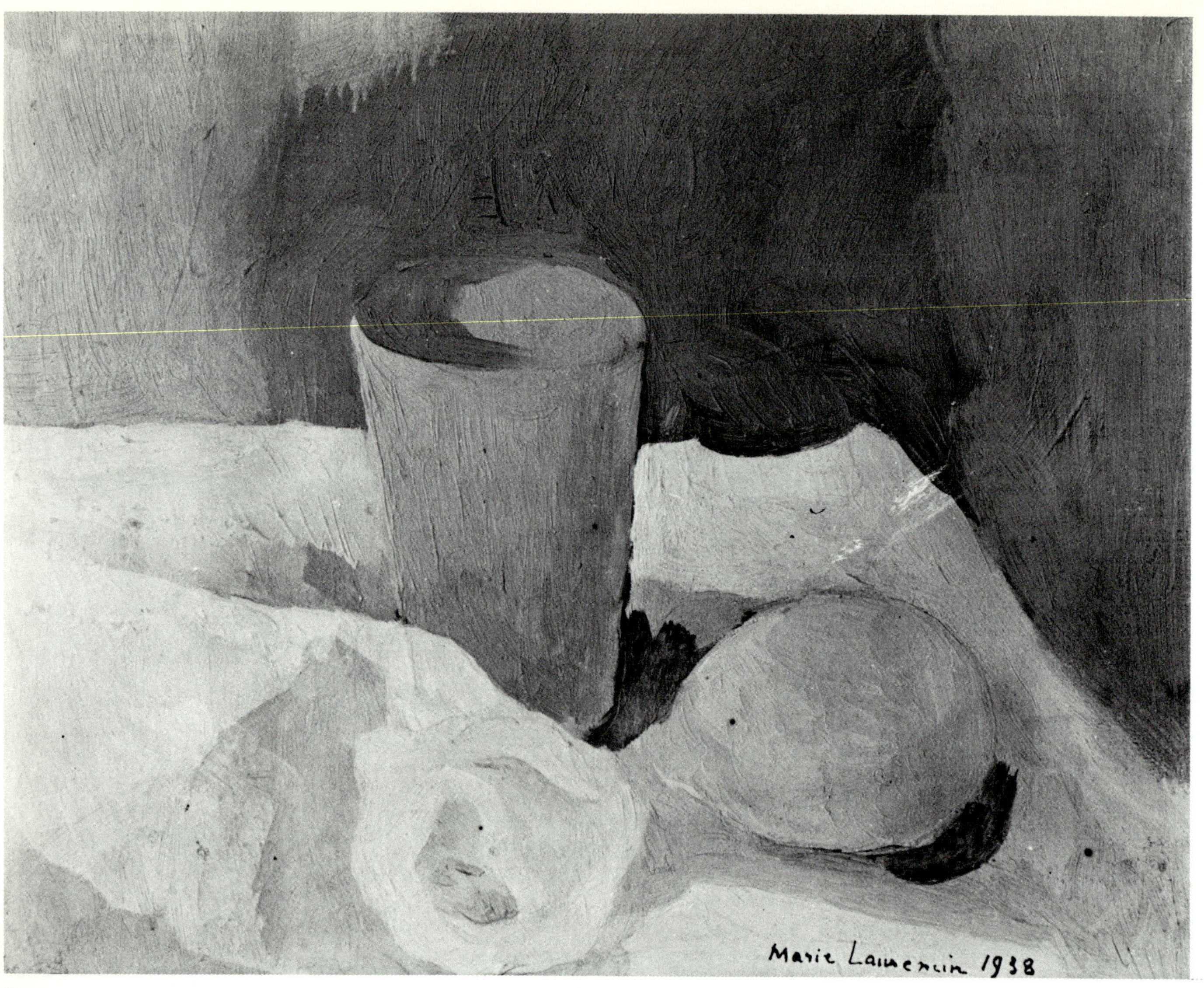

Marie Laurencin
Nature morte au citron/Still life with a lemon, 1938
Oil on canvas (Private collection)

ory terms. André Salmon implied in his short account of her career which was included in Bénézit's *Dictionnaire des Peintres, Sculpteurs, Dessinateurs et Graveurs* that the whole of her artistic development took place after her rescue from the dismal academic purlieus of the Académie Humbert, engineered by Braque in 1907, and that anything of value that she knew about painting was learned from the artists of the *bateau-lavoir* group. In fact Marie Laurencin was too strong willed and independent minded to play the role in this circle which custom decreed – that of admiring female neophyte and hanger-on. She later recorded her wish that had she been able to choose a master from the great painters of the previous generation, she would have selected Renoir. This seems to have been a perceptive choice given their many common sources of inspiration, and represented the very antithesis of the Cubist world into which she was thrust by force of circumstances. She was also accustomed to point out that it was at the Académie Humbert that she acquired the ability to draw.

In 1910 Apollinaire described Marie Laurencin's *Salon des Indépendants* exhibits as Cubist, and in the following year two of her pictures were hung in the famous Cubist exhibition in room 41 of the *Salon* of that year, two pictures which, to judge from their titles, *Portrait de Mme Fernande X* and *Jeunes Filles,* were no more nor less Cubist than any of her other works of the same date. Her involvement with the Cubist movement continued in the next year, when she worked on the decoration of the *Maison Cubiste* designed by Raymond Duchamp-Villon and André Mare. She had already worked with André Mare, assisting him with the decoration of the dining room and study shown at the *Salon d'Automne* in1911. To judge from the surviving photographs of the *Maison Cubiste* neither of these early decorating projects was

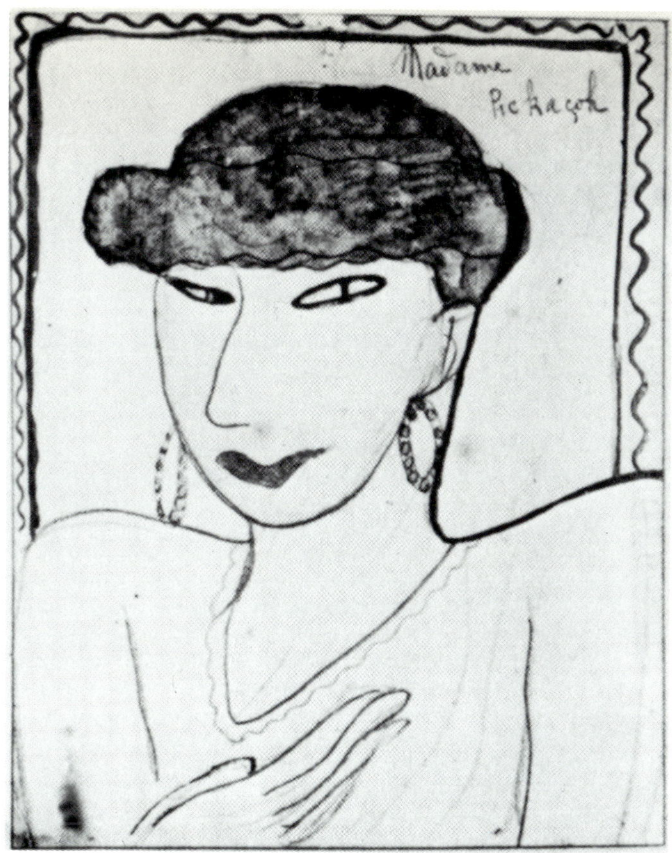

Marie Laurencin
'Mme. Pickaçoh' (Fernande Olivier), *c.* 1908
Ex. collection Apollinaire (M. Boudard)

particularly startling. The proportions of the façade of the *Maison Cubiste* are very conventional, differing little from the innumerable bourgeois houses in the environs of Paris. It would hardly stand out from its neighbours as in any way experimental even amongst the remaining traditional suburban villas in Le Vésinet or Saint-Germain-en-Laye. The interior is similarly unremarkable and the furniture is Biedermeier in derivation, with the addition of some unexceptionable 'Modern-style' decorative motifs. In spite of this cautious approach the project was greeted with cries of horror and alarm, one critic even fearing decapitation as the result of a falling cube. Charles André Gautier wrote in *L'Architecture* (26th October, 1912) the following: 'Je passe précipitamment sous la porte du petit hôtel présenté par André Mare et ses douze collaborateurs, dans le crainte qu'un cube ne se détache de sa façade et ne m'écrabouille; à l'intérieur, je suis accablé par l'odeur de moisissure qui se dégage de ses ensembles, vieillots, tristes, pauvres et prétentieux' (I passed quickly through the doorway of the little house presented by André Mare and his twelve collaborators, in the fear that a cube might detach itself from the façade and brain me; inside I was overcome by the smell of mustiness which rose from these arrangements, dated, sad, poverty-stricken and pretentious). The roll-call of the artists involved certainly suggests that the project would display startling originality in both conception and execution. The three rooms were equipped from top to bottom with specially designed furniture and accessories, including *boiseries* by Roger de la Fresnaye, a coffee-service by Jacques Villon, furniture by André Mare and pictures and sculpture by leading Cubist artists such as Léger, Metzinger, Marcel Duchamp and Albert Gleizes. Marie Laurencin provided the design for a porcelain vase, and painted four oval panels which surmounted the four pierglasses in the corners of the *salon.* The Cubist house attracted insults and criticism out of all proportion to its likely impact on architectural design, protestations even coming from the floor of the Chambre de Députés. The exhibit was attacked by members of the public who were heroically fended off by Marie Laurencin, Villon's wife Gaby, and Mare's wife, Charlotte, who kept guard daily armed with umbrellas.

1912 was a year of concentrated activity for

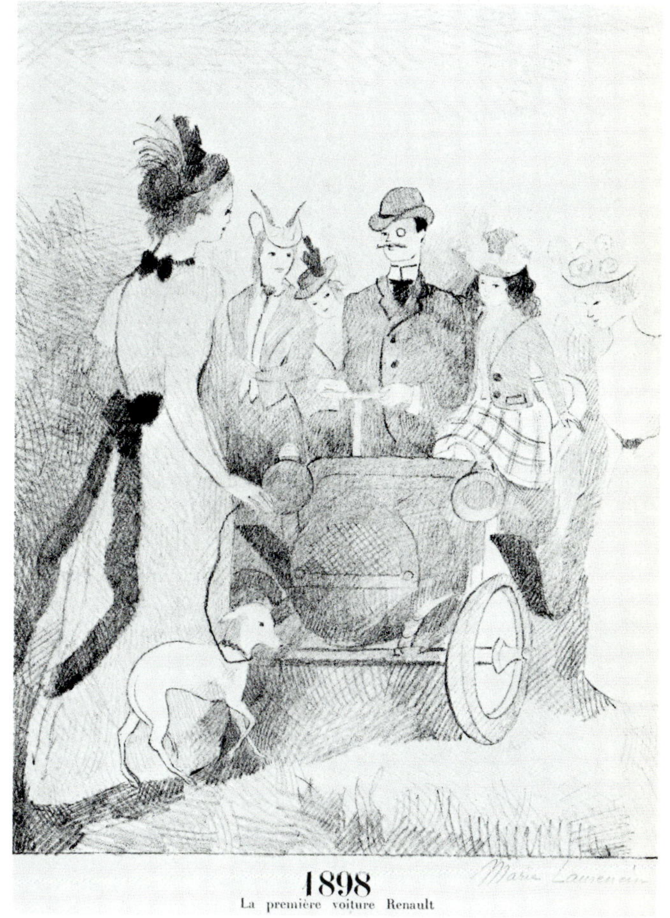

Marie Laurencin
The First Renault Car 1898, c. 1930
Lithograph, printed in colour (The Museum of Modern Art, New York, Lillie P. Bliss Bequest)

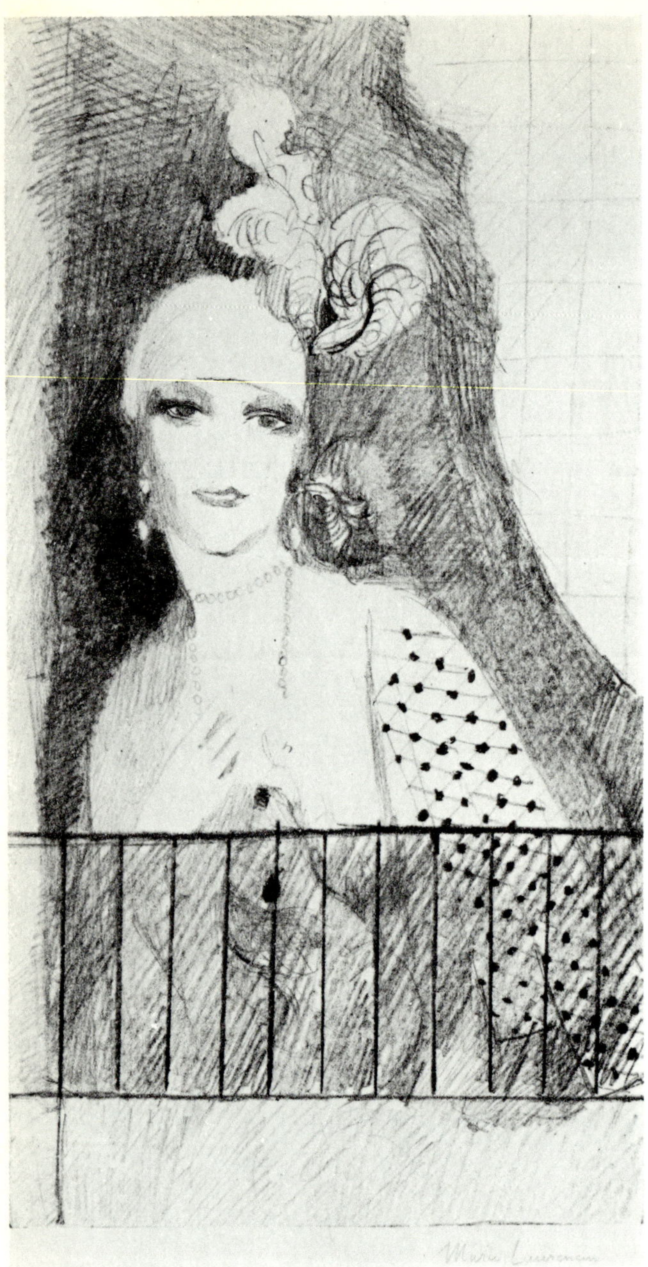

Marie Laurencin
Portrait de la baronne Gxxx/Portrait of Baronne Gxxx, *c.* 1925
Lithograph, 32 × 17 cm. (Photo John R. Freeman & Co)

Marie Laurencin, for as well as the work on the *Maison Cubiste* she participated with Léger, Marcel Duchamp, Raymond Duchamp-Villon, Juan Gris, Picabia, Robert Delaunay, André Lhote and Marcoussis in the *Section d'or* exhibition at Galerie La Boëtie. At the same time she was preparing for an exhibition at the Galerie Barbazanges, the gallery which occupied part of the ground floor of the premises at 109 faubourg St. Honoré, acquired in that year by her friend Paul Poiret, the couturier. Meanwhile the long and crucially influential liaison with Apollinaire was coming to an end, leaving a project to illustrate one of Apollinaire's volumes of poetry unrealised. (The manuscript of *Le Médaillon toujours fermé* is inscribed:- 'pour être illustré par Marie Laurencin'; this would have been her first commission for book illustration). Apollinaire was deeply distraught and was only able to accept the finality of Marie's decision when she married, on June 21st 1914, a fellow student at the Académie Humbert, the German painter Otto von Waëtjen. The outbreak of war a few weeks later forced Marie Laurencin and her husband to seek refuge in Spain, where they spent the whole of the war. Marie only returned to Paris in 1920 after a year spent in Düsseldorf, when she filed for a divorce from von Waëtjen.

Otto von Waëtjen was born in Düsseldorf in 1881 of good – even noble – German lineage (the dedication in Apollinaire's *Le Médaillon toujours fermé* of 1915 reads 'A la baronne von Waëtjen', and Marie Laurencin was apt to refer to her right to this title). On his mother's side he was related to a family of Swiss artists of which the best known member was his grandfather, the landscape painter Benjamin Vautier. Both his uncle Otto and his cousin Benjamin also became painters, and his own choice of vocation seems thus to have been pre-ordained. He studied in Munich and then with his uncle Otto Vautier, before going to Paris to attend the Académie Humbert. His work was once described by a friend of his wife's as *'pitoyable'*, a view very much in conflict with his own estimate of his ability. He believed himself to be an artist of great talent, certainly of greater talent than his wife, and that the future would see justice done to his reputation. The truth, as usual, lies somewhere between these two extremes. He was little more than a competent plagiarist, without originality of imagination, doing at one time a Dufyesque coast-scene, then a Marquet-like factory, or a mannered and old-fashioned 'Laurencin'. His greatest competence lay in the field of straightforward portraiture for he was not entirely lacking in a sense of design, but it was the ambition to paint in a manner far in advance of his natural ability which

Opposite above
Les Biches/The Hinds, 1921
Oil on canvas 65 × 81 cm. (Photo courtesy Acquavella Galleries Inc., New York)

Opposite below left
Jeune Fille au chat et au chien/Young Girl with a Cat and a Dog, *c.* 1918
Oil on canvas, 100 × 73 cm. (Galerie Motte, Geneva)

Opposite below right
Femmes dans la forêt/Women in the Forest, 1920 (detail)
Oil on canvas, 81 × 100 cm. (Armand Hammer Coll., U.S.A.)

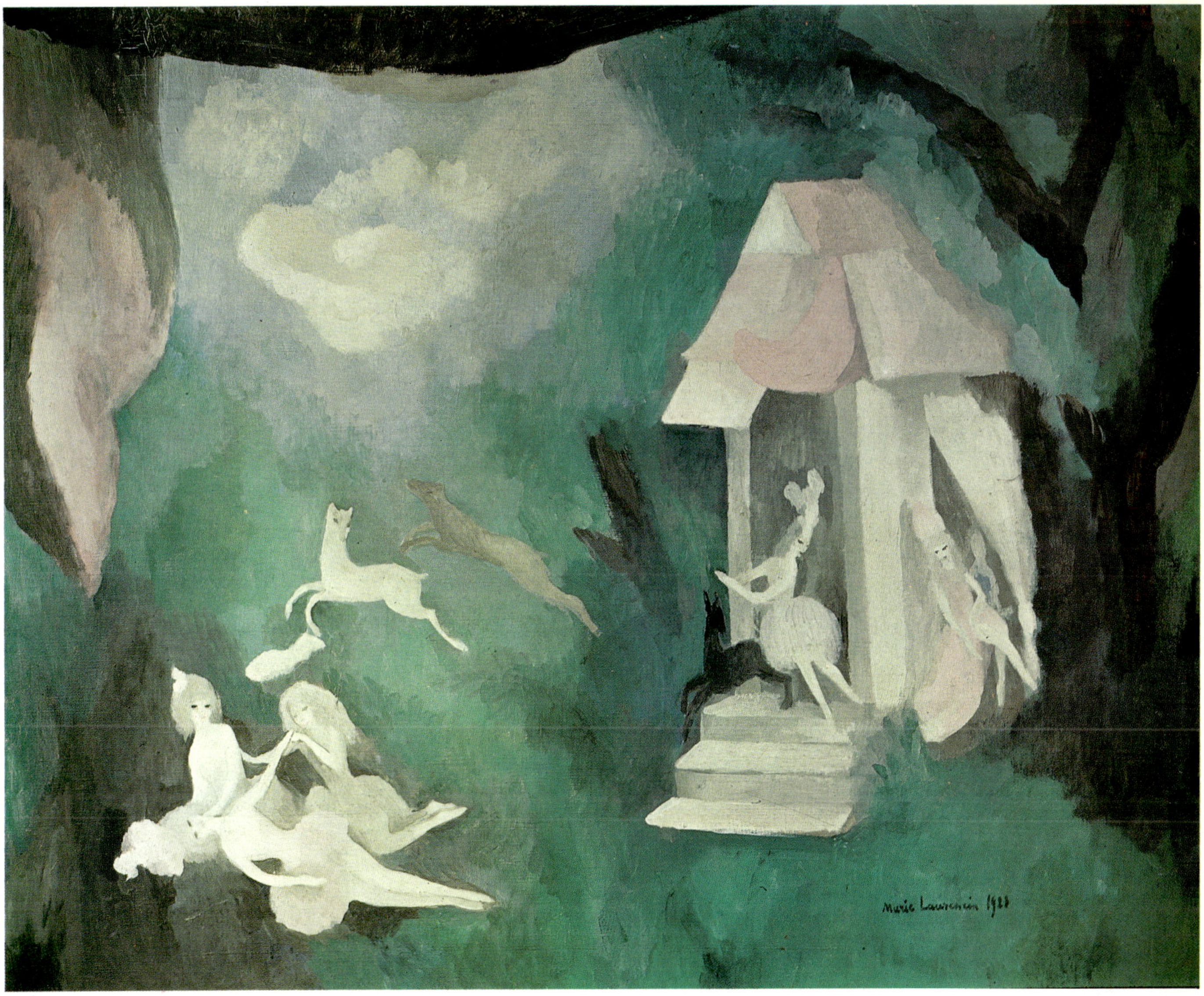

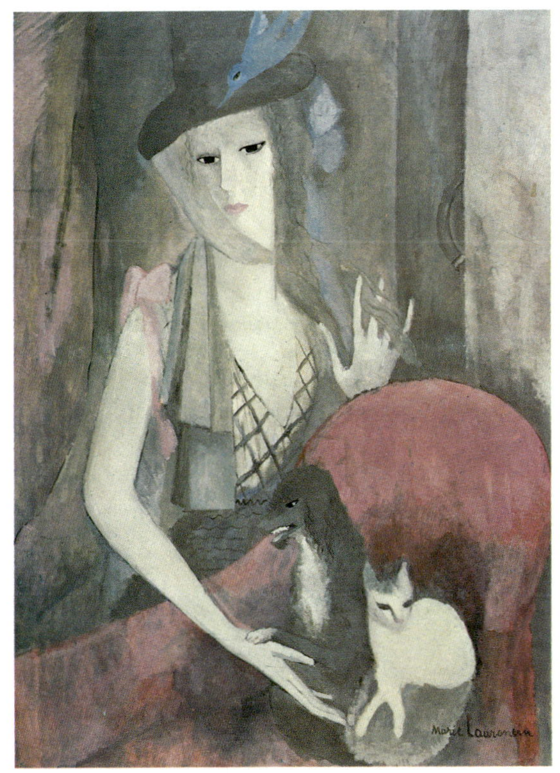

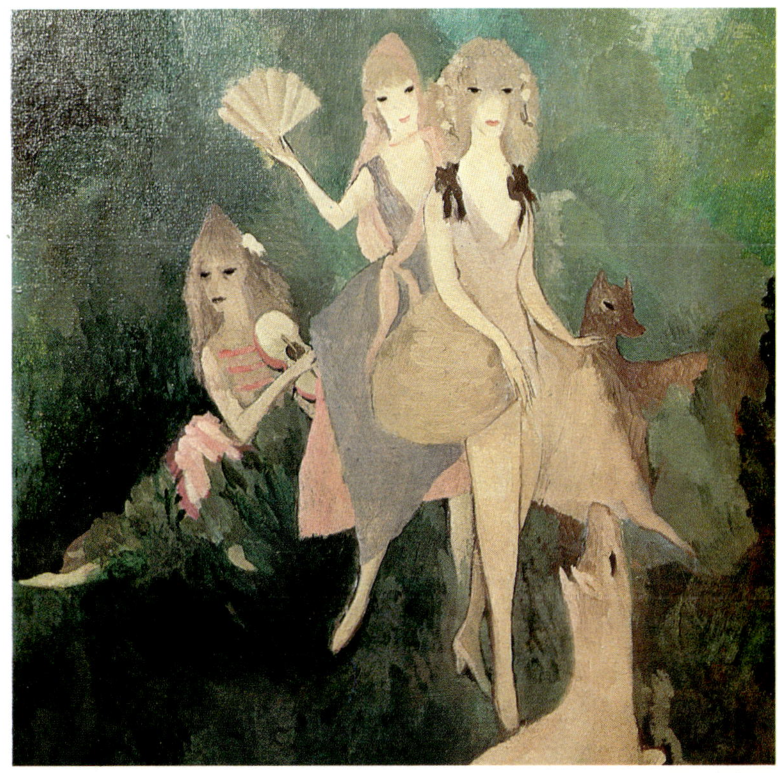

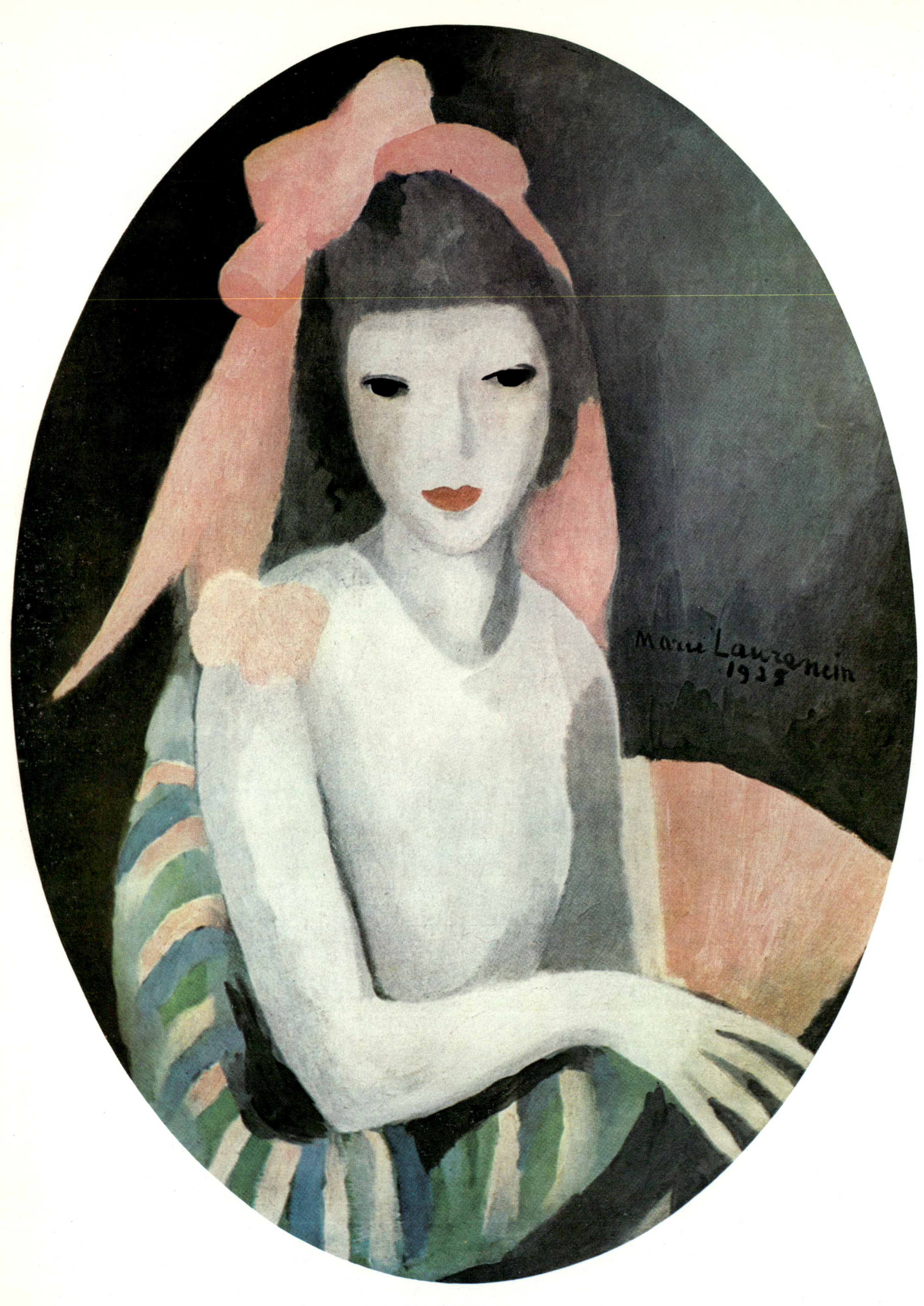
Marie Laurencin
1925

ultimately made his work deserve the harsh epithet given to it. He was quite active in the 1920s and his work was reproduced with some regularity in German art periodicals, notably in *Der Querschnitt* (in which a certain number of his wife's works also appeared), the magazine edited by Daniel Kahnweiler's brother Gustave.

Marie Laurencin's action in marrying a German at this inopportune moment was the subject of a certain amount of comment. She was even identified with the character in the novel by Jean Giraudoux, entitled *Siegfried et le limousin,* a woman artist who marries a German just before the outbreak of the war. Other aspects of this character were not in the least like Marie. They were certainly displeasing to her and she vigorously denied the connection. René Gimpel's wife even asked her if she had divorced von Waëtjen because he was a German, but she in fact revealed that it was for the more prosaic reason that he had become an alcoholic. The whole von Waëtjen family were very much impoverished by the war. Marie Laurencin kept in touch with them, helping with money when she could. Her husband lived in considerable poverty in Paris for a period between the wars, and she remained on friendly terms with him throughout this time in spite of the divorce, keeping in touch with him until his death in 1942.

By 1921 Marie Laurencin had been exhibiting for fourteen years. She was by now a well established artist with a growing reputation and a large number of admirers. She must have felt that the time had come to make a private life for herself which would give her the stability and continuity necessary to the successful pursuit of her career. The whole of the preceding period of her professional life had been devoted to two relationships. Both of these relationships had ended disastrously for her and the demands on her tolerance – of Apollinaire's compulsive philandering on the one hand, and of von Waëtjen's excessive drinking on the other – had made inroads on her spiritual energy which inevitably interfered with her work. In addition to this her marriage to von Waëtjen had involved her in a long exile from her natural habitat. From the date of her re-establishment in Paris she seems to have decided to protect her privacy more carefully, and her greatest pleasure at this time certainly came from the company of her most intimate women friends, those whom she saw frequently, like Nicole Groult, the wife of André Groult and sister of Paul Poiret, herself a distinguished dress-designer. Marie Laurencin saw her almost every day, but Nicole Groult's loving interest made no demands on her privacy.

Opposite
Rosette, 1925
Oil on canvas (Ex. coll. Albert Flament)

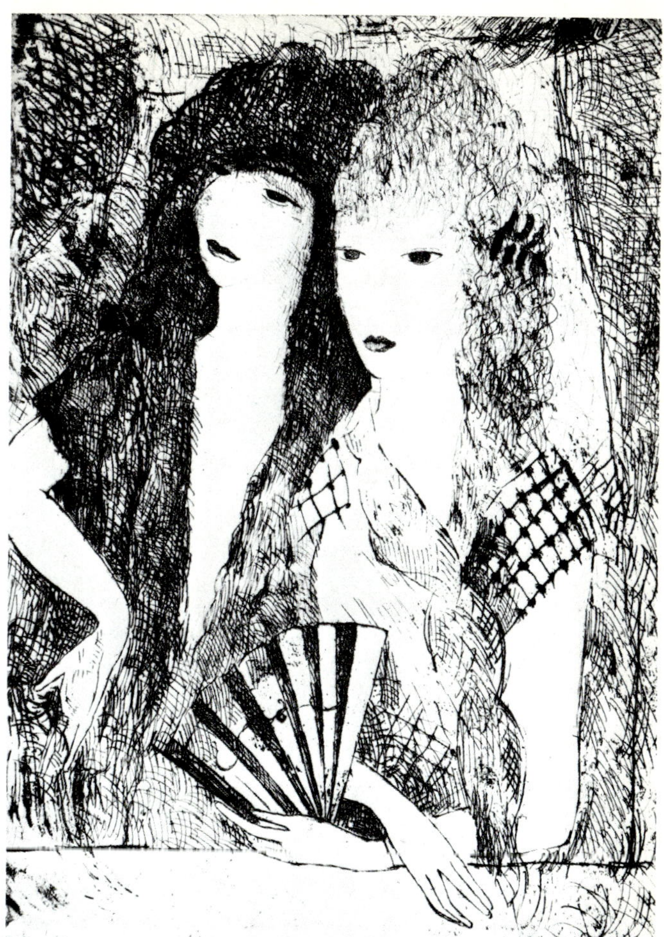

Marie Laurencin
Les Espagnoles/The Spanish Girls, *c.* 1920
Etching (Victoria and Albert Museum)

Marie Laurencin had the reputation of never being without a lover, probably a misreading of her expansive and loving personality. Somerset Maugham, content to perpetuate this myth, assumed that the young man who accompanied her on a visit was the current favourite. In fact this was probably Armand Lowengard, her devoted and constant companion for many years. Marie Laurencin met Armand in the early 1920s through her recently acquired friend René Gimpel, the art dealer. Gimpel was Lowengard's uncle by marriage, his wife being the sister of Lowengard's mother, both of whom were sisters of Lord Duveen. Inevitably Armand, a brilliant scholar who had obtained a degree after only few months at Oxford in 1914, was destined to be employed in the influential and profitable art dealing empire built up by the Duveen brothers. After distinguished service in the army, imprisonment by the Germans, and being wounded in the First World War, he joined the House of Duveen in 1919 as an assistant to Edward Fowles in the 'little palace'

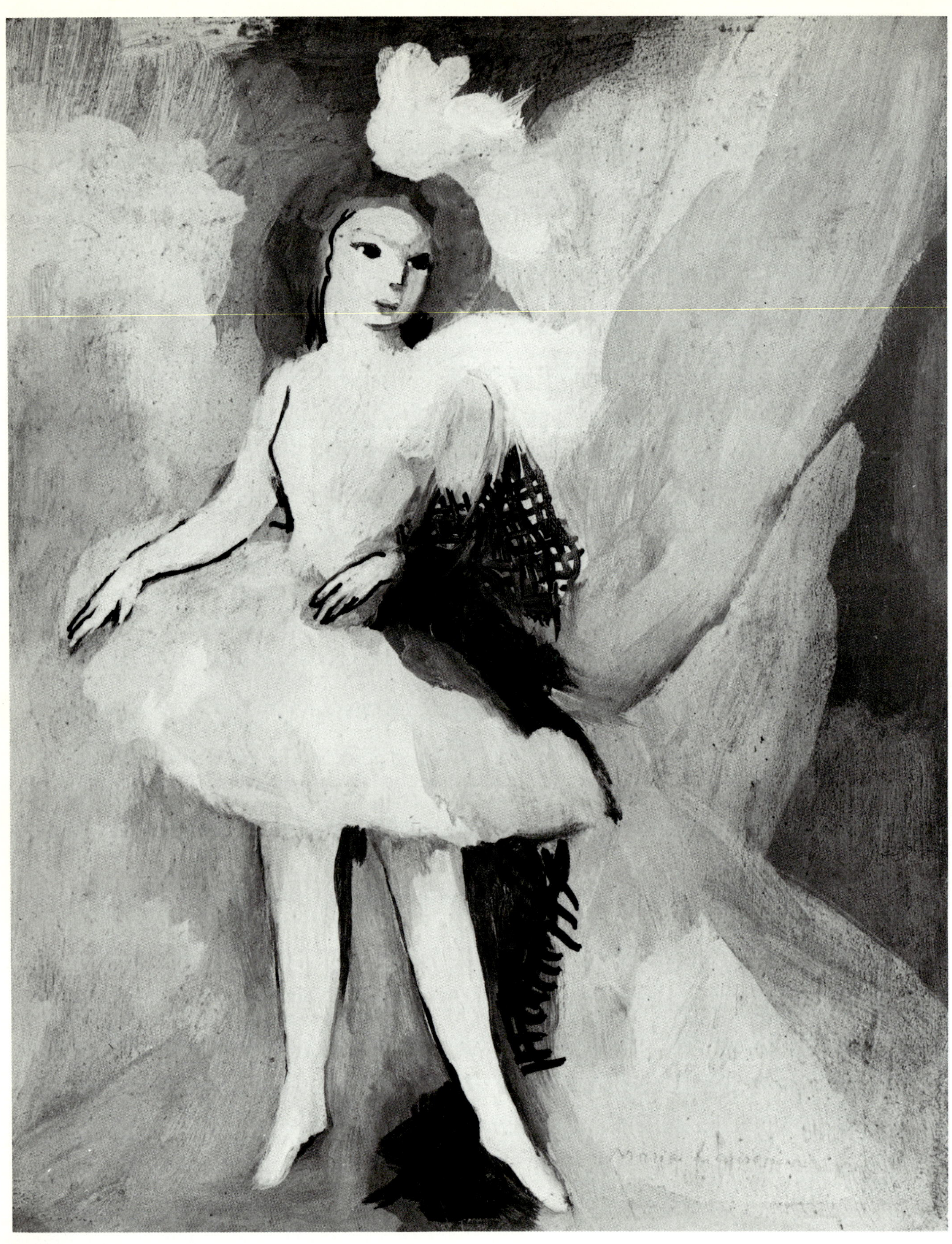

Marie Laurencin
Danseuse au châle noir/Ballet dancer with a black shawl, *c.* 1946
Oil on panel, 26.5 × 22 cm.

which was the Duveen gallery in the place Vendôme in Paris. After a year spent training his naturally excellent visual memory by sending him on a prolonged tour of the museums of Europe as well as on a visit to the now legendary Berenson in Florence, Armand was set to work. He was found to be quite without any business sense and was thereafter used as a 'scout' at auction sales. He developed a knowledgeable interest in modern art which, in spite of his enthusiasm, he did not succeed in communicating to Duveen. It was therefore highly probable that he would have met Marie Laurencin sooner or later in the enclosed world of the modern movement in Paris, but his relationship to Gimpel made the encounter inevitable. Armand Lowengard became passionately devoted to Marie, in spite of her often capricious treatment of him. This included involving him in complicated dealings with the families of her cats, which landed him almost invariably in humiliating situations, and her response to telephone calls which was entirely unpredictable (she, on the other hand, seems to have tolerated without embarrassment Armand's compulsion to show his war wound whenever it was mentioned however inconvenient the occasion). He longed to marry her, although the difference in their ages was thought by the Gimpels to be an impediment – Armand was born in 1893 and was thus Marie's junior by eight years – and this may indeed have strengthened Marie's decision to refuse his repeated proposals. But it is also possible that, consciously or unconsciously, she had made up her mind not to marry again after the failure of her marriage to von Waëtjen.

After the death of Joseph Duveen in 1939 the House of Duveen passed into the joint ownership of Armand and Edward Fowles. With the closure of the London and Paris branches early in the war they were obliged to move to New York, where they had few contacts in spite of the fact that many of Duveen's best customers were wealthy American collectors. The fortunes of Duveen suffered as a result of this, only to be rectified through the intervention of the eminent scholar and critic Robert Langton Douglas. Armand Lowengard died in America in 1944, but the firm remained in business until 1969.

The years of exile in Spain were to see a consolidation of Marie Laurencin's mature style, and produced one of the characteristic figures of the group pictures of the 1920s, the *Jeune femme au châle noir* who features in many of the scenes of ballet and dancers. She is developed from the mantilla-draped figure of *Les Espagnoles,* of which more than one version exists.

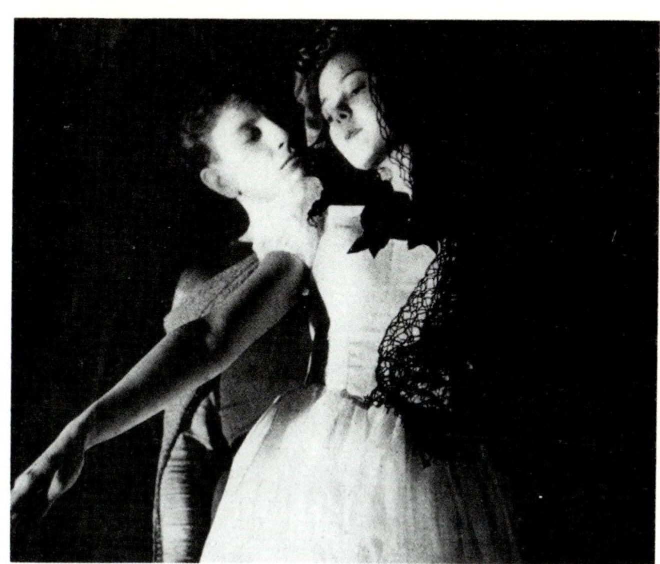

Irène Skovik and Christian Foye in *Déjeuner sur l'herbe,* music by Joseph Lanmer, décor and costumes by Marie Laurencin. Les Ballets du théâtre des Champs-Elysées, 1945

While Marie Laurencin was in Madrid she was once again involved in an *avant-garde* art movement, this time with the emergent Dadaism. With Picabia, Albert Gleizes and Arthur Cravan she co-edited the Dada magazine *391,* a follow-up to the defunct *291* which Picabia had been editing in New York. As with Cubism she remained untouched by Dada influence, and her work shows no trace of this contact with one of the most daring of artistic innovators. The only legacy with this involvement with Dadaism is the strange 'portrait' of her by Max Ernst, which he made in 1919. It was intended as an illustration to Tristan Tzara's *Dadaglobe,* which never appeared. Max Ernst explained this curious vision to W. S. Liberman in a conversation held twenty years later when the print become part of the collection of the Museum of Modern Art in New York. Ernst said that he was trying at the time (in 1919 that is) to obtain a visa to visit Paris, and that Marie Laurencin did her best – but in vain – to help him. The exact significance of some of the details by then escaped him, notably the reiterated cries for help, but he believed that the print 'exprime assez bien la nonchalance et l'absence volontaire de toute ambition *artistique,* qui sont parmi les caractéristiques de l'époque dada' ('explains well enough the nonchalance and the volontary absence of all *artistic* ambition, which is amongst the characteristics of the Dada period').

Marie Laurencin did not return to Paris until 1920, the time of the breakup of her marriage. While she was in Düsseldorf after the war she maintained certain contacts in Paris, designing wallpapers for André Groult, the famous Art Deco

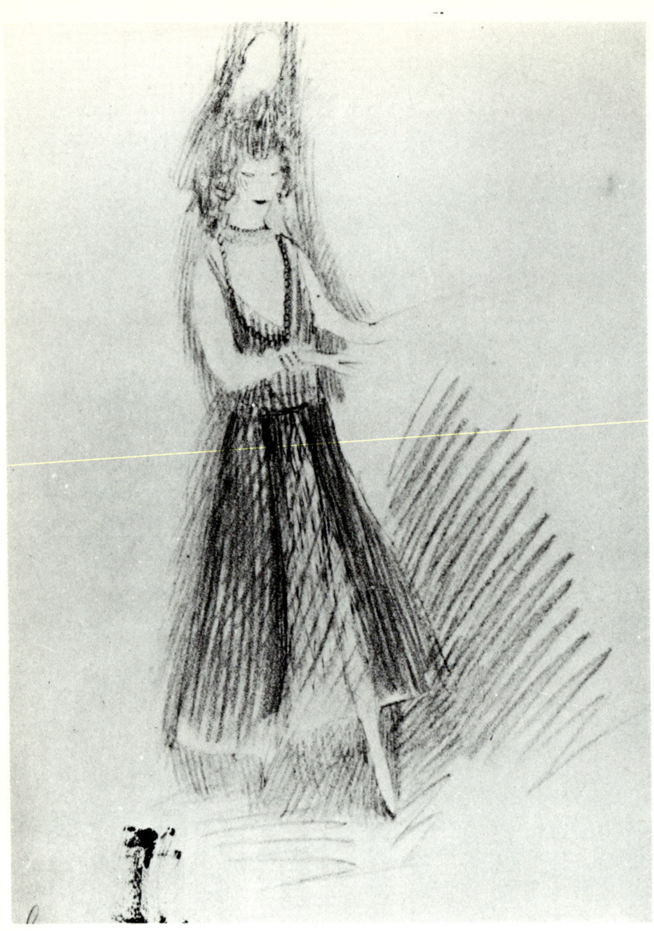

Marie Laurencin
Costume design for the hostess in *Les Biches,* 1924

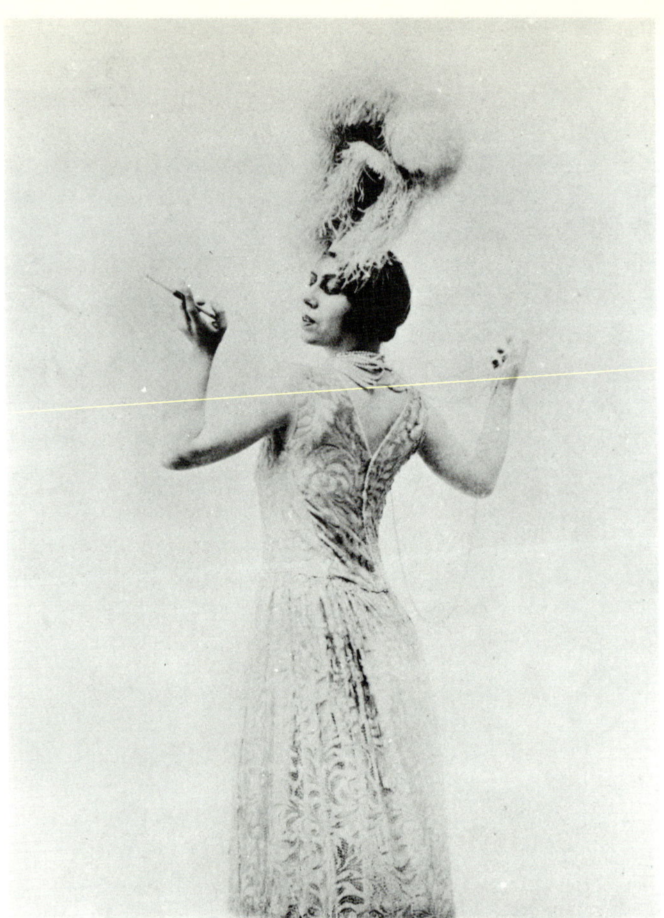

Nijinska as the hostess in *Les Biches* by Francis Poulenc
Diaghilev ballet, 1924

designer and decorator who was the brother-in-law of the couturier, Paul Poiret, and illustrating a novel by an old friend, Louise Fauve-Favrier, *Les Choses qui seront vieilles* published in 1919, but the productive period between the wars dates from her re-establishment in Paris with Paul Rosenberg. She returned to find that her pre-war work had been sequestered at the outbreak of hostilities and sold off for pitiably small sums, an additional reason for welcoming the arrangement with Rosenberg, which allowed the great luxury of freedom from financial anxieties.

In the autumn of 1923 she started work on the designs for the décor and costumes of Francis Poulenc's ballet *Les Biches,* commissioned by Diaghilev for the following season. During the final period of his career Diaghilev took up the suggestion made by Boris Kochno, and began to stage a number of experimental modern ballets written mainly by the composers connected with the group known as *Les Six,* which included Eric Satie, Georges Auric, Ibert and Poulenc himself. The designers were also chosen from among the ranks of the *avant-garde,* and included Picasso, Matisse, Larionov and Gontcharova, Gris and Derain. The happy synthesis of the mood and subjects of *Les Biches* with the costumes and scenery makes it impossible to imagine any choice other than Marie Laurencin for the designer. It is possible that her name was suggested by Poulenc himself, as she was already known to him. She made contact with him in 1921, writing to compliment him on his musical settings for Apollinaire's poems from *Le Bestiaire ou cortège d'Orphée,* containing early works, some written before 1908, which had first appeared in 1911. As her correspondence with Poulenc during 1923 shows, she was painfully aware of the burdensome responsibilities which fall on the designer, who provides the one contribution to the production which cannot be altered or improved as the show proceeds.

In the event the production was a great success, being received with considerable critical acclaim and enthusiasm on the part of the audience. The ballet was first performed in Monte Carlo on January 6th 1924, where it was the most successful production of the season. The first London performance took place in the following year on the 25th May and was given in Berlin early in 1926, adding to Marie Laurencin's reputation in each place. Her work was already known in Berlin where

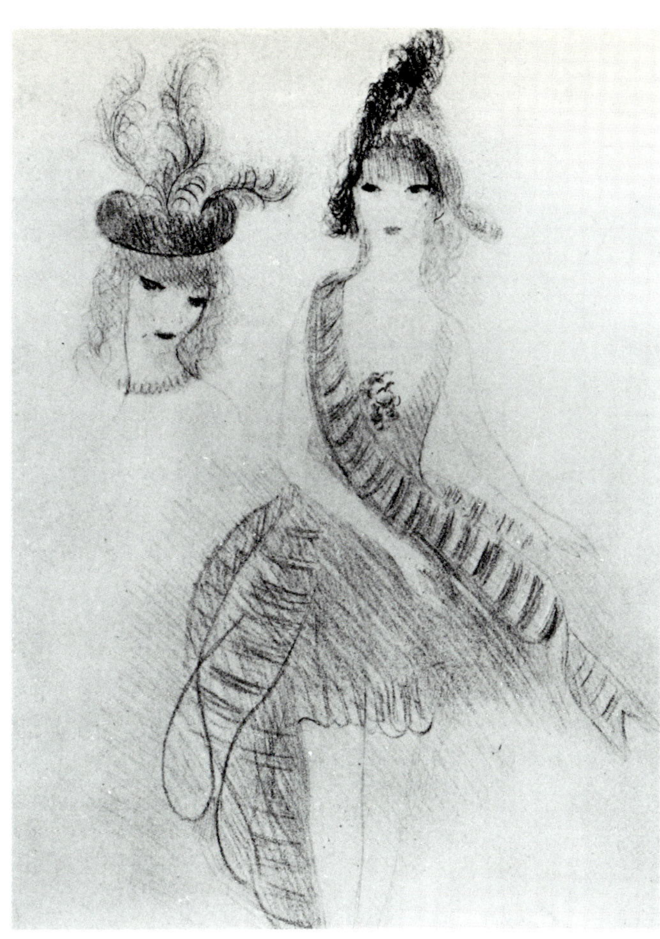

Marie Laurencin
Costume designs for *Les Biches,* 1924

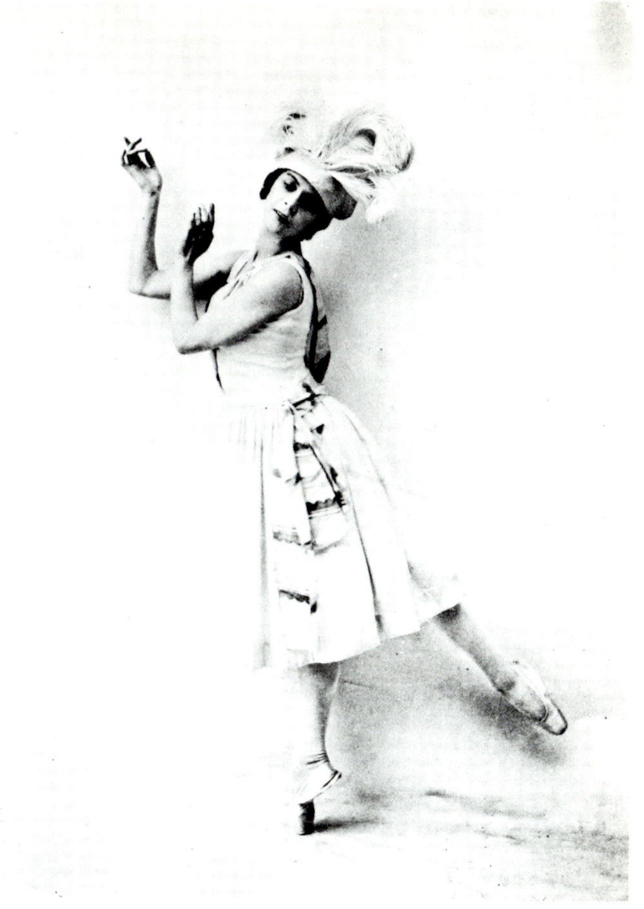

N. Devalois in *Les Biches* by Francis Poulenc
Diaghilev ballet, 1924

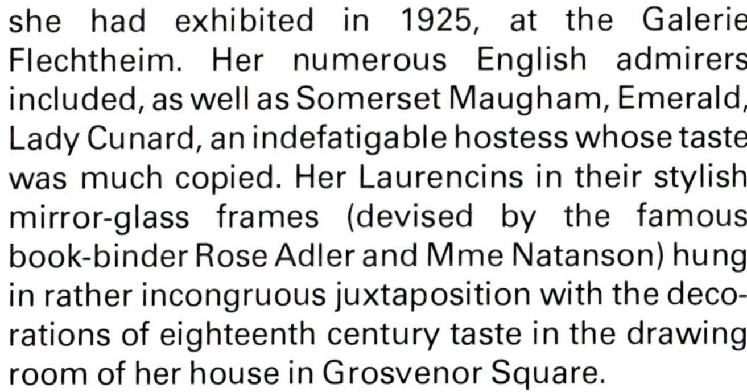

she had exhibited in 1925, at the Galerie Flechtheim. Her numerous English admirers included, as well as Somerset Maugham, Emerald, Lady Cunard, an indefatigable hostess whose taste was much copied. Her Laurencins in their stylish mirror-glass frames (devised by the famous book-binder Rose Adler and Mme Natanson) hung in rather incongruous juxtaposition with the decorations of eighteenth century taste in the drawing room of her house in Grosvenor Square.

Les Biches was one of the ballets staged by Diaghilev in the last years of his life illustrating a theme from modern life, in this case the 'modern woman'. Although so well received by the public, the ballet was not without its detractors. Cyril Beaumont considered the subject unsavoury – there is an unmistakeable suggestion of homosexuality in the relationships of the members of the house-party of both sexes, and the fashionable attire and modish *ennui* of the guests could hardly be expected to recommend themselves to him. Arnold Haskell immediatly spotted the dangers inherent in such a theme treated with such relentless topicality, and in his opinion the ballet was doomed to occupy only a temporary place in the repertoire, a judgement which was echoed by Harold Acton in his *Memoires of an Aesthete,* which appeared in 1948. He wrote some acutely perceptive comments, describing it as the 'quintessence of the nineteen twenties'. He also doubted its ability to survive for long in the repertoire, but foresaw the possibility of its revival as a period piece, an accurate prediction which was to come true in the 1964 production at Covent Garden. Here all Marie Laurencin's original designs were most faithfully reproduced, and the whole scheme can be seen to retain the freshness and originality which made both the décor and the costumes so influential on the fashion of their own time. In the same passage which contains his comments on *Les Biches,* Harold Acton also says that Marie Laurencin's paintings expressed the mood of the period in the same way as Chanel's dress designs; it is perhaps of only marginal interest to record that the costumes for *Les Biches* were momentarily as influential on fashion as any of Chanel's designs, a curious irony since Marie Laurencin herself was not particularly interested in fashion. She dressed with great regard for neatness, often in black, relieved only by hand-embroidered collars and cuffs. Her portrait sitters were often somewhat disconcerted to find that

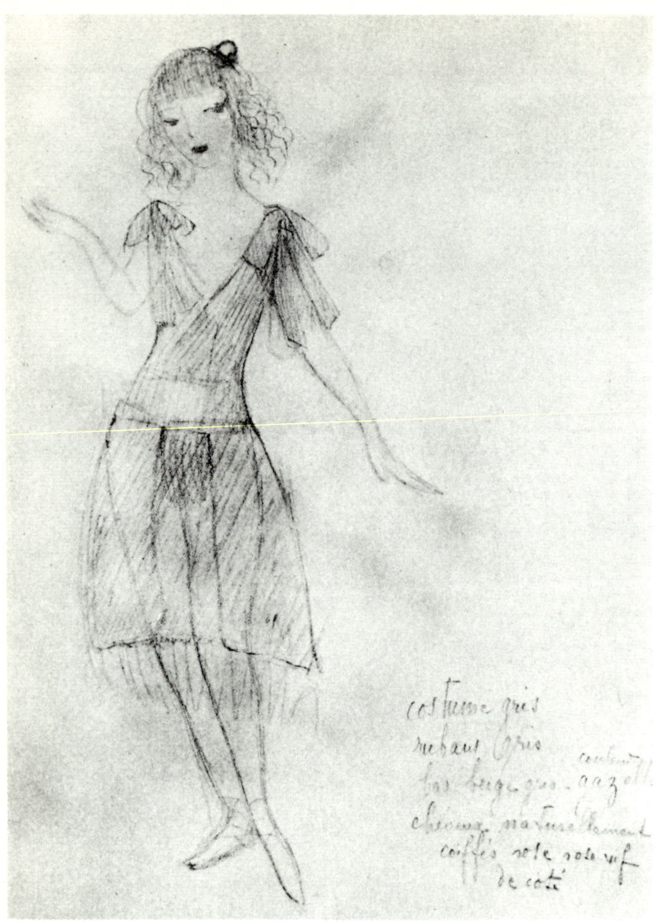

Marie Laurencin
Costume design for Diaghilev ballet, *Les Biches,* 1924

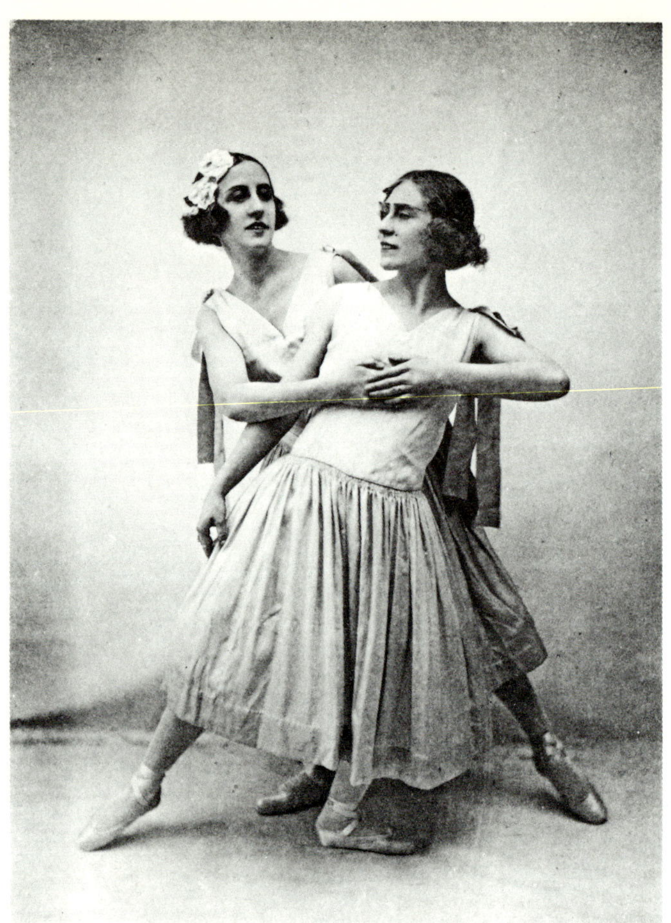

L. Tchernicheva and L. Sokolova
in *Les Biches* by Francis Poulenc
Diaghilev ballet, 1924

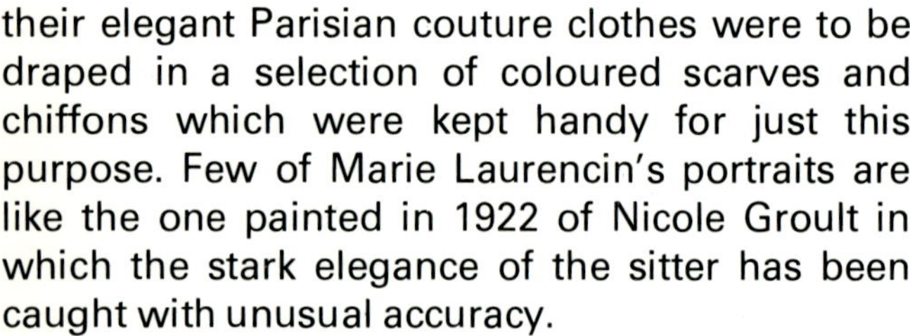

their elegant Parisian couture clothes were to be draped in a selection of coloured scarves and chiffons which were kept handy for just this purpose. Few of Marie Laurencin's portraits are like the one painted in 1922 of Nicole Groult in which the stark elegance of the sitter has been caught with unusual accuracy.

In the summer of 1924 comte Etienne de Beaumont took advantage of the receptive mood created by the success of Diaghilev's modern ballets to mount a short season of similarly experimental modern works. The *Soirées de Paris* were given at the Théâtre de la Cigale in the aid of the Russian refugees and the widows and orphans of the First World War. Marie Laurencin designed one of the ballets, called *Les Roses,* and a poster. These commissions were quickly followed by another ballet, *L'Eventail de Jeanne* in 1927, and décor for the revival of de Musset's *A quoi rêvent les jeunes filles,* given at the Comédie Française in 1928. *Un jour d'été,* given at the Opéra Comique in 1940, followed after a gap of twelve years. Towards the end of her career, her inspiration as fresh as ever, she designed the costumes for the *Déjeuner sur l'herbe* for the company started in 1944 by Irène Lidova, with Roland Petit and Janine Charrat (later metamorphosed into Les Ballets Roland Petit), which opened to an enthusiastic reception in October 1945. Two years later she painted the screen-panels with the château of the Sleeping Beauty for the Marquis de Cuevas, who had taken over the Ballets de Monte Carlo from Lifar on his return to Paris.

Although Marie Laurencin's principal activity throughout her career was painting, at the same time she completed a remarkable number of decorative commissions other than the ballet and theatre designs already mentioned. She was involved in the decorations for the famous *Ambassade Française* for the Exposition Internationale des Arts Décoratifs held in Paris in 1925, providing pictures for André Groult's *Boudoir de Madame l'Ambassadrice.* A comprehensive record of this remarkable group effort by the Société des Artistes Décorateurs exists in a handsome souvenir volume published by Charles Moreau. She also contributed illustrations to more than twenty books, encompassing a wide variety of subjects, some obviously more suited to her imaginative range than others. Janet Flanner

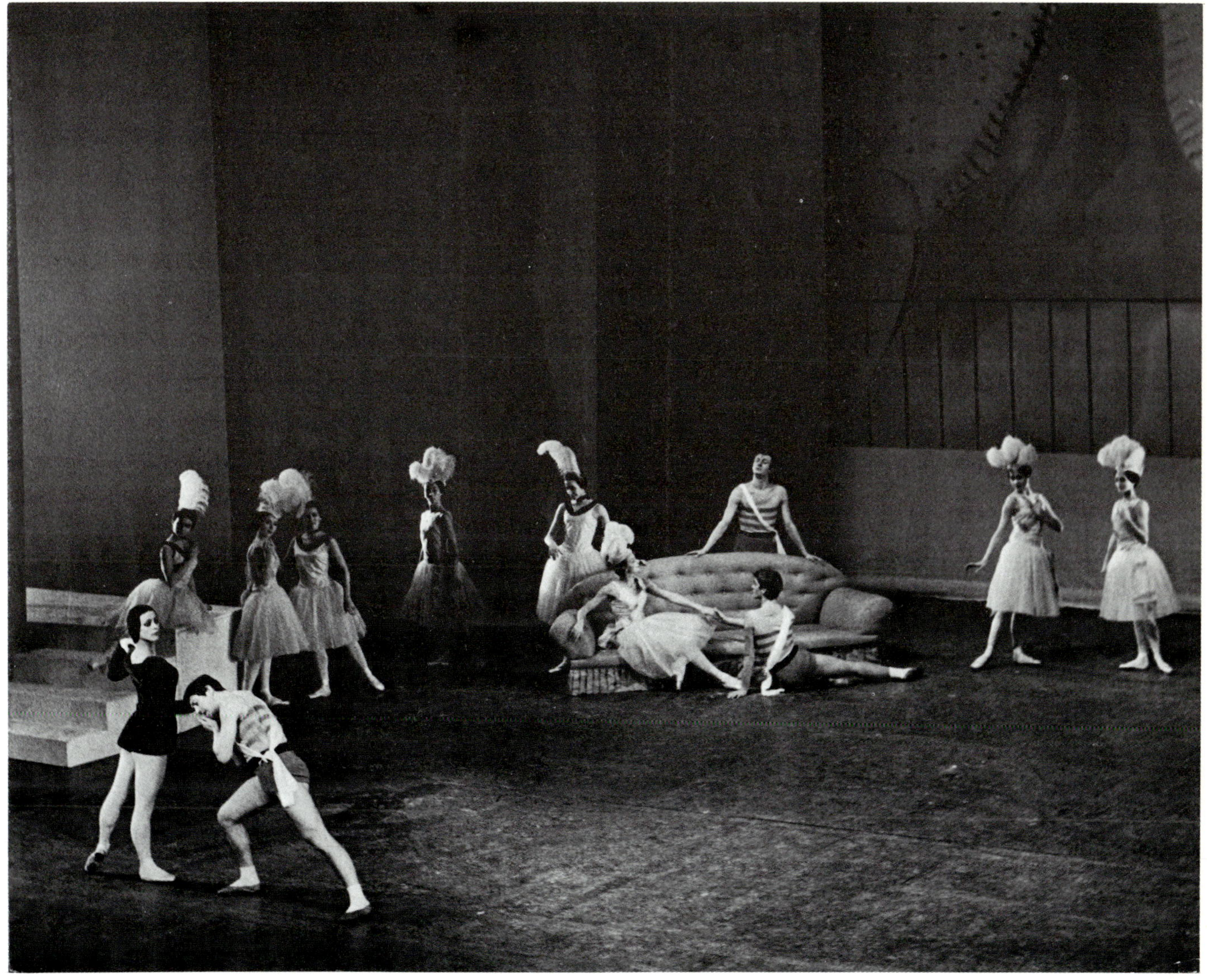

Georgina Parkinson, David Blair and the corps de ballet in *Les Biches*
Royal Ballet, Covent Garden 1964. (Photo Houston Rogers)

remarked rather dismissively of her version of *Alice in Wonderland* which appeared in an *édition de haut luxe* in 1931, that the rabbit in its little pink hat and the hatless Alice were both just like Marie Laurencin. Nonetheless the book, published in English, did exceedingly well. The Verona Press *Garden Party,* by Katherine Mansfield, was much more suited to Marie Laurencin's talents, and the delicate coloured lithographs complement the text perfectly. Of all the illustrated books the one which gives most exactly the flavour of her work is probably *Les Petites Filles de Marie Laurencin,* a series of seventeen watercolours of young girls most faithfully reproduced which was published by Paul Rosenberg in the early days of her relationship with the gallery. The plates are so precisely like watercolours that the temptation to detach them from the book is hard to resist, the more so as the book is without text, and it is now rare to find a copy intact.

Apart from the book illustrations Marie Laurencin produced a large body of graphic work, both in etching and lithography. The lithographs are almost uniform in quality as it was evidently a medium which suited her imagination. The etchings are much more variable, some verging on the trivial, though the best show a depth of visual expression which exploits the medium to the full. Etching requires a degree of planning and organisation which was foreign to her sources of inspiration; it is not readily adapted to delicate and suggestive atmospheric subjects, and was thus more suitably exploited in the intense vision of *Les Espagnoles* than in the dancing figures which feature so frequently in the graphic work.

In 1927 Marie Laurencin undertook some of the decoration of the newly acquired premises of Boulestin's restaurant in Southampton Street, two panels, one of a seated girl which fitted over the door of the restaurant, and the other of a standing

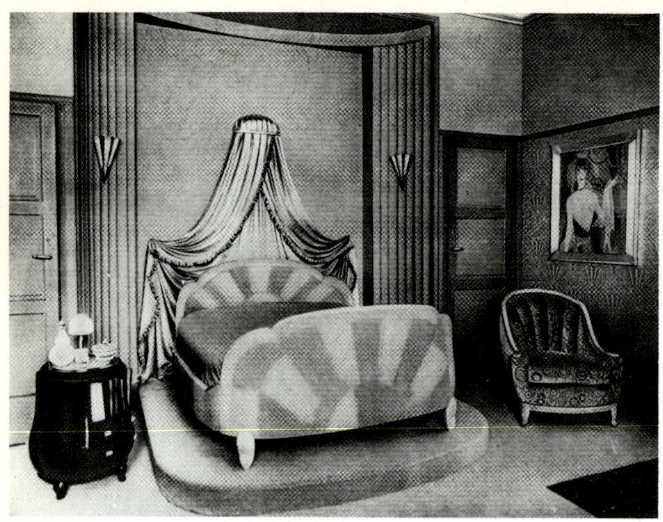

Chambre de dame/Lady's Bedroom
Designed by André Groult, with paintings by Marie Laurencin for the Exposition Internationale des Arts Décoratifs, Paris 1925

athlete. Other panels were painted by J. E. Laboureur (a large circus scene in the foyer), and Allan Walton, who provided a stylised still life for the main restaurant. The fabrics were designed by Raoul Dufy. Marie Laurencin claimed that she executed this commission free, which would not be uncharacteristic, and Marcel Boulestin presented her with a chair as a gesture of gratitude. The chair must have been quite remarkable as it cost £50, a considerable sum of money at that date, and allegedly came from Mappin and Webb.

Marie Laurencin also designed a number of posters. Though easily recognisable as her work, they retain all the stylish quality that is the hallmark of the decorative commissions of this period but the demands of legibility and impact have in some way altered the concept and the emphasis of the designs. With the exception of the amusing promotional material she designed for Renault, they are among her least successful productions.

Marie Laurencin's most characteristic pictures were produced after her re-establishment in Paris in 1920. At this date all her flirtations – which were never very serious – with the experimental aspects of the Modern Movement were abandoned in favour of her private vision of the world. The consistency of this vision and her own belief in the validity of her artistic contribution were her greatest assets in the vortex of the *avant-garde* world of the 1920s, but these same assets were to become liabilities in the last years of her career. By the time of the exhibition of her work at Agnew's Gallery in London in 1936 her work was described dismissively by the critic of *The Studio* as 'dated'. For the insatiable aesthetic appetite of the art buying public custom had indeed staled the beauty of her work. It is perhaps significant that prices for her paintings were very low during the Second World War, but in the early 1950s they began to rise quite rapidly and are now far beyond the reach of the modest collector to whom her work has always appealed so greatly. If the gay and illusive world of her *biches* and elegant young women is found to be anachronistic in contrast to the grim reality of total war, there is no doubting the pleasure which her work has given and still gives in the more congenial atmosphere of peace and prosperity.

Marie Laurencin continued to paint until she was nearly seventy. She suffered from a certain amount of ill-health throughout the whole of the period after her return to Paris in 1920, but her death came unexpectedly on the 8th June 1956. This followed the briefest of illnesses which seemed to be an attack of her recurrent stomach trouble no more serious than any other that she had suffered throughout the years. Her final years were marred by an unpleasant legal wrangle over the ownership of her appartment, but this was resolved in her favour before she died. It was thus with a sense of outrage that her friends heard of her untimely death following a heart attack just at the moment when her affairs were in such good order.

BOOKS ILLUSTRATED BY MARIE LAURENCIN

1919 *Les Choses qui seront vieilles* by Louise Faure-Favier illustrated with 13 lithographs by Marie Laurencin. La Renaissance du Livre, Paris 1919.

1920(?) *Sommer,* poems by René Schickélé and an essay by André Salmon, illustrated with four lithographs by Marie Laurencin.

1921 *La Tentative amoureuse* ou *Le Traité du vain désir, Les Poésies d'André Walter,* by André Gide, illustrated with 9 wood-engravings in colour by Jules Germain and L. Petitbarat after watercolour drawings by Marie Laurencin. Editions de la Nouvelle Revue Française, Paris 1921.

1922 *L'Eventail de Marie Laurencin,* poems dedicated to Marie Laurencin with ten etchings by Marie Laurencin. Editions de la Nouvelle Revue Française, Paris 1921.

1924 *Les Biches,* Théâtre Serge Diaghilev by Boris Kochno, Introduction by Jean Cocteau. Cover and 14 lithographs by Marie Laurencin. Paris 1924.

Les Petites Filles by Marie Laurencin, ed. Paul Rosenberg, illustrated with 17 hand coloured blocks by Marie Laurencin, Daniel Jacomet et Cie, Paris 1924.

1925 *Brigitte, ou la belle au bois dormant* by Marcel Jouhandeau, illustrated with 4 lithographs by Marie Laurencin. Editions de la Galerie Simon (D. H. Kahnweiler), Paris 1925.

1926 *Petit Bestiaire,* Poèmes inédits de Marie Laurencin, illustrated with 2 lithographs by Marie Laurencin. Editions François Bernouard, Paris 1926.

Lettres Espagnoles by Jacques de Lacretelle, illustrated with 11 etchings by Marie Laurencin. Société d'édition, 'Le Livre', Paris 1926.

Dix filles dans un pré, by Jean-Richard Bloch, illustrated with 4 etchings by Marie Laurencin. Au Sans-Pareil, Paris 1926.

Les Belles à table, by Maurice des Ombiaux, including 1 etching by Marie Laurencin. Paris 1926.

1928 *Finette* ou *L'Adroite princesse,* by Marie-Jeanne L'Héritier de Villandon, illustrated with 5 coloured lithographs by Marie Laurencin. Paris 1928. Editions P. Trémois, Paris 1928, (seventeenth century fairy story, attributed to the niece of Charles Perrault).

Naissance précédée de *Changer d'étoile,* Marcelle Auclair, Paris 1934.

Nœuds coulants, Paul Morand, Collection Les Panathénées No 11, Paris 1928.

L'Age de l'Humanité, by André Salmon (editor of *Vers et Prose), Paris 1928.*

1930 *Alice in Wonderland,* by Lewis Carroll, illustrated with 6 lithographs by Marie Laurencin. The Black Sun Press, Paris 1930.

1930 *Les Sœurs Brontë, filles du vent,* René Crevel, illustrated with 5 lithographs (27 x 37.5 cm.). Editions des Quatre Chemins, Paris 1930.

1931 *Luce ou l'enfance d'une courtisane,* Jacques de Lacretelle, illustrated with 6 drawings *clichés au trait* after Marie Laurencin. Editions P. Trémois, Paris 1931.

Antarès, Marcel Arland, illustrated with 5 etchings by Marie Laurencin. Editions du Pavois, Paris, N.D.

1937 *Camille,* by Alexandre Dumas, illustrated with reproductions in stencil of watercolours by Marie Laurencin. Limited Editions Club of America, 1937.

Paris 1937, album of 62 etchings produced to coincide with the decorative art exhibition of that year by the Municipality of Paris, including one work by Marie Laurencin.

1939 *The Garden Party,* by Katherine Mansfield, illustrated with 6 lithographs by Marie Laurencin. The Verona Press (printed by L'Officina Bodoni in Italy).

1944 *Fêtes Galantes,* by Paul Verlaine, illustrated with 10 etchings by Marie Laurencin. Albert Messein, Paris, 1944.

1946 *Le Carnet des nuits,* by Marie Laurencin, Ecrits et documents de peintres, 3 illustrations. Geneva 1946.

1947 *Du cubisme,* ed. Albert Gleizes and Jean Metzinger, including one etching by Marie Laurencin. Compagnie Française des Arts Graphiques, 1947.

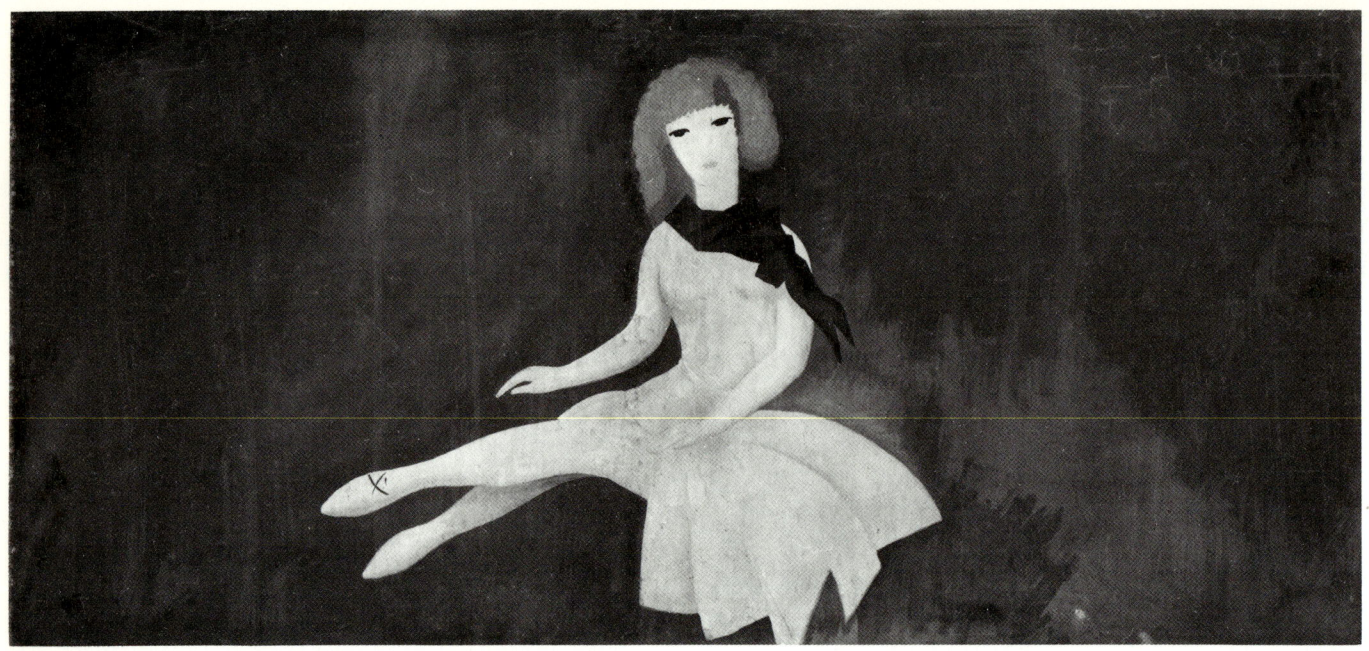

Marie Laurencin
Femme assise/Woman sitting (Mural for Boulestin's Restaurant), 1927
Tempera and oil on canvas, 80 × 176 cm.

BIBLIOGRAPHY

Adéma, Marcel, *Apollinaire le mal-aimé*, Librairie Plon, Paris, 1952.

Allard, Roger, *Marie Laurencin,* Editions de la Nouvelle Revue Française, 1921.

Apollinaire, Guillaume, *Méditations esthétiques, les peintres cubistes,* Paris, 1913.

Breunig, L.-C. (ed.) *Guillaume Apollinaire, chroniques d'art (1902-1918)* Gallimard, Paris, 1960.

Chavance, René, *Une Ambassade française,* Editions Charles Moreau, Paris, 1925.

Cooper, Douglas, *The Cubist Epoch,* Phaidon, London, 1971.

Day, George, *Marie Laurencin,* Paris, 1947.

Fels, Florent, *L'Art Vivant de 1900 à nos jours,* Pierre Cailler, Geneva, 1950.

Flament, Albert, 'Arabesques sur Marie Laurencin', *La Renaissance de l'Art Français,* 1924.

Garland, Madge, 'The World of Marie Laurencin', *The Saturday Book,* No. 23 (ed. John Hadfield), Hutchinson, 1963.

Gimpel, René, *Journal d'un collectionneur,* Paris, Calmann-Lévy, 1963

Golding, John, *Cubism: A History and an Analysis, 1907-1914,* Wittenborn, New York, 1949.

Jouhandeau, Marcel, *Marie Laurencin,* (1000 copies), Editions Quatre Chemins, Paris, 1928.

Kahnweiler, D. H. (ed.) *Der Querschnitt,* Berlin, 1921-25.

Kochno, Boris, *Les Biches,* Théâtre Serge Diaghilev, 2 vols., Paris, 1924.

Picabia, Francis, (ed.) *391* (1917-1924), Barcelona, New York, Zurich, Paris.

Poiret, Paul, *En habillant l'époque,* Editions Grasset, Paris, 1930.

Pradel, Marie-Noëlle, 'La Maison cubiste en 1912', *Art de France* (vol.1) p.177, 1966.

Roger-Marx, Claude and Albert Skira, *Anthologie du livre illustré,* Paris, 1946.

Warnod, Jeannine, *Le Bateau-Lavoir,* Presses de la Connaissance, Paris, 1976.

Opposite
Above left
Femme dans un décor féerique/Woman in an Enchanted Setting, 1908
Watercolour, gouache, pen and ink, 16 × 12 cm.

Above right
Jeune Fille aux fleurs/Young Girl with Flowers, *c.* 1908
Pen and ink, 26 × 19.5 cm.

Opposite
Below left
Femme assise/Woman Sitting, *c.* 1908
Pen and ink and wash 15 × 10 cm.

Below right
Auto-portrait/Self-portrait, *c.* 1908
Black crayon, 31.5 × 25 cm.

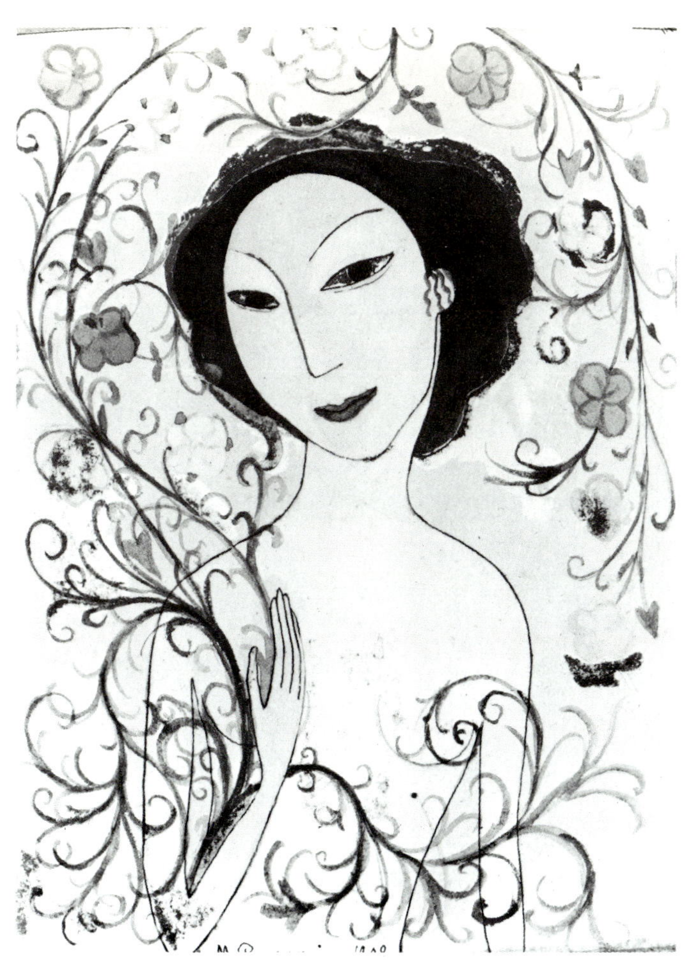

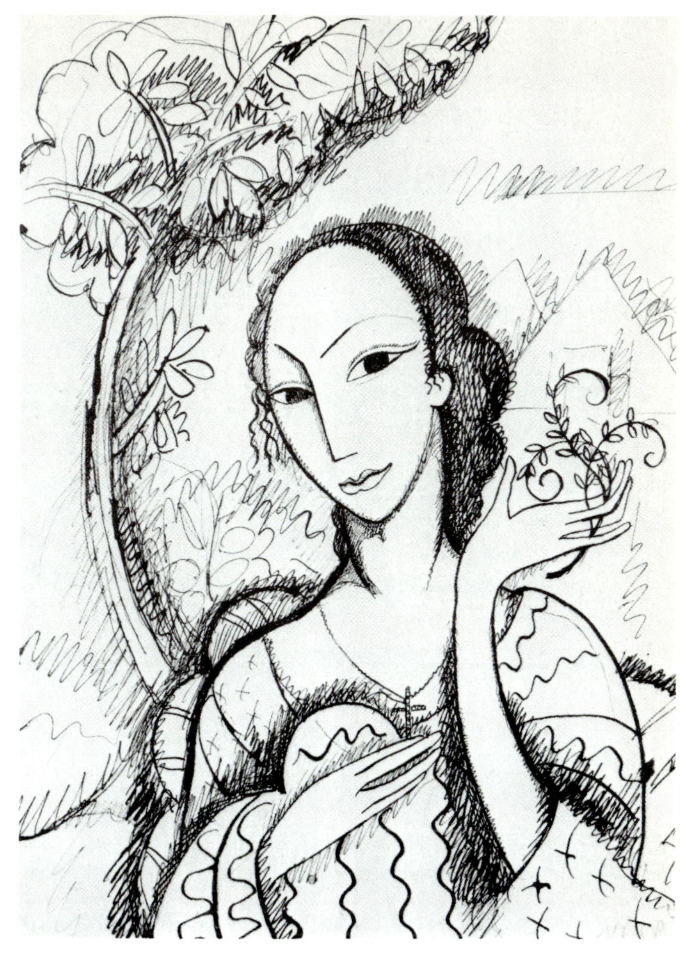

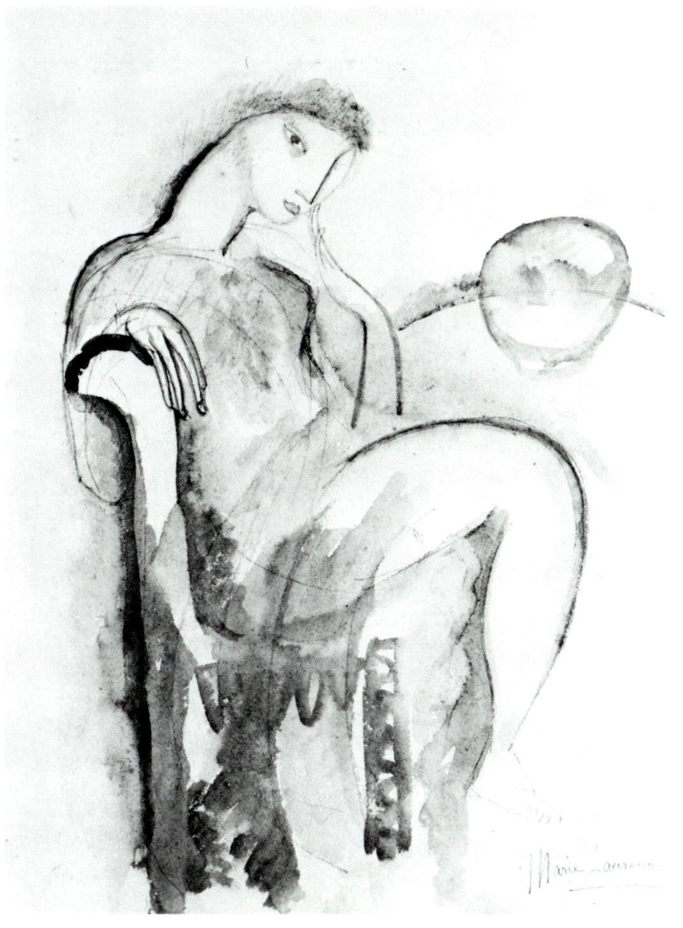

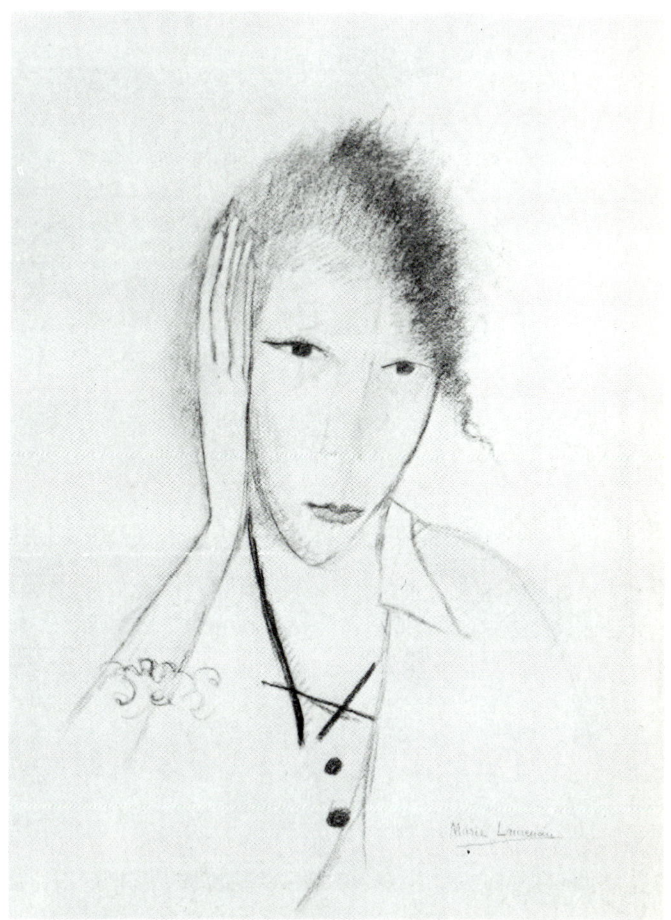

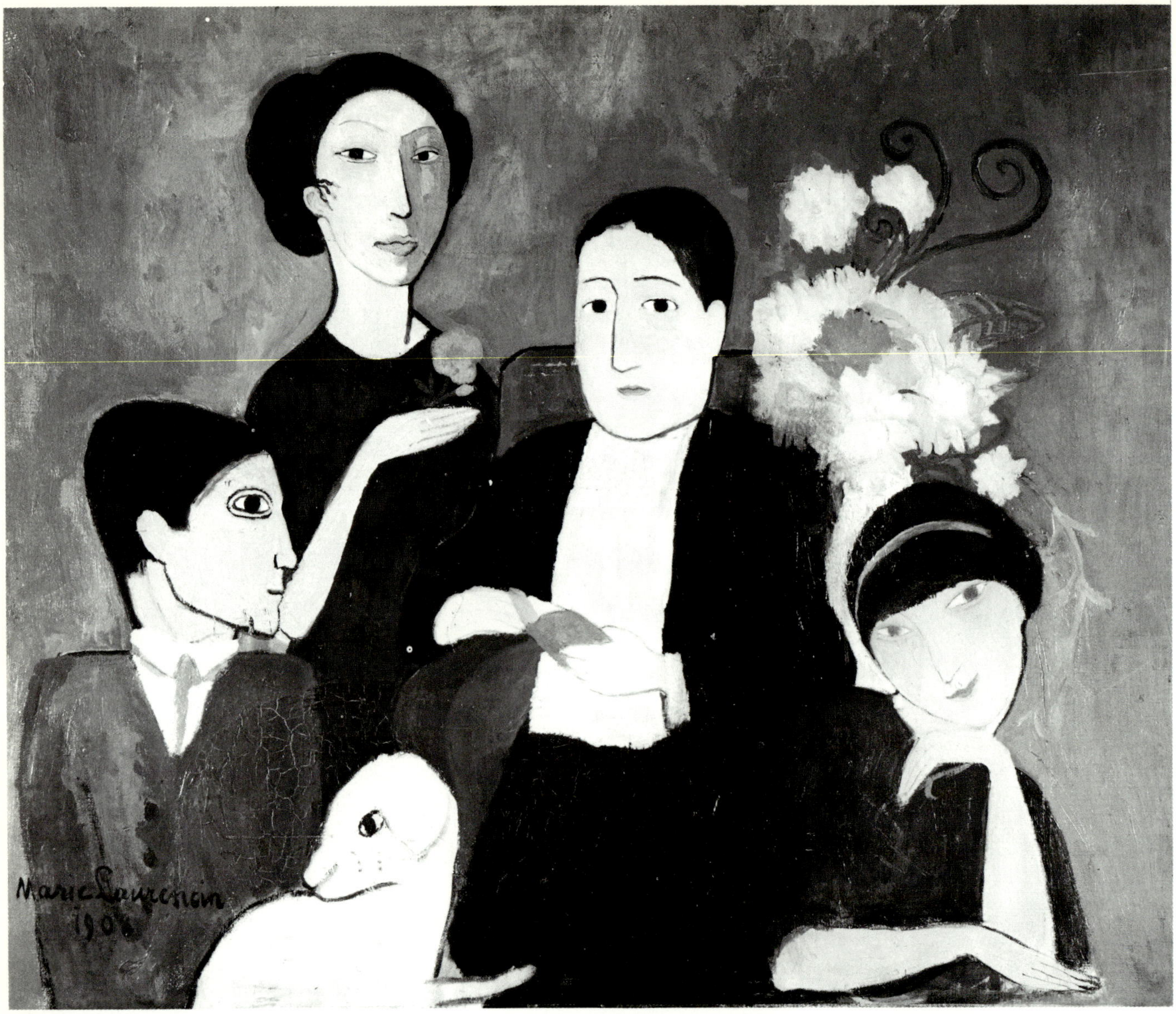

Groupe d'artistes/Group of Artists, 1908
Oil on canvas, 62.8 × 79 cm. (Cone Collection, Baltimore Museum of Art)

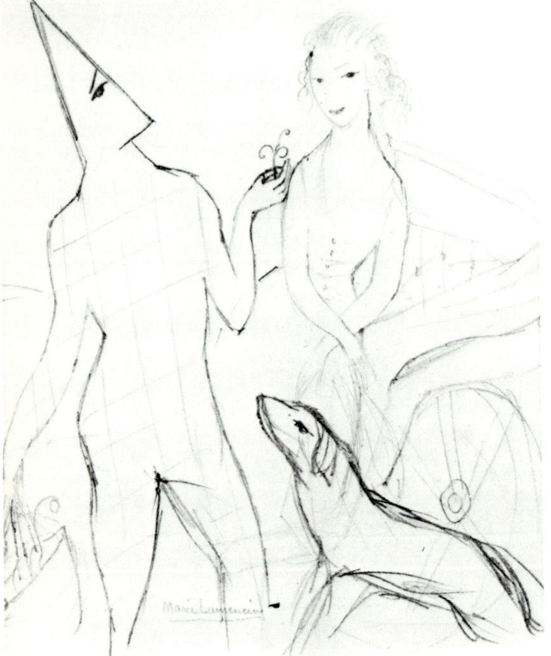

Left
Carnaval/Carnival, *c.* 1908
Pencil, 19 × 16.5 cm.

Opposite above
Jeune Femme au chapeau/Young Woman with a Hat (from the Maison Cubiste), 1912
Oil on canvas, 38.7 × 30.5 cm.

Opposite below
Tête de jeune fille/Head of a Young Girl (from the Maison Cubiste), 1912
Oil on canvas, 38.7 × 30.5 cm.

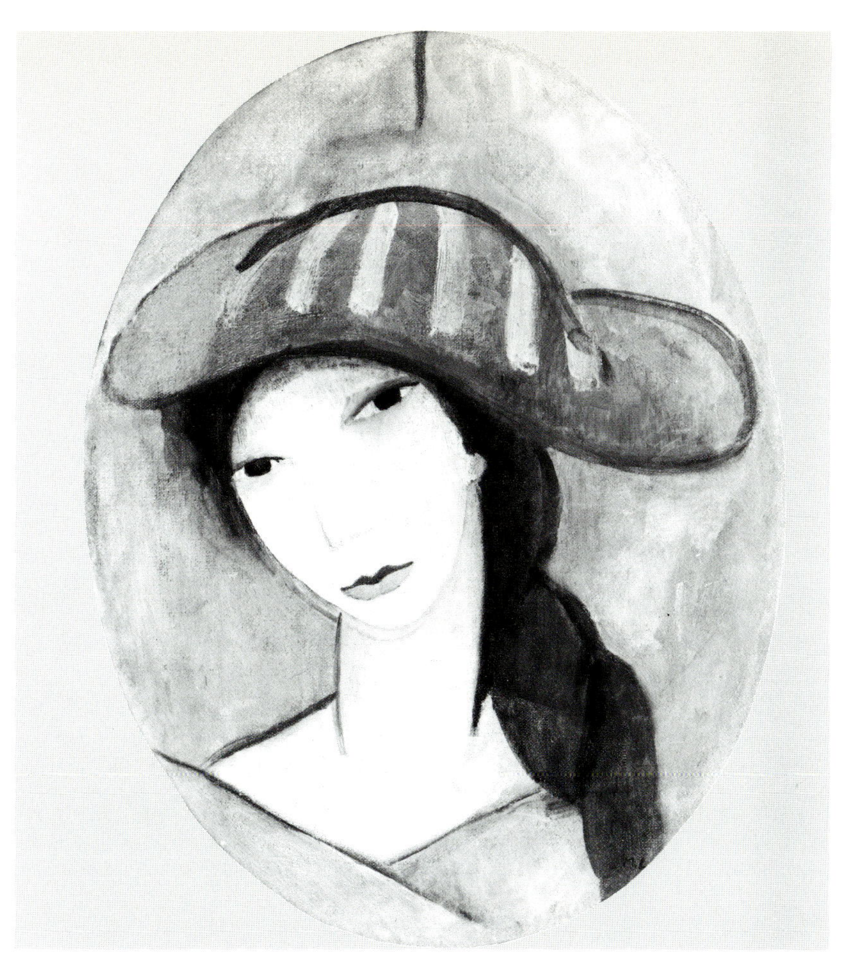

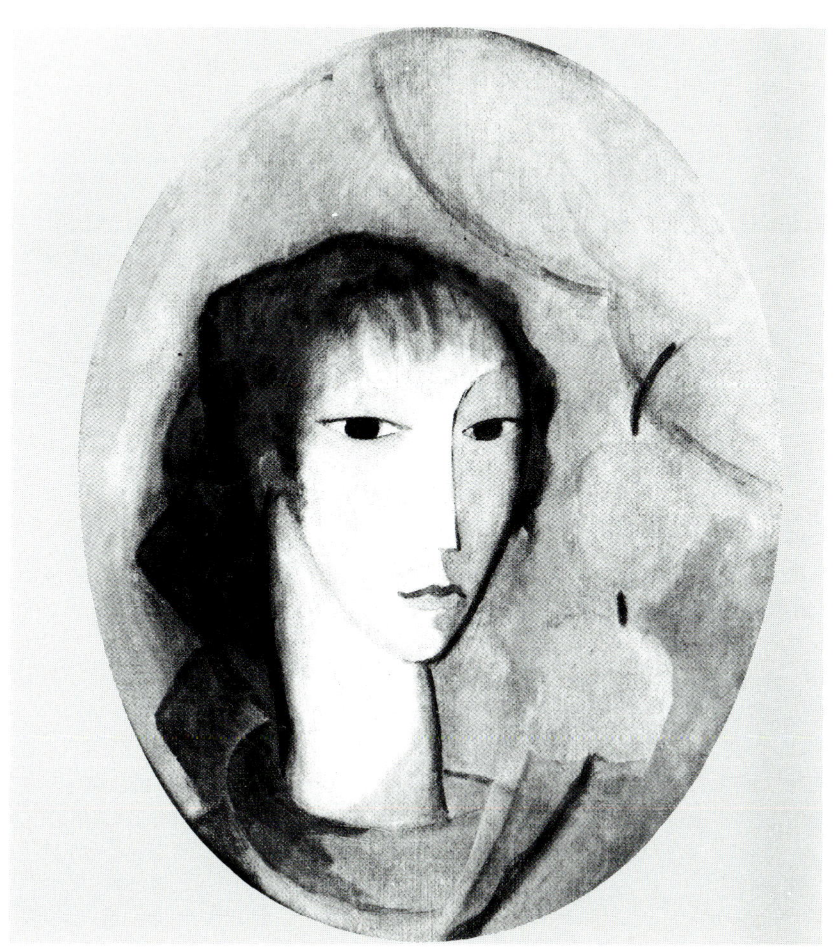

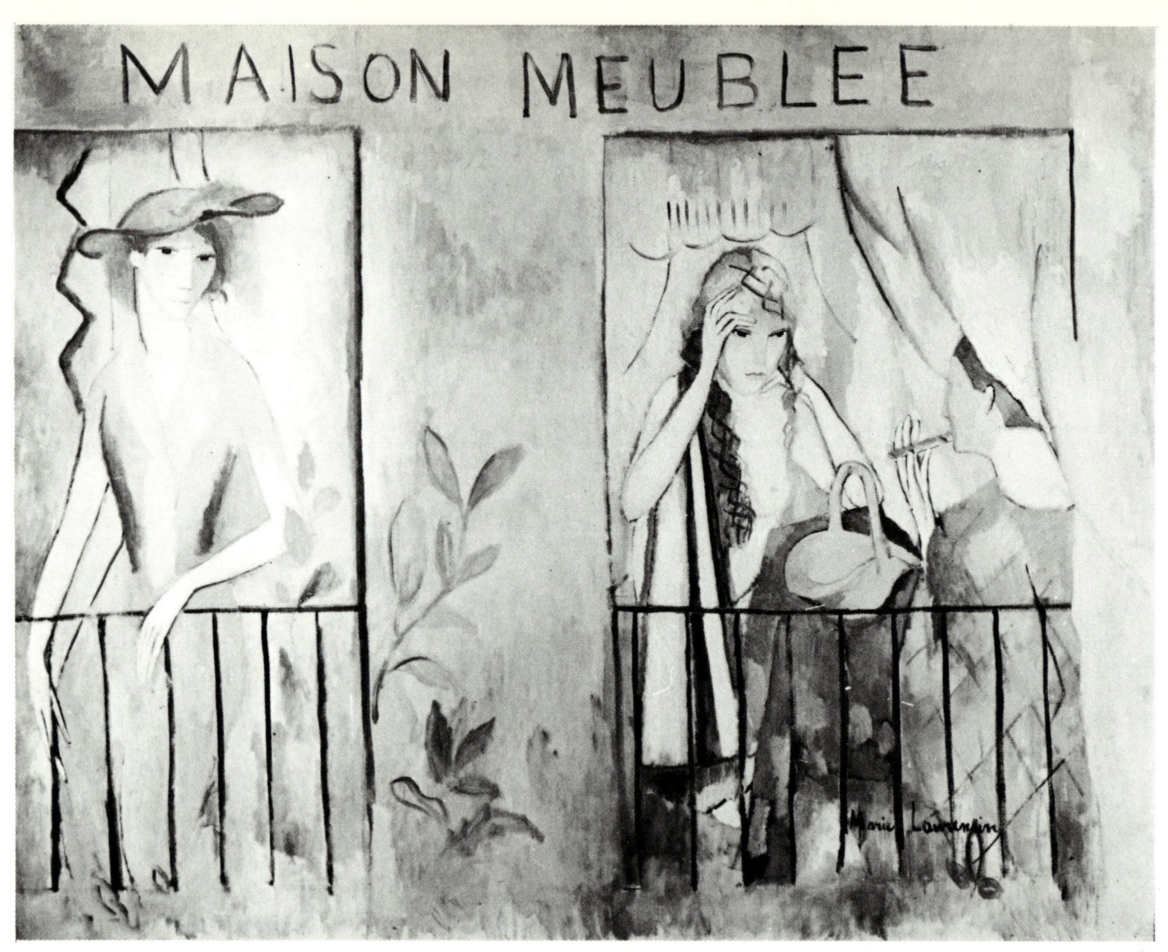
MAISON MEUBLEE
Marie Laurencin

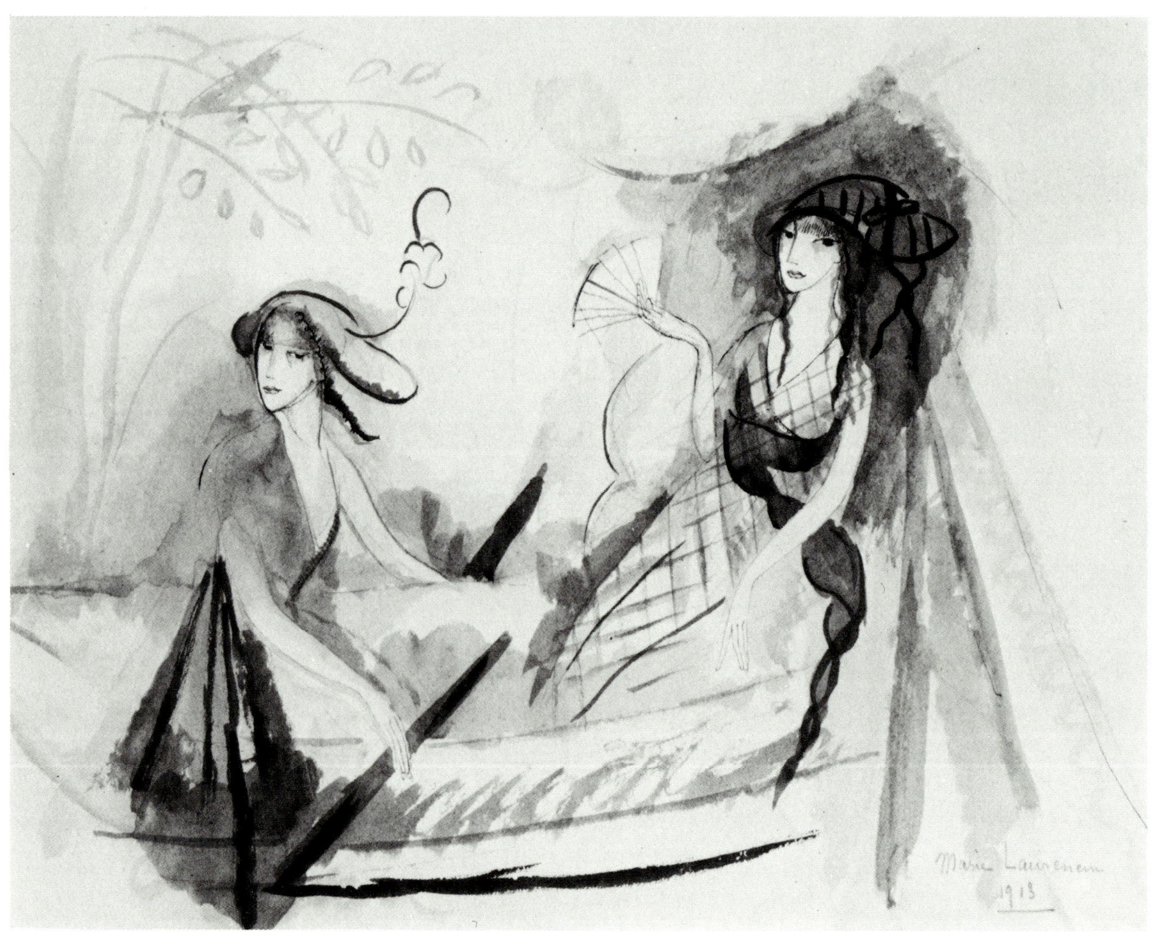
Marie Laurencin
1913

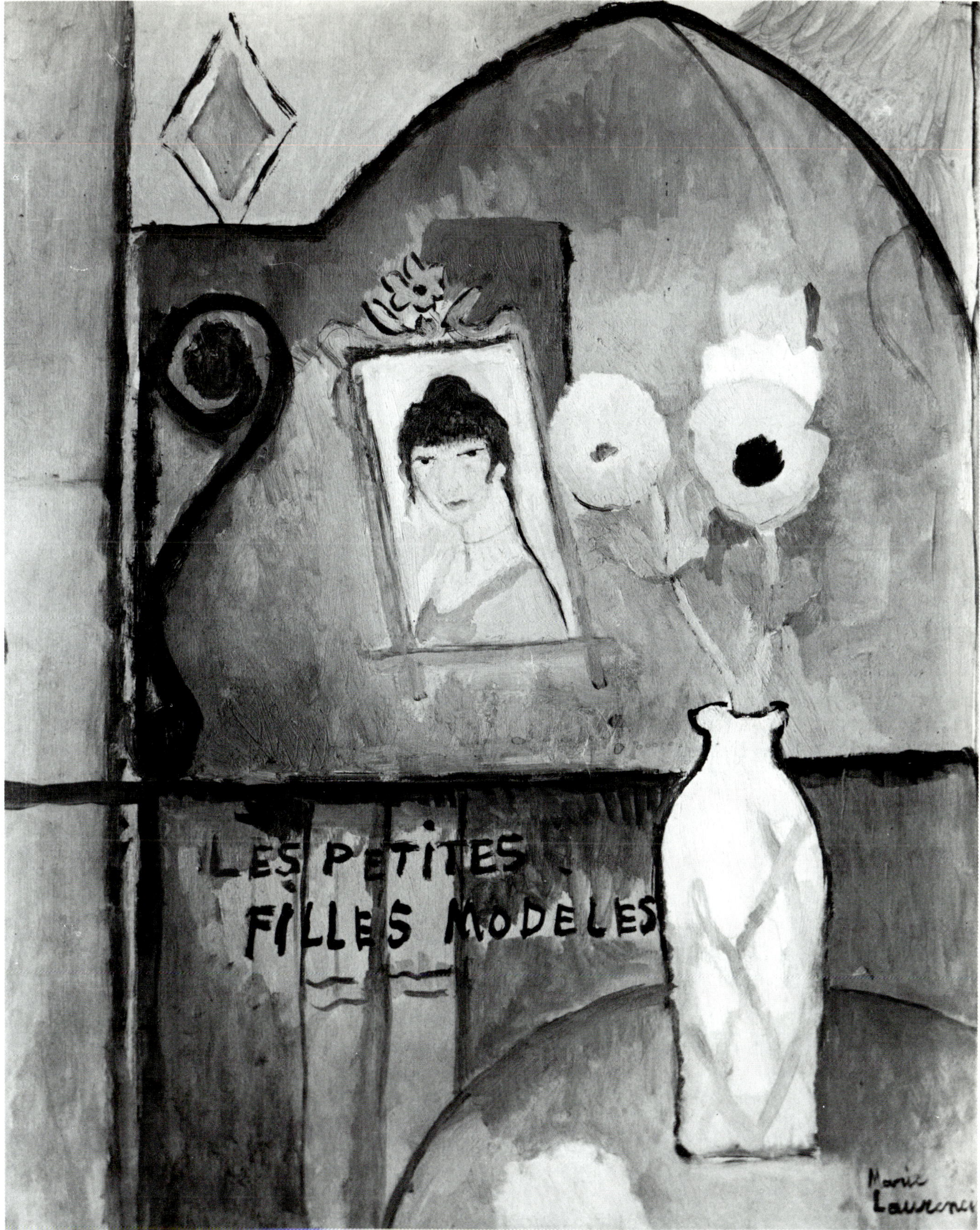

Opposite above
Maison meublée
Oil on canvas, 114.2 × 146 cm. (Ex. coll. Armand Lowengard)

Opposite below
Deux jeunes filles au bateau/Two Young Girls in a Boat, 1913
Watercolour, 19 × 22.8 cm. (Sotheby Parke Bernet & Co.)

Above
Les Petites Filles Modèles/Little Girl Models, 1913
Oil on canvas, 53.3 × 41.9 cm. (Philadelphia Museum of Art, A. E. Gallatin Coll.)

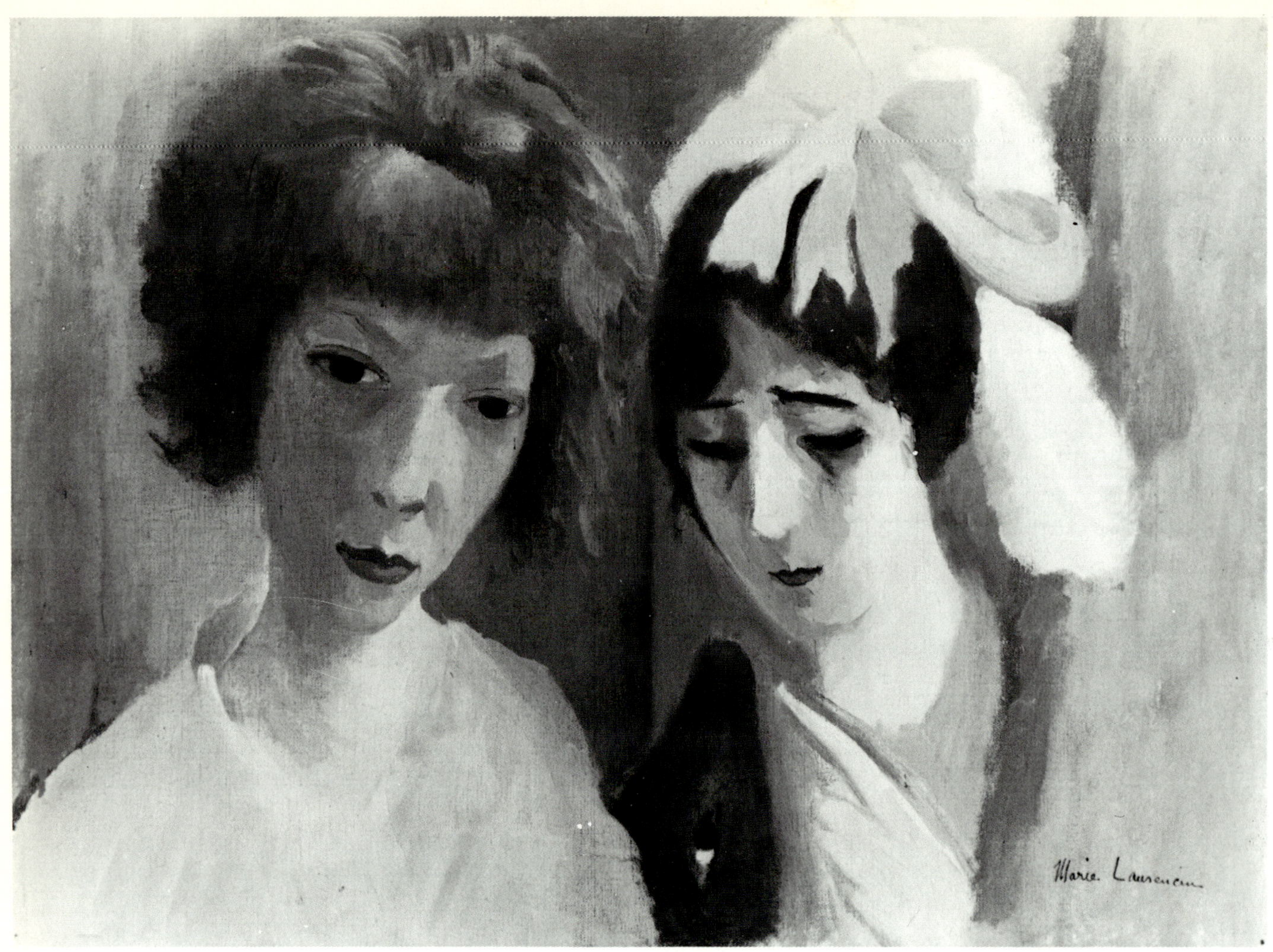

Deux filles/Two Girls (Cecilia de Madrazo and the artist), 1915
Oil on canvas, 33 × 46.9 cm. (Tate Gallery, London)

Opposite
L'Italienne/The Italian Girl, 1925
Oil on canvas (Ex. coll. Albert Flament)

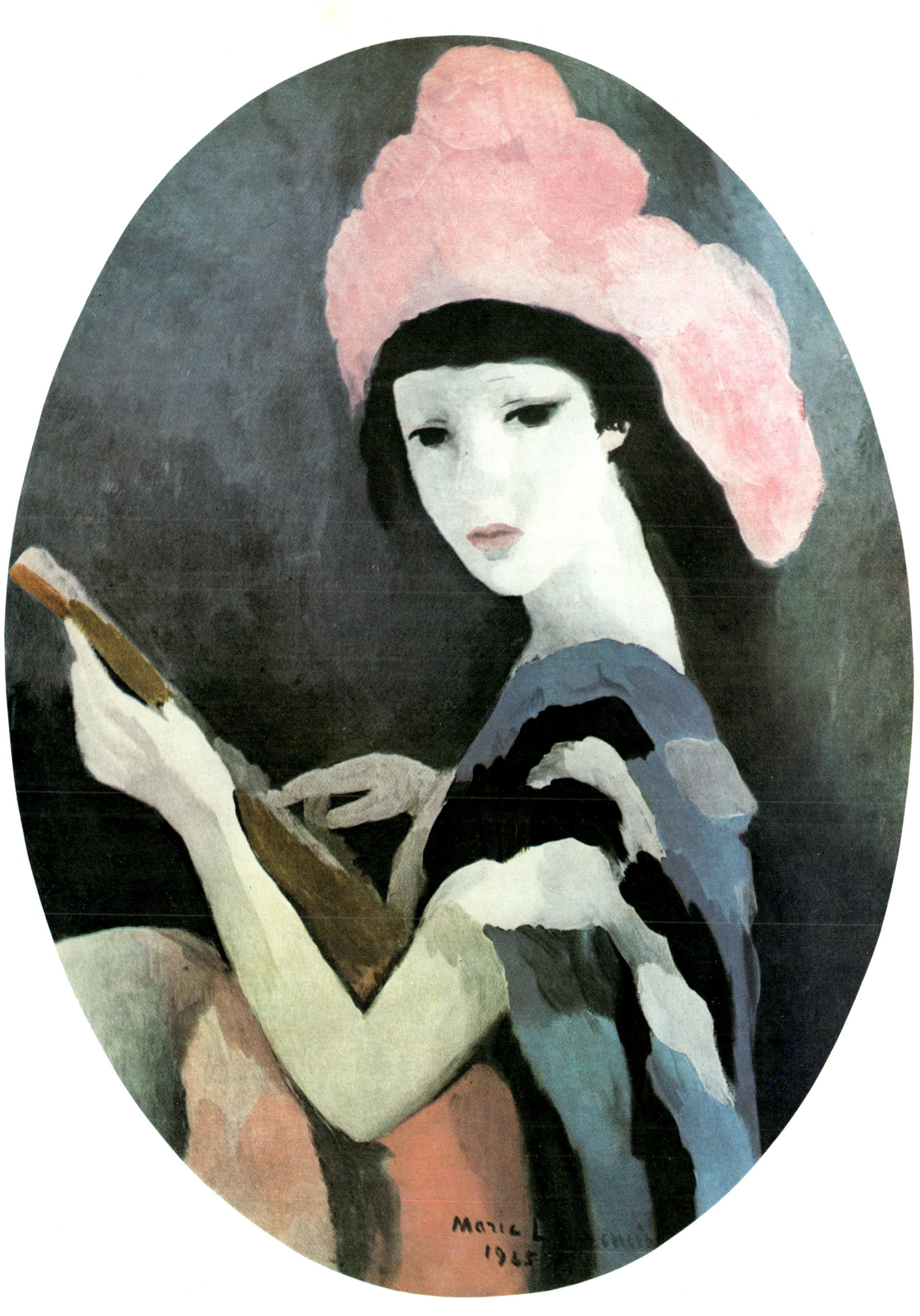

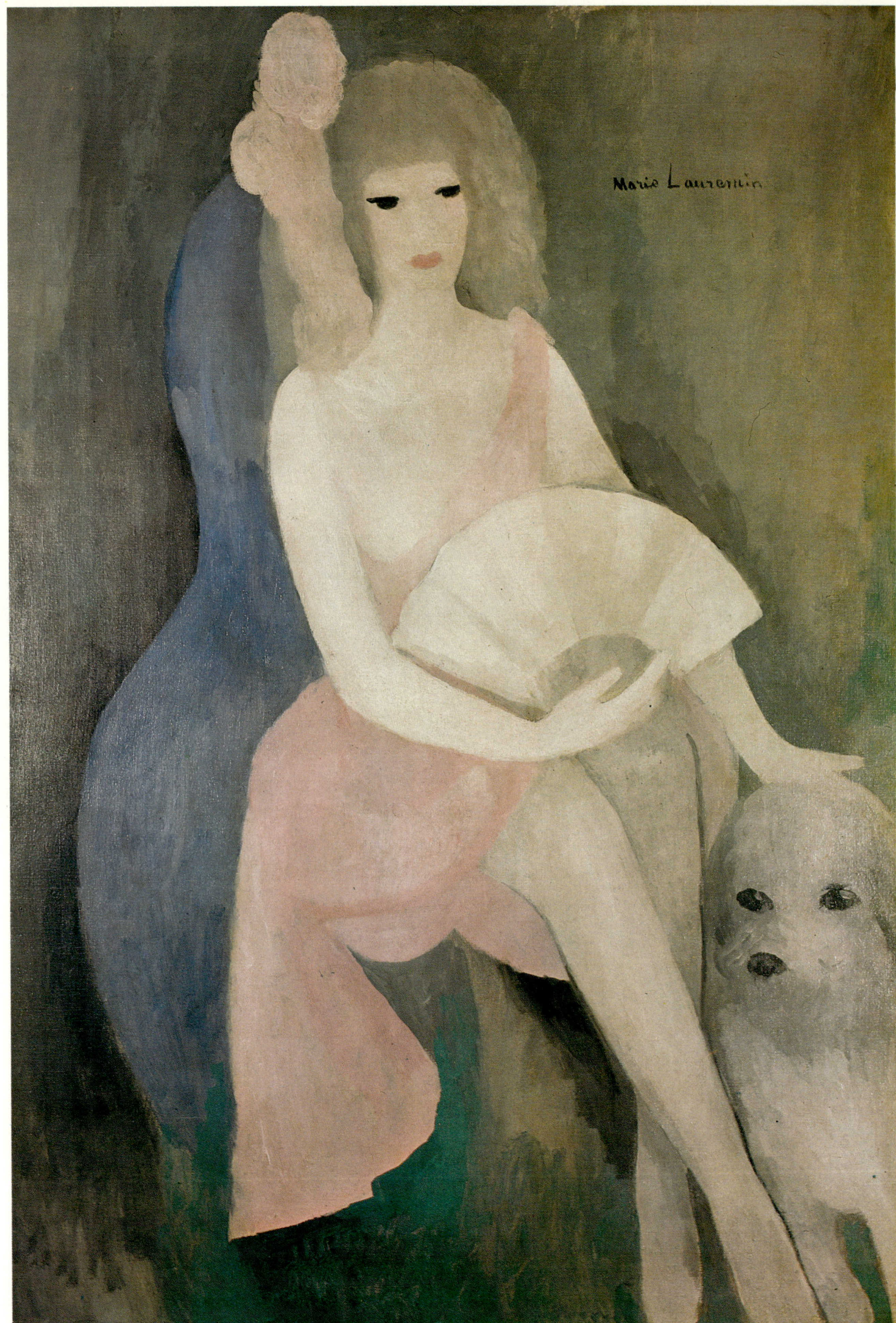
Marie Laurencin

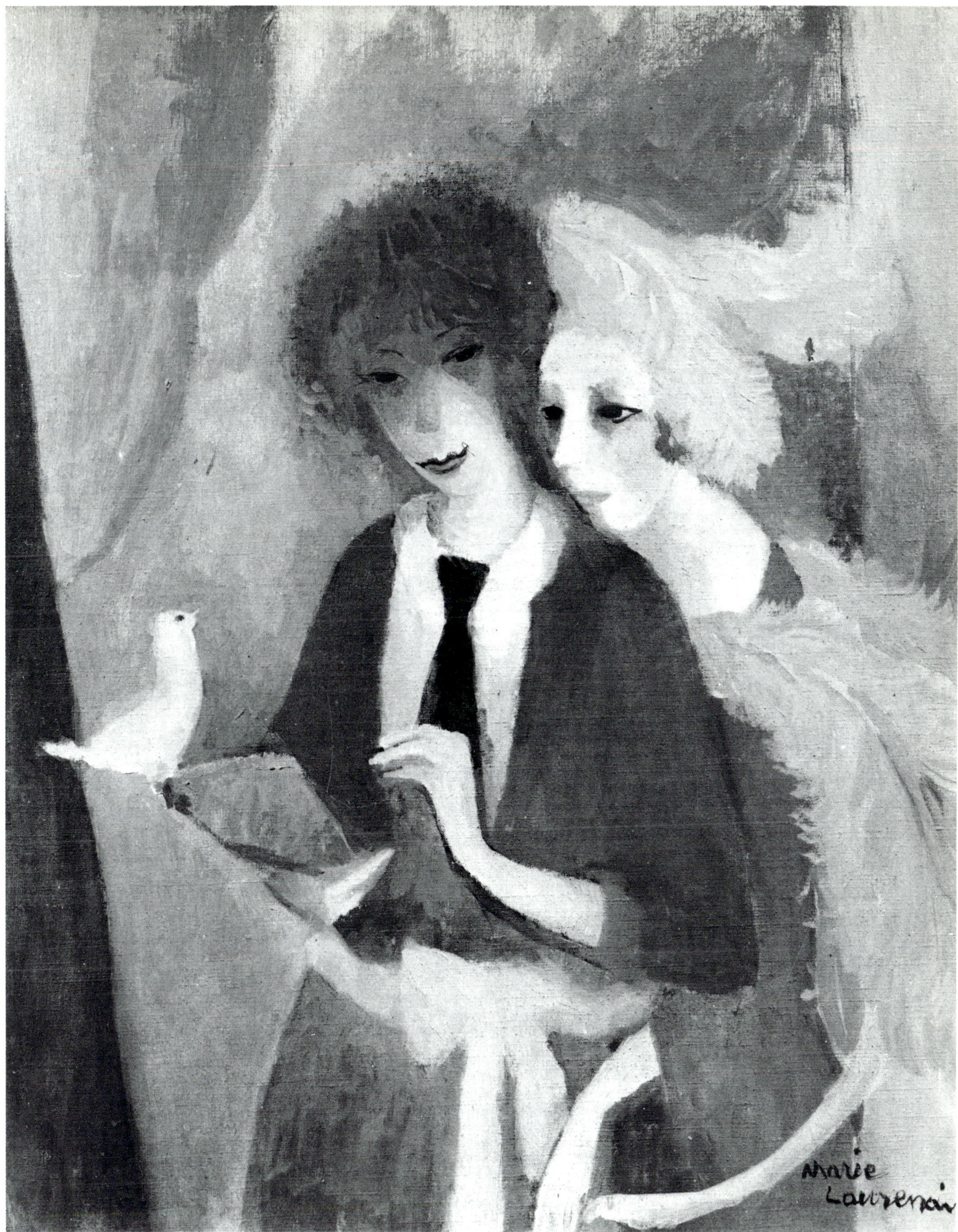

Opposite
Jeune Femme à l'éventail/Young Woman with a Fan, 1924
Oil on canvas (Coll. of the late Robert Oppenheim)

Above
Femme à la colombe/Two women with a Dove, *c.* 1918
Oil on canvas (Musée National d'Art Moderne, Paris)

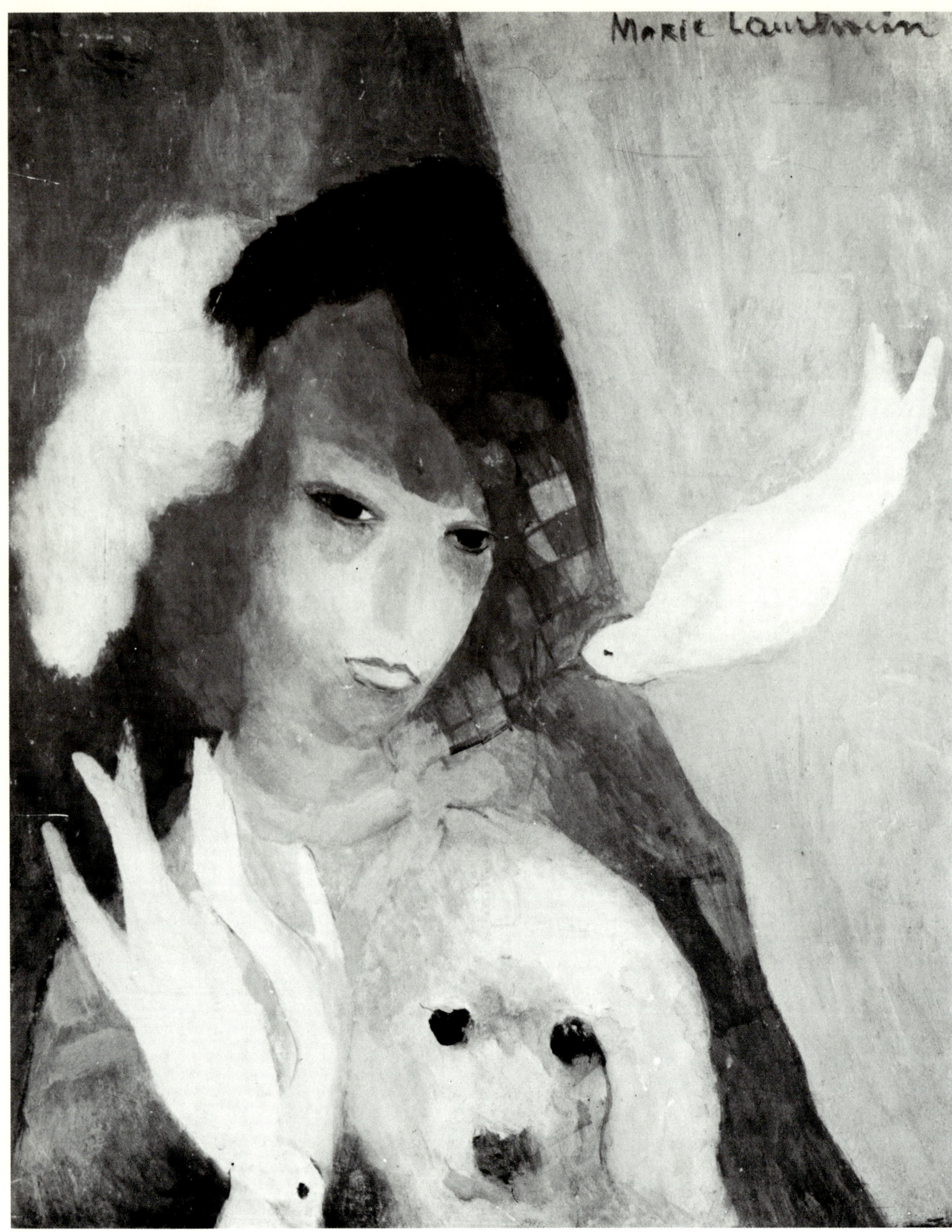

Jeune Fille au chien et aux colombes/Young Girl with a Dog and Doves, *c.* 1920
Oil on panel, 44.5 × 36.8 cm.

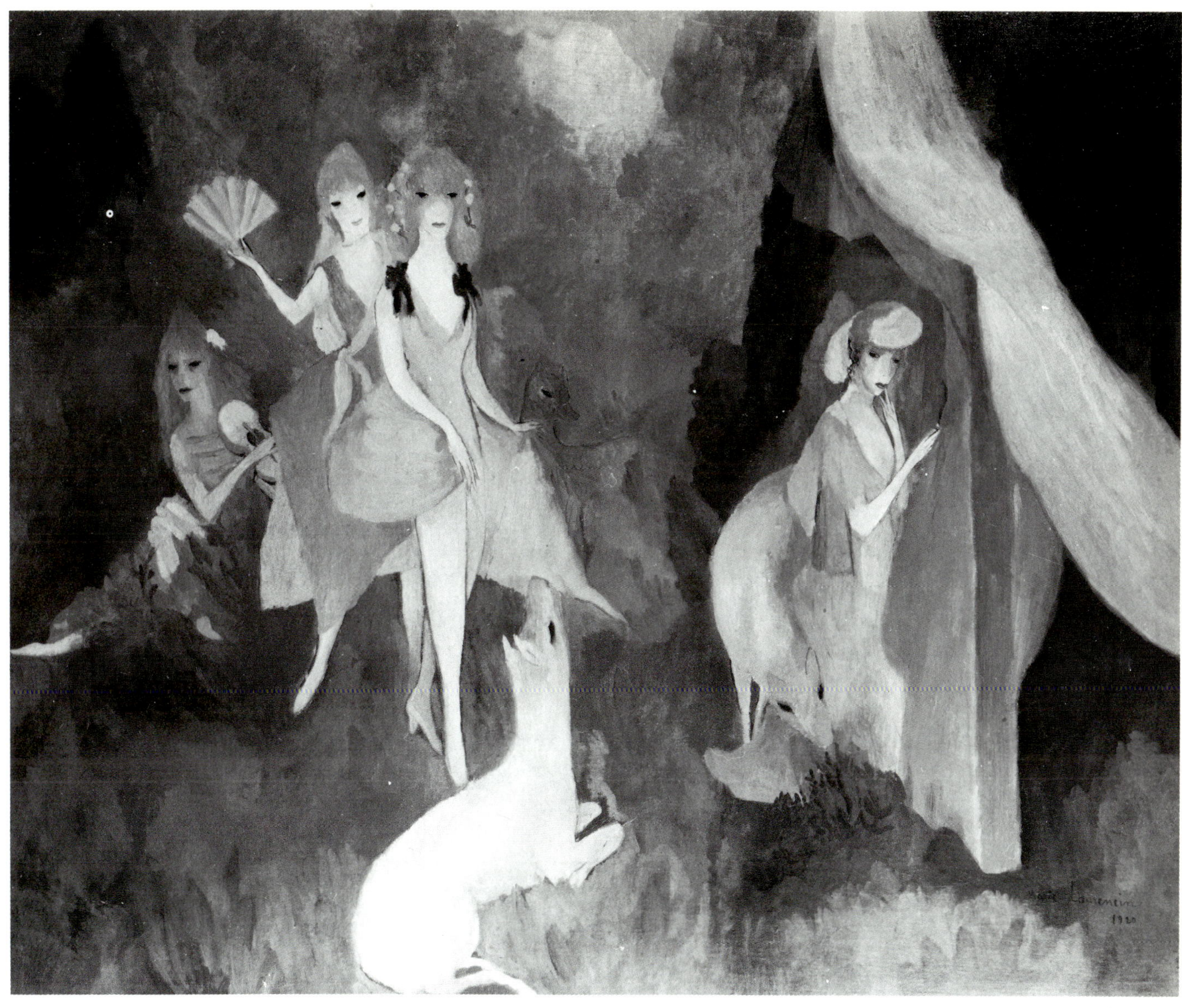

Femmes dans la forêt/Women in the Forest, 1920
Oil on canvas, 81 × 100 cm. (Armand Hammer Coll., U.S.A.)

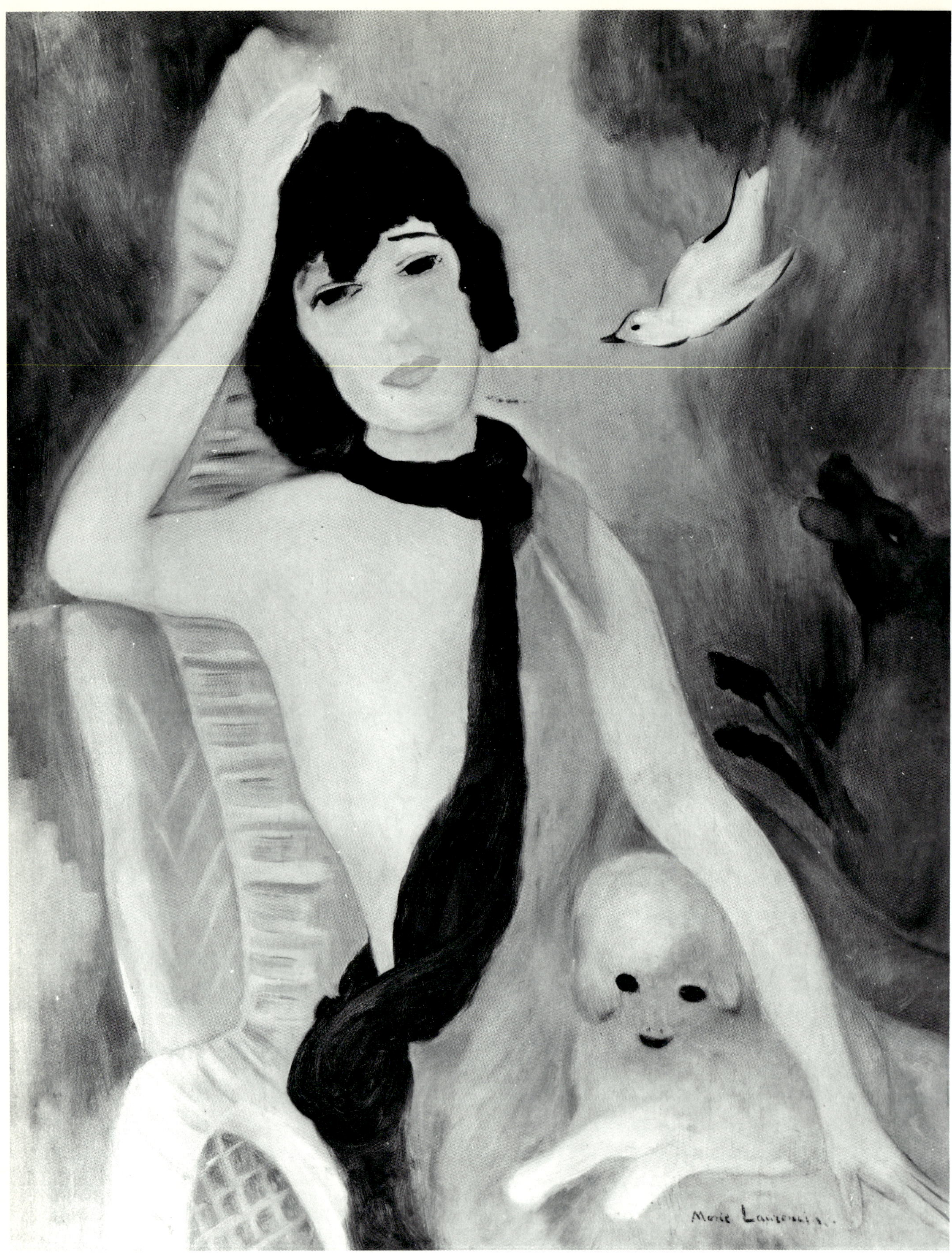

Femme au foulard brun/Woman in a Brown Scarf (Version of the portrait of Mlle. Chanel), 1922
Oil on canvas, 81 × 59.5 cm. (Christie's, London)

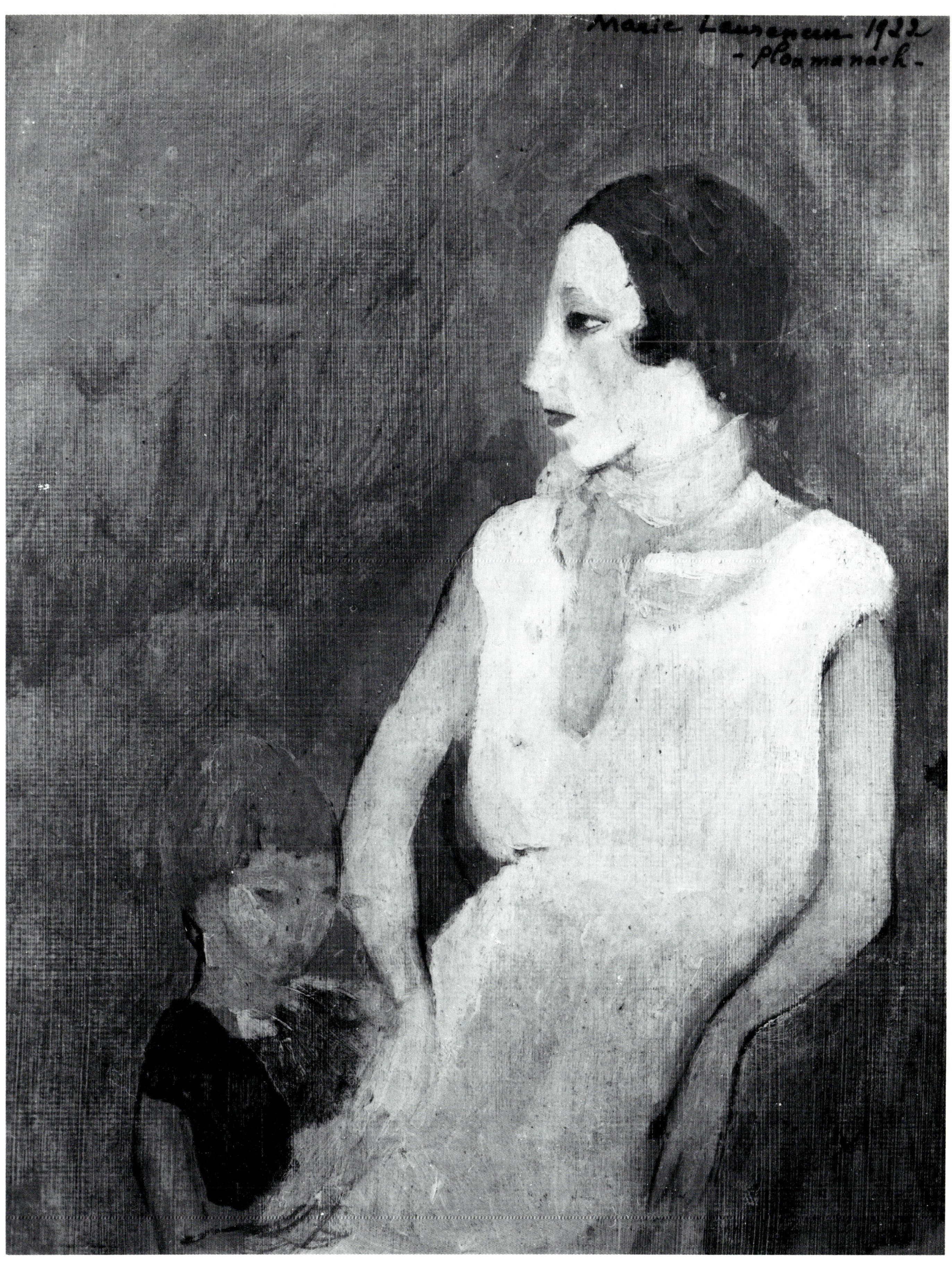

Portrait of Mme. Nicole Groult/Portrait of Mme. Nicole Groult, 1922
Oil on canvas, 25.5 × 21 cm. (Christie's, London)

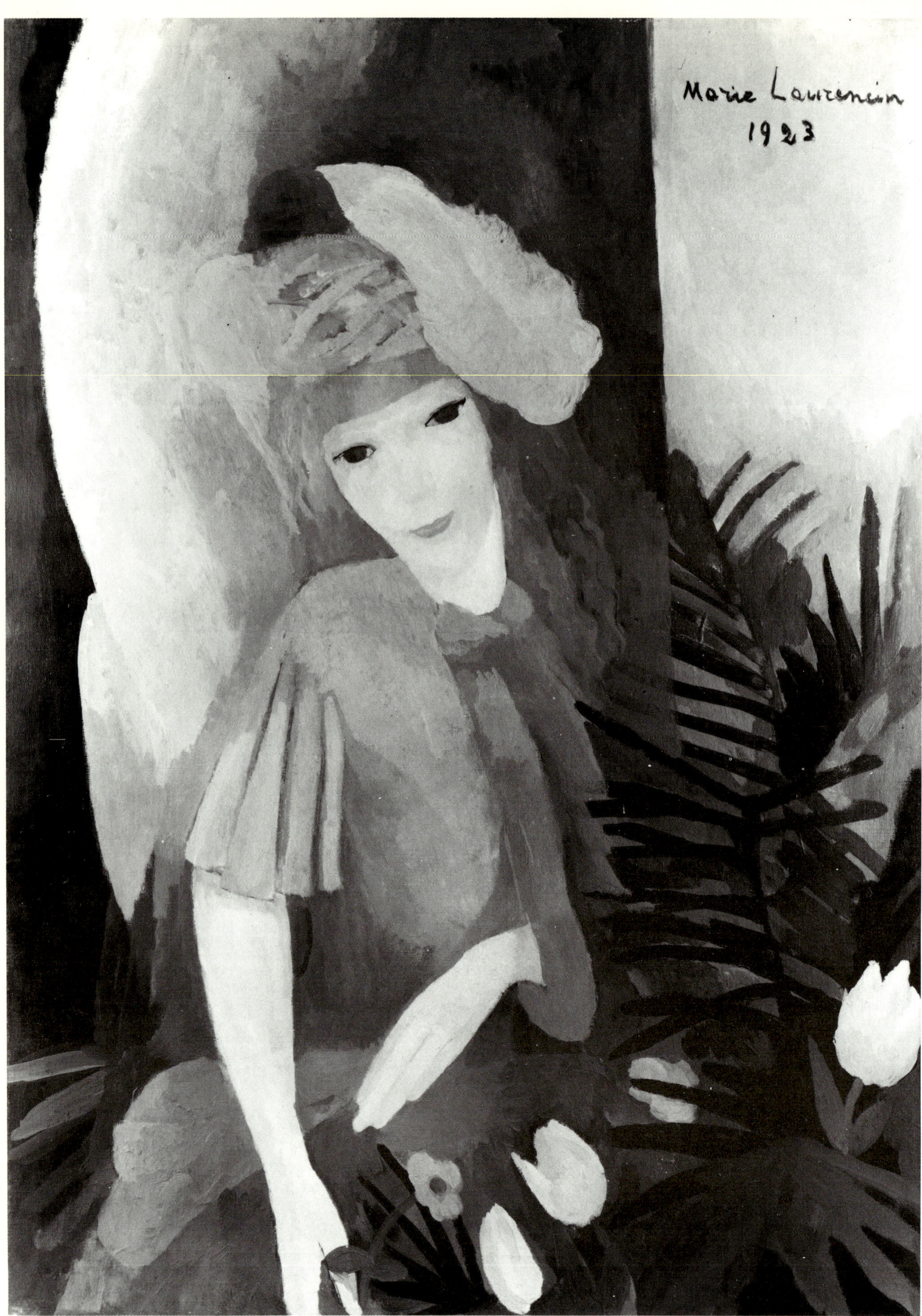

La Sultane/The Sultana, *c.* 1923
Oil on canvas, 80 × 58.5 cm.

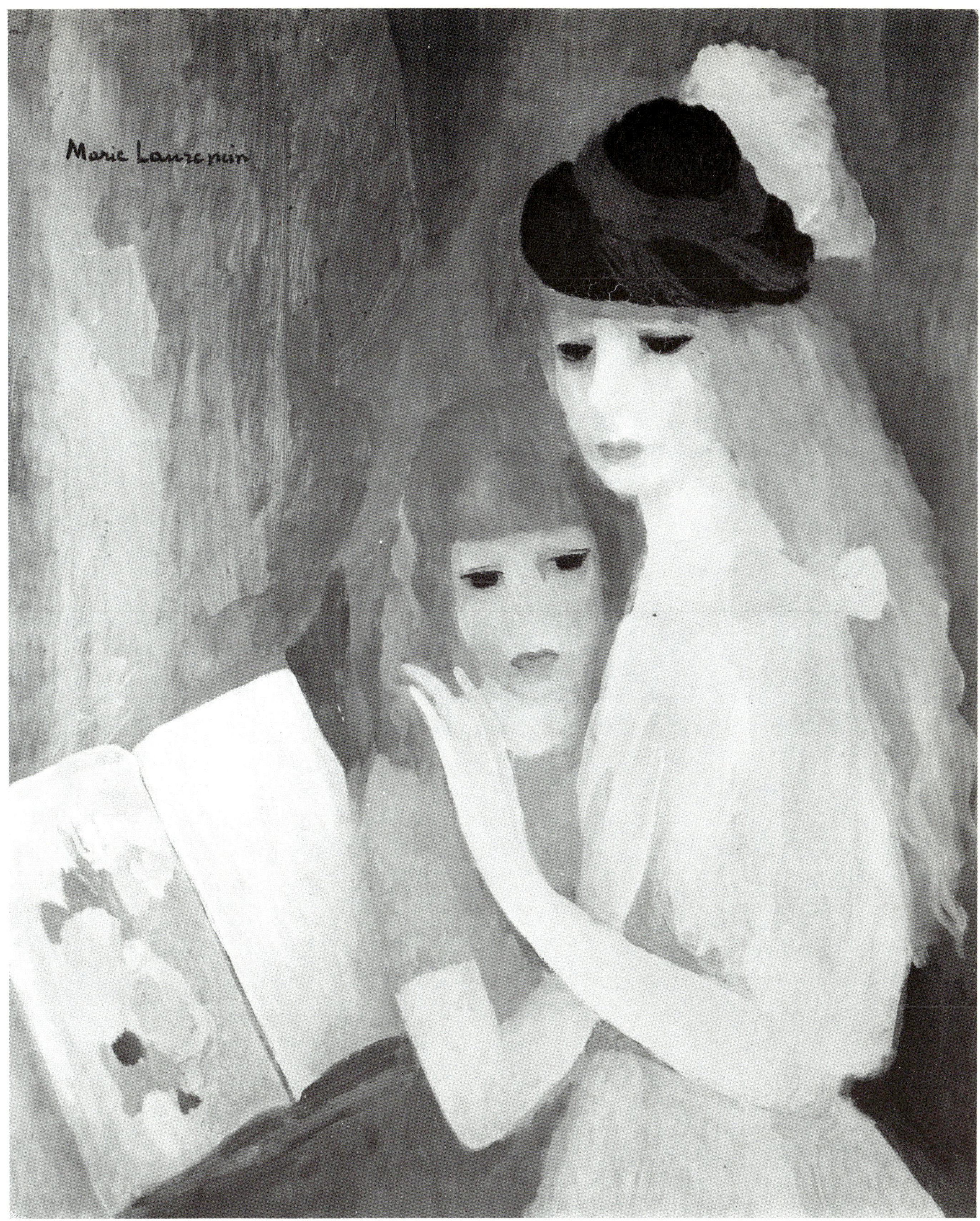

La Lecture/Reading, 1924
Oil on canvas, 64 × 54 cm. (Christie's, London)

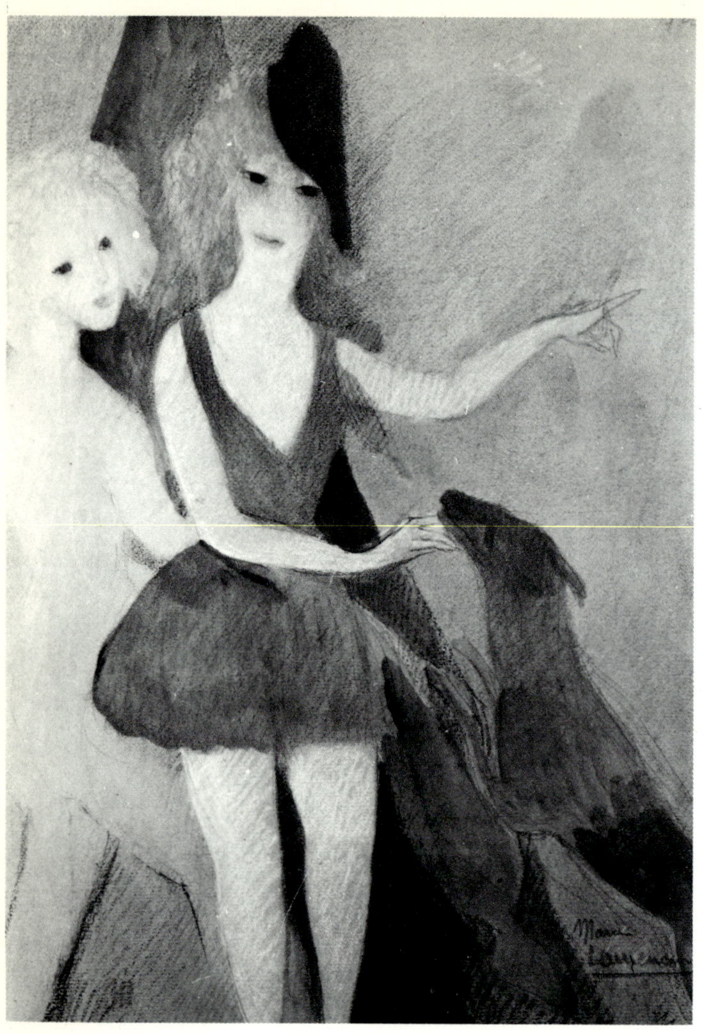

Deux jeunes filles jouant avec leurs chiens/Two Young Girls playing with their Dogs, *c.* 1923
Coloured crayons and wash, 33.6 × 24 cm.

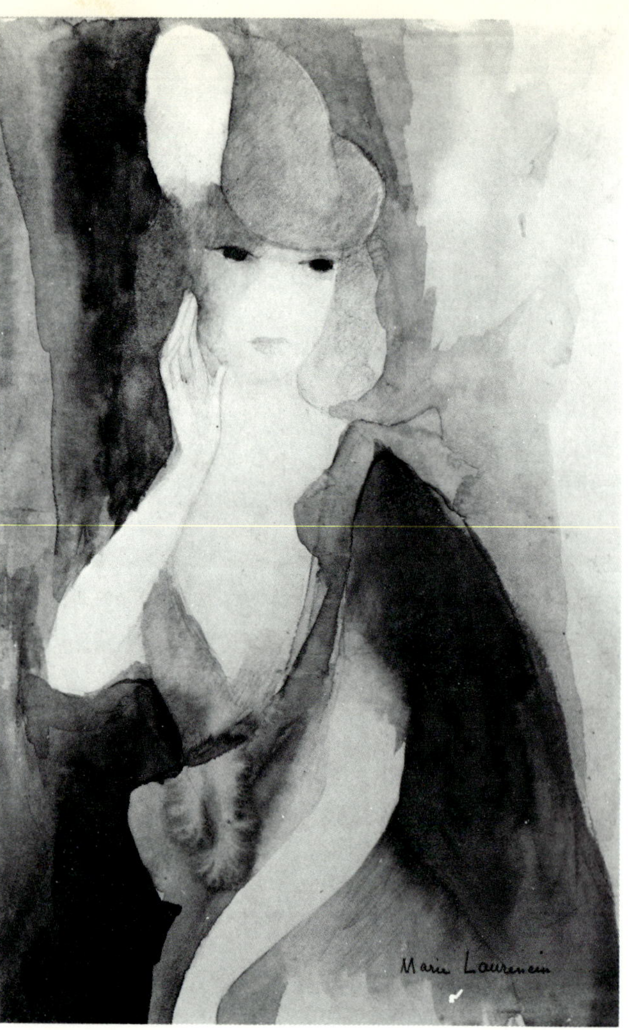

Jeune Fille/Young Girl, *c.* 1923
Watercolour, 31 × 26 cm.

Opposite
Vase de fleurs/Vase of Flowers, 1925
Oil on canvas (Galerie Motte, Geneva)

Pages 46–47
Jeune Fille aux anémones/Young Girl with Anemones, *c.* 1928
Oil on canvas, 54 × 81 cm. (Galerie Motte, Geneva)

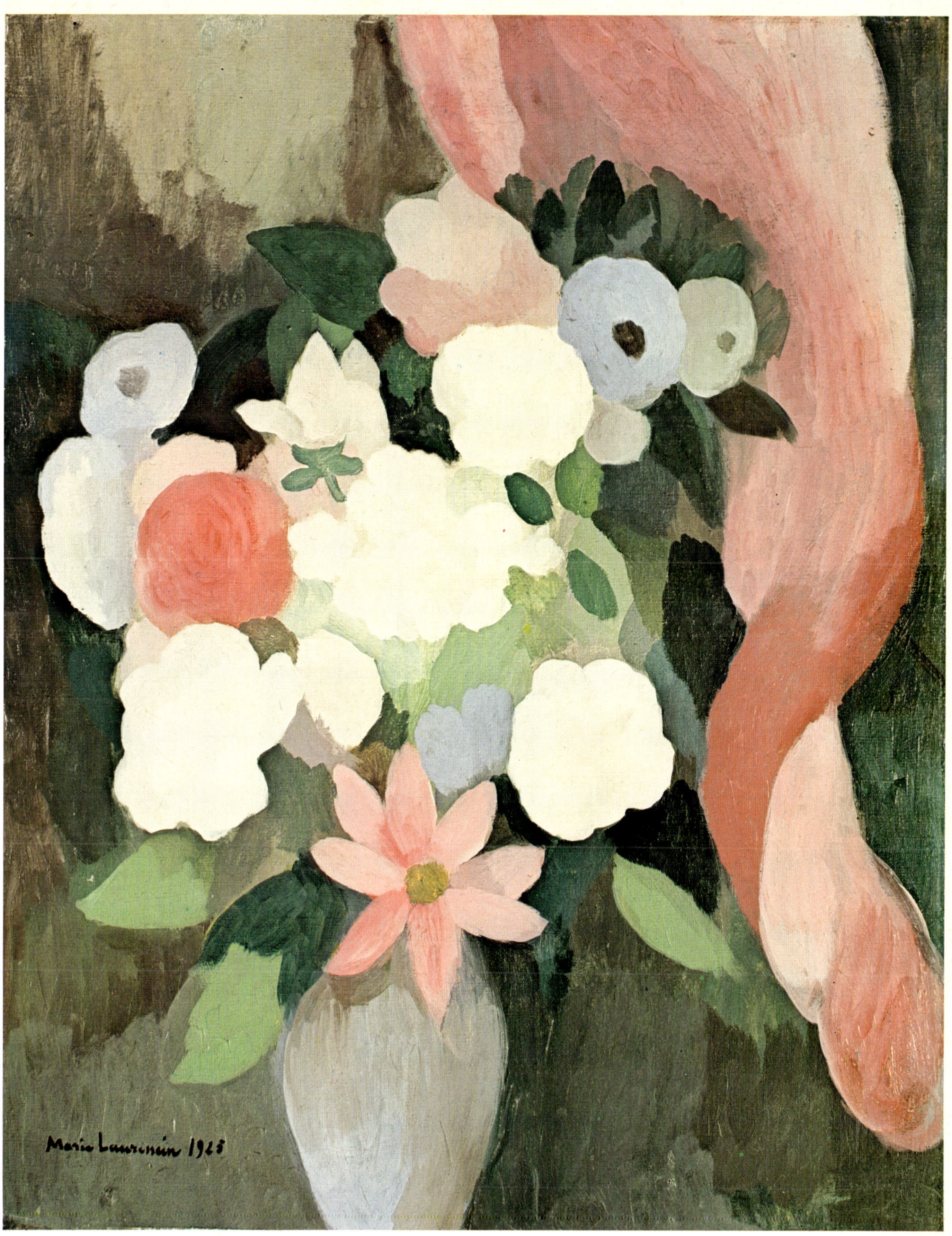
Marie Laurencin 1925

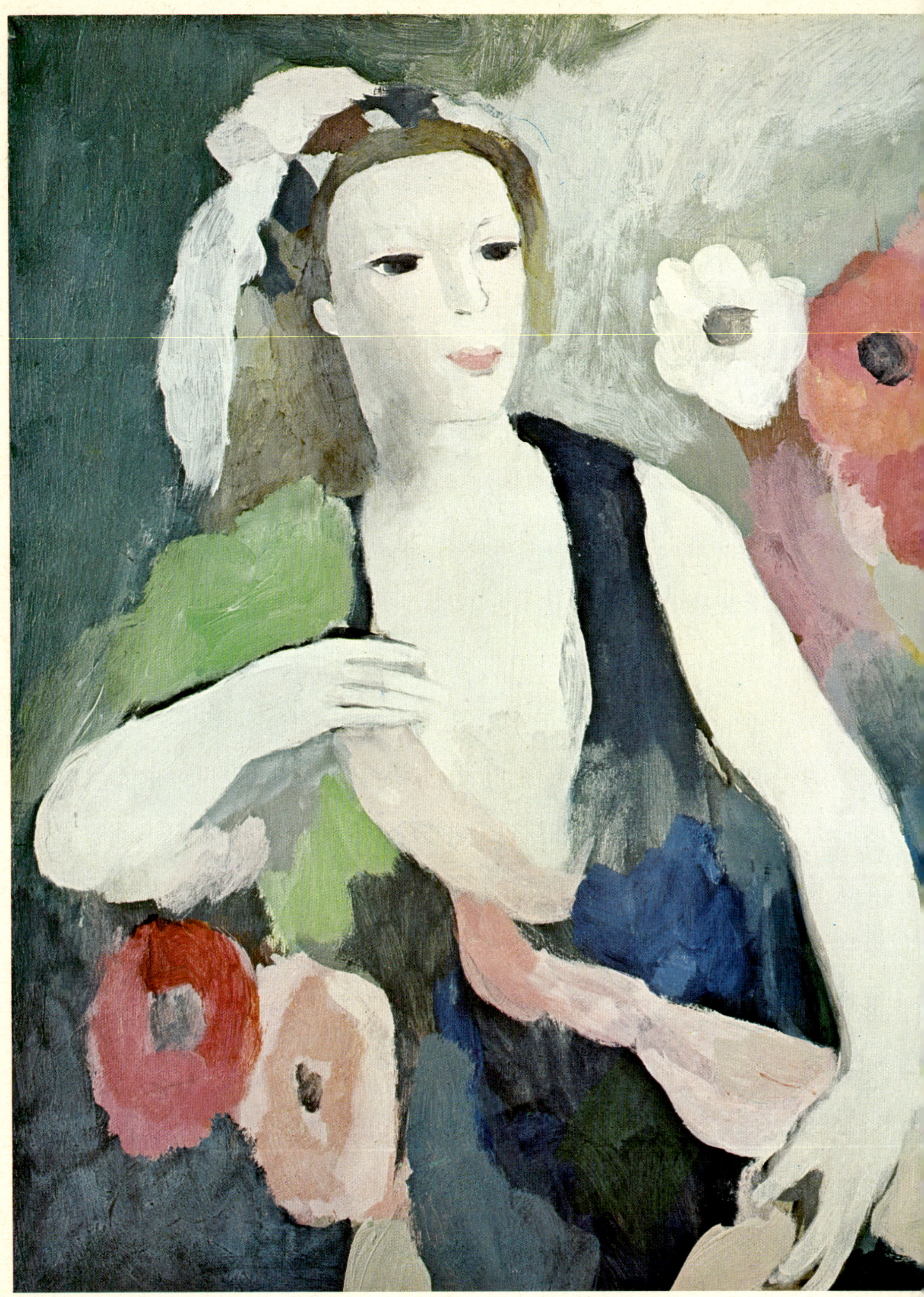

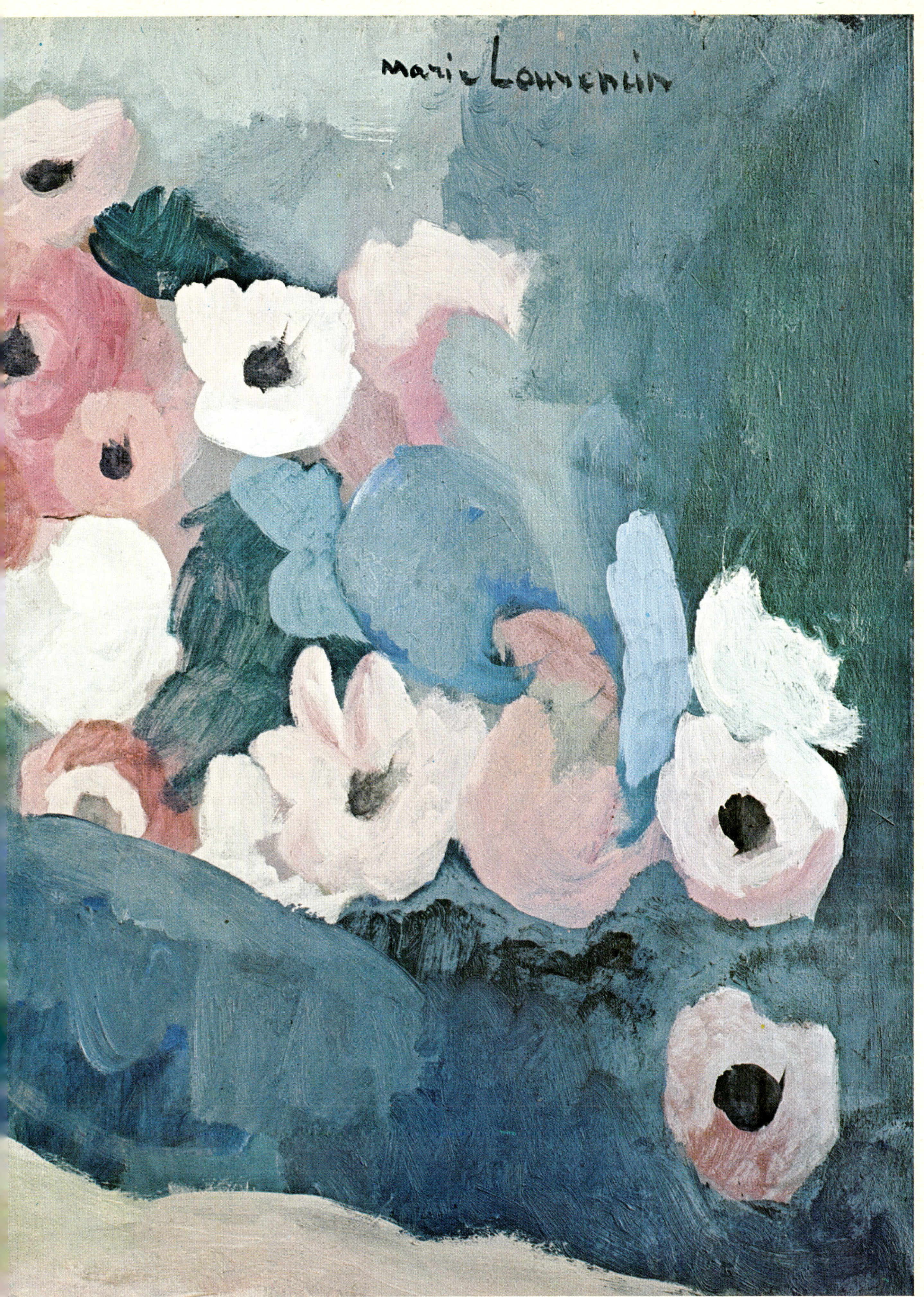
marie Laurencin

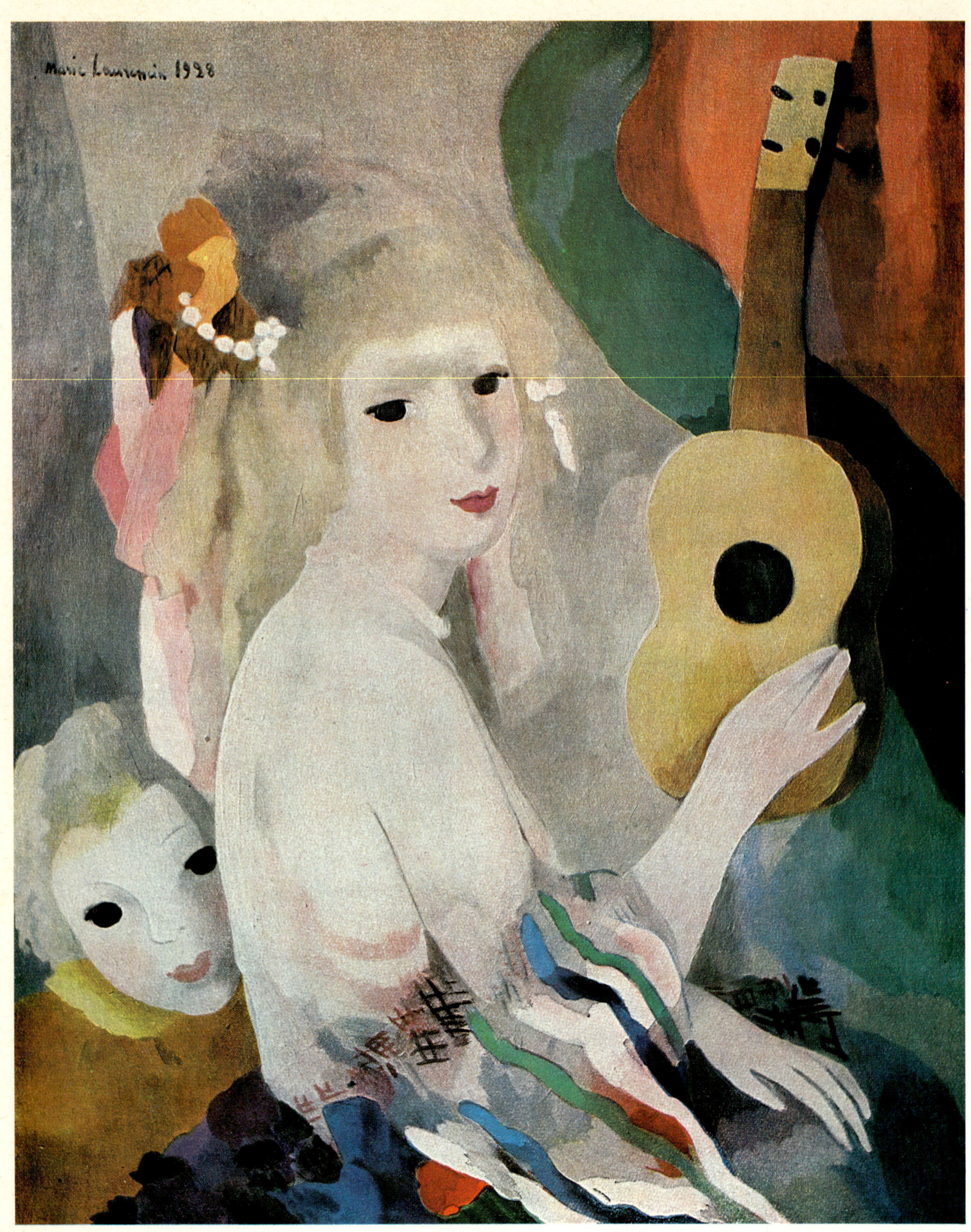
Marie Laurencin 1928

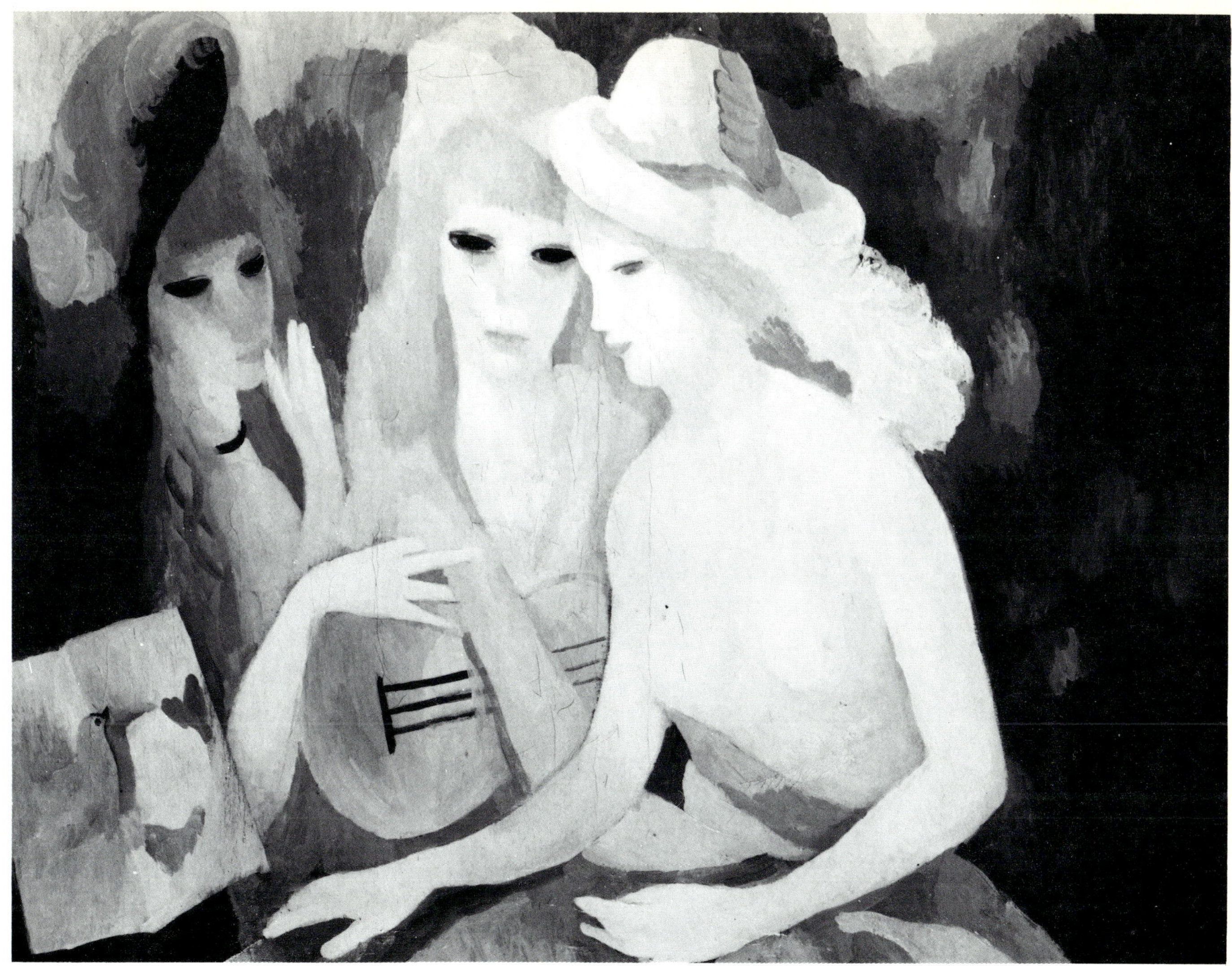

La Musique/Music, 1924
Oil on canvas, 70.5 × 91 cm. (Ex. Leicester Galleries)

Opposite
Arabesque, 1928
Oil on canvas

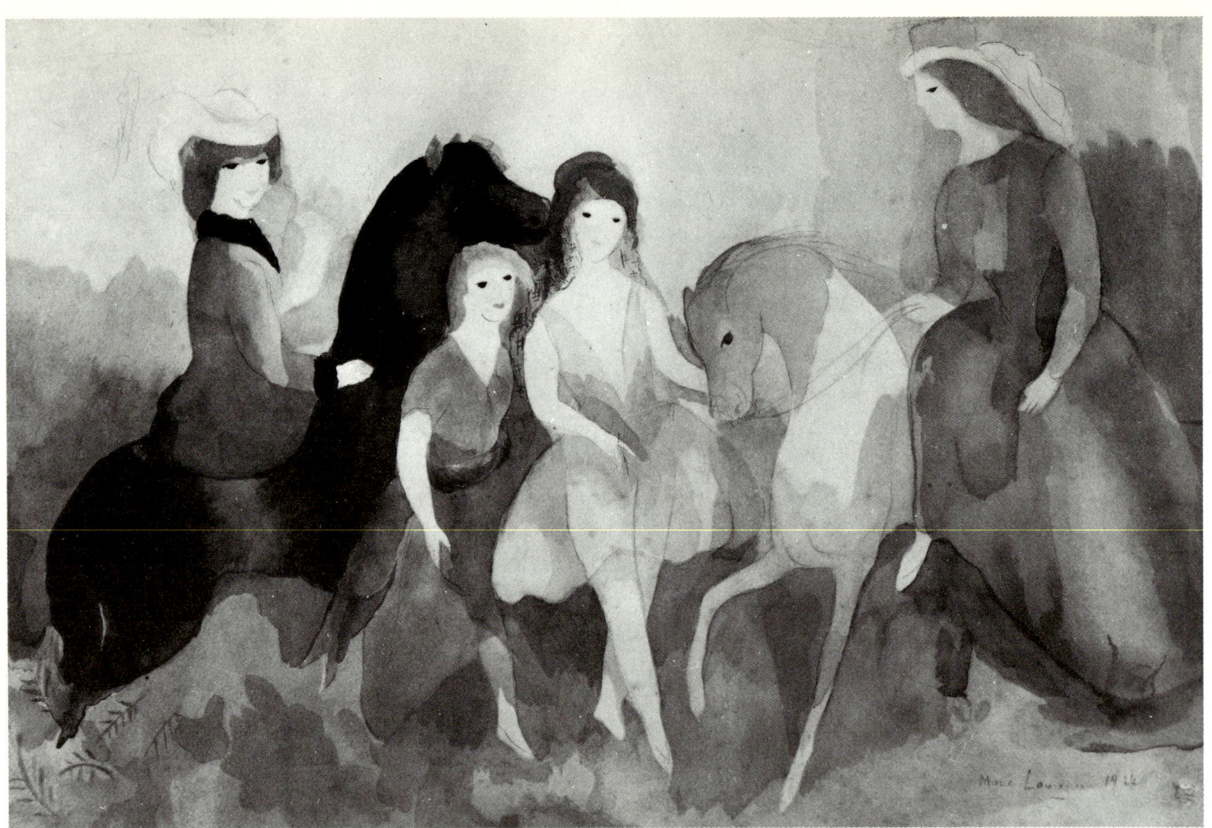

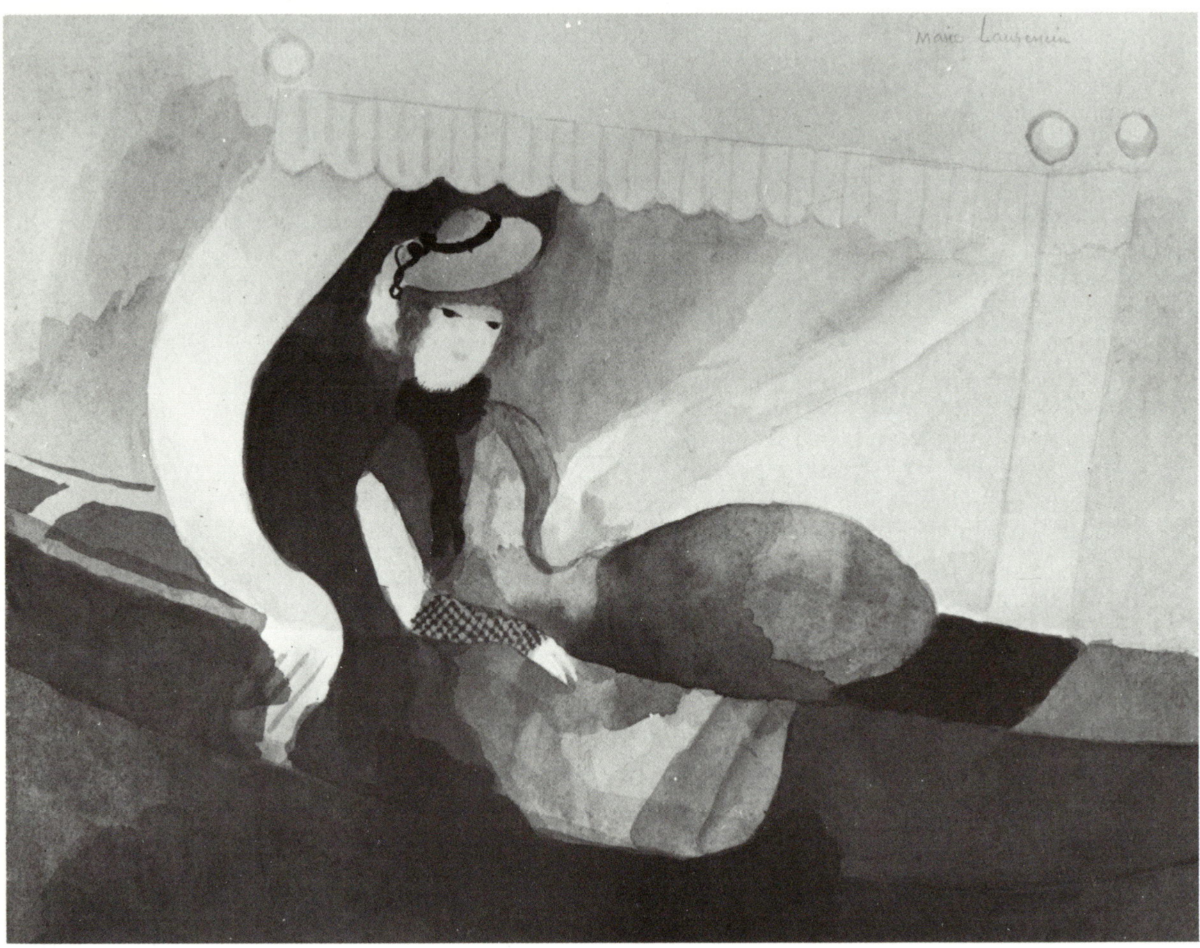

Deux jeunes filles et deux amazones/Two Young Girls and Two Women on Horseback, 1924
Watercolour, 25.5 × 37.5 cm. (Christie's, London)

Jeune Fille au bateau/Girl in a Boat, *c.* 1925
Watercolour over pencil, 18.8 × 24.8 cm. (The Metropolitan Museum of Art, New York, Bequest of Miss Adelaide Milton de Groot (1876–1967), 1967)

Opposite
Nymphe et biche/Nymph and Hind, 1925
Oil on canvas, 71 × 52 cm. (Philadelphia Museum of Art, gift of Mr & Mrs Herbert Cameron Morris)

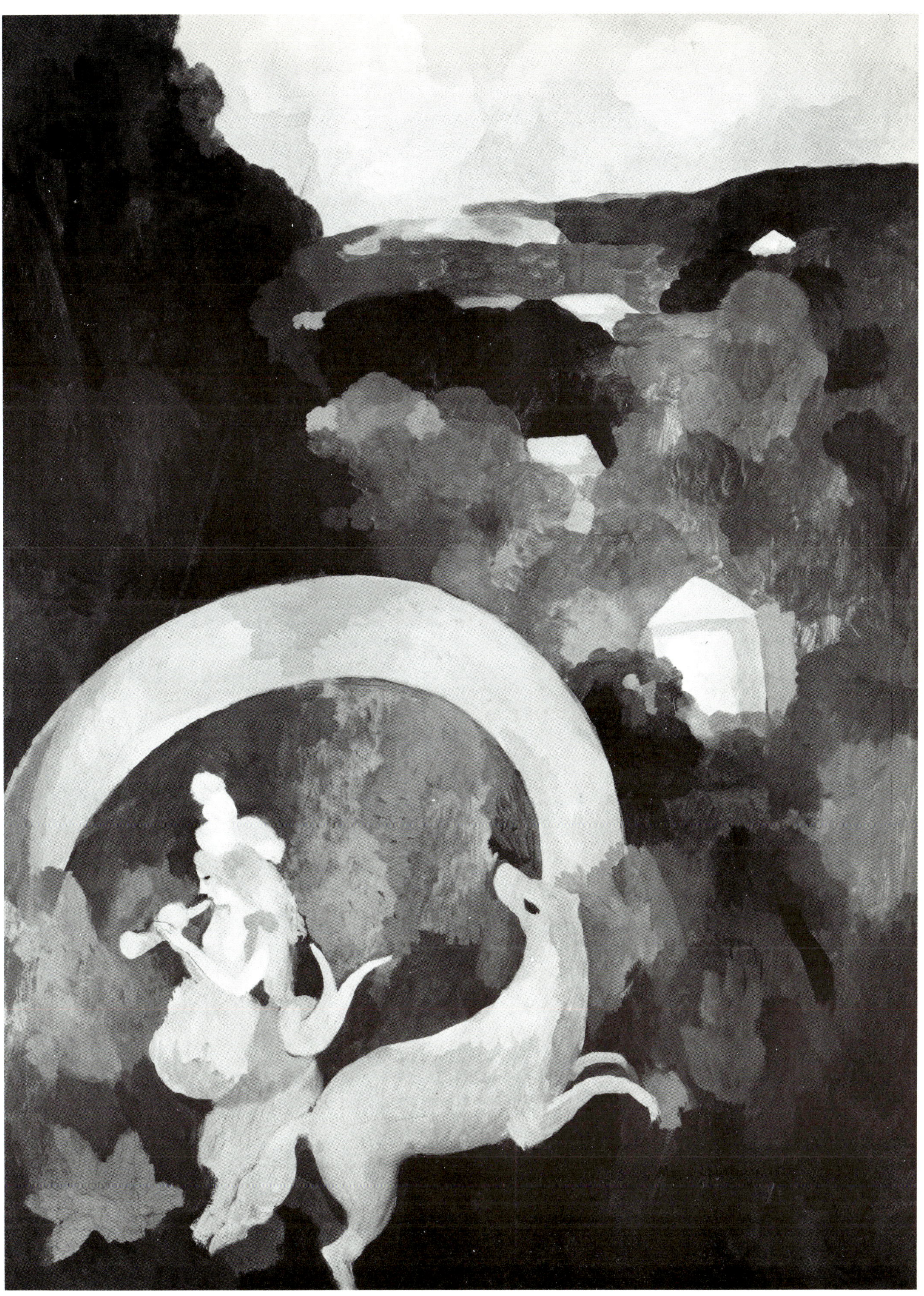

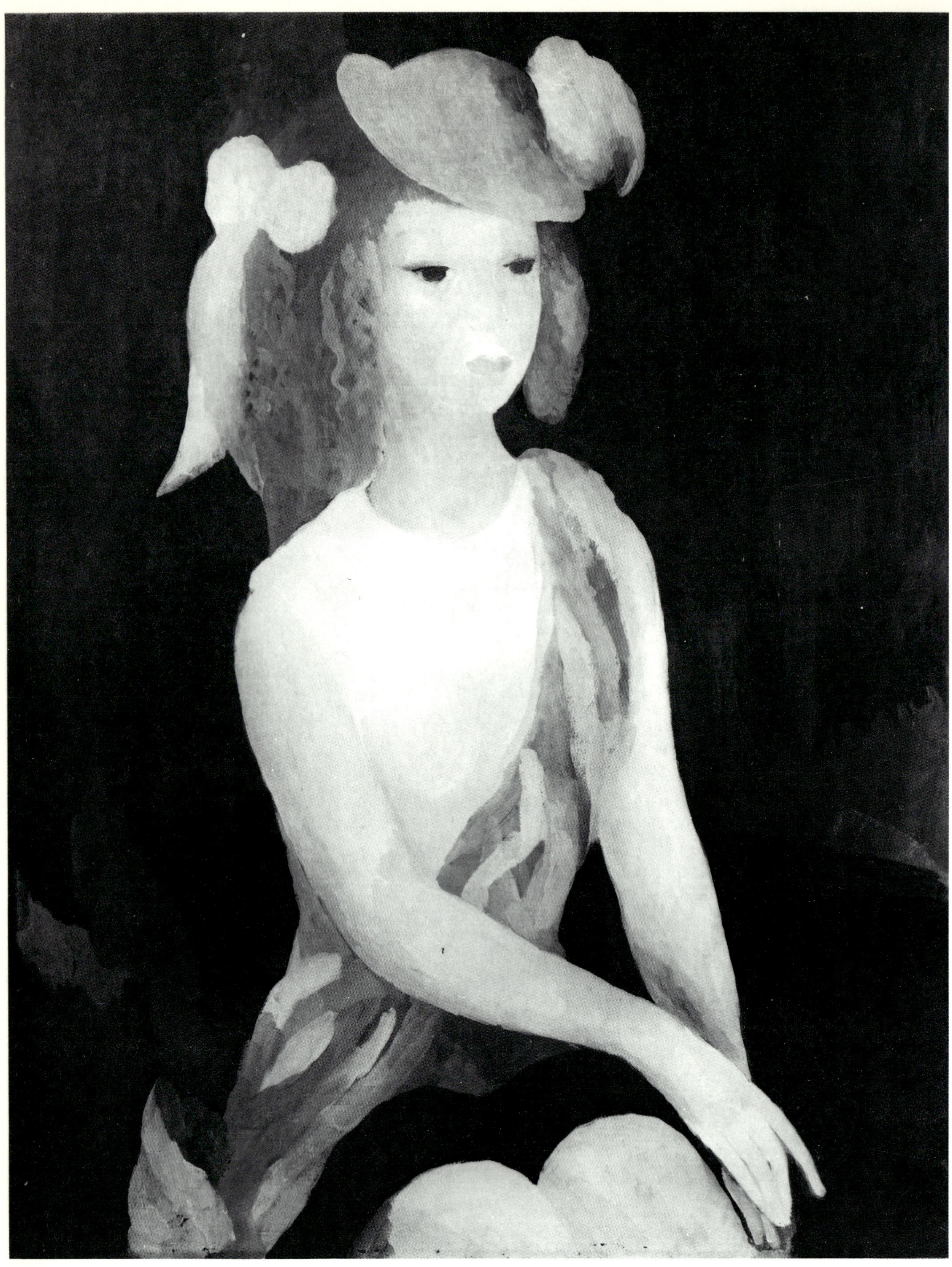

Jeune Fille assise/Young Girl Seated, 1925
Oil on canvas, 79 × 63.5 cm.

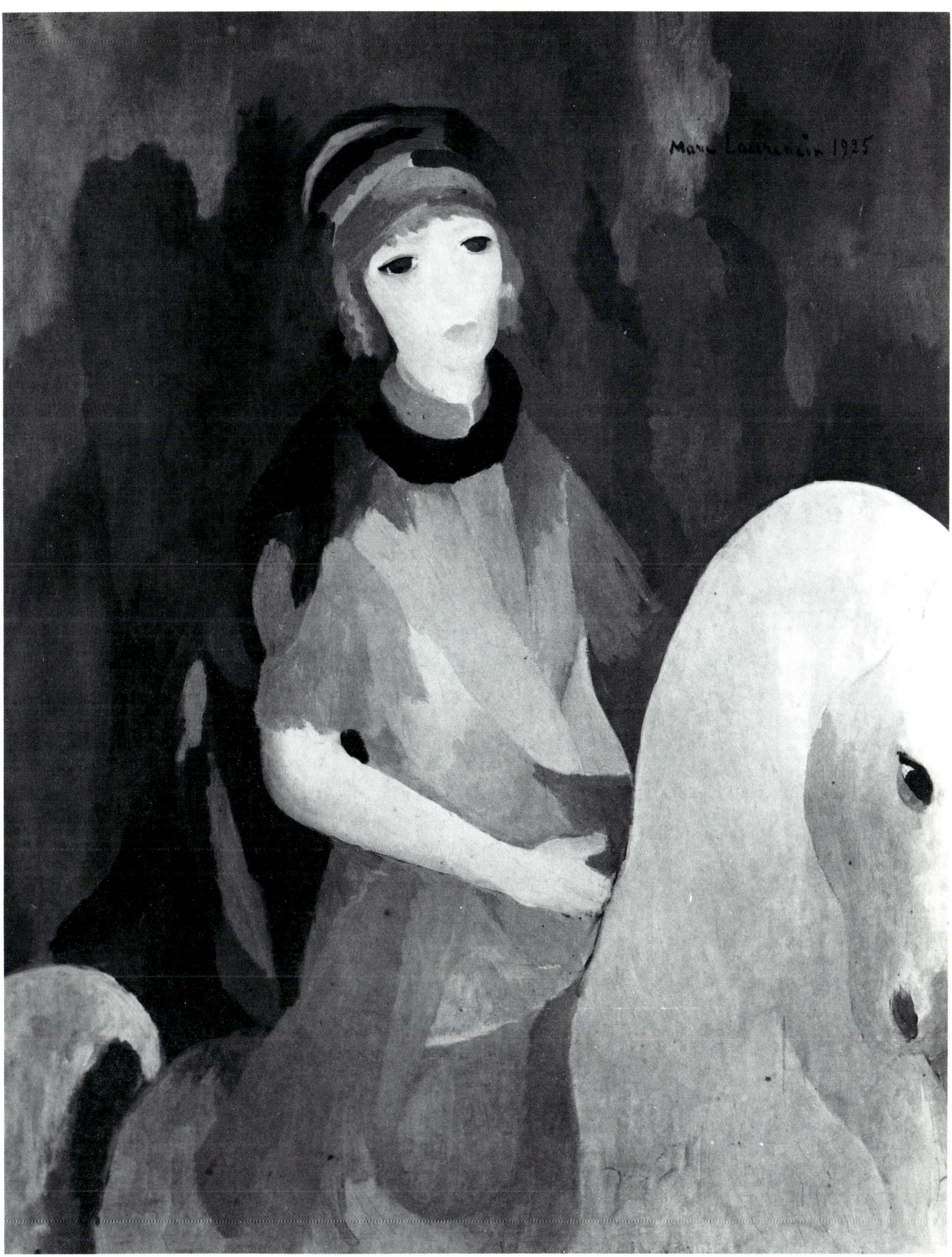

Emerald, Lady Cunard, 1925
Oil on canvas, 90 × 70 cm. (Ex. coll. Armand Lowengard)

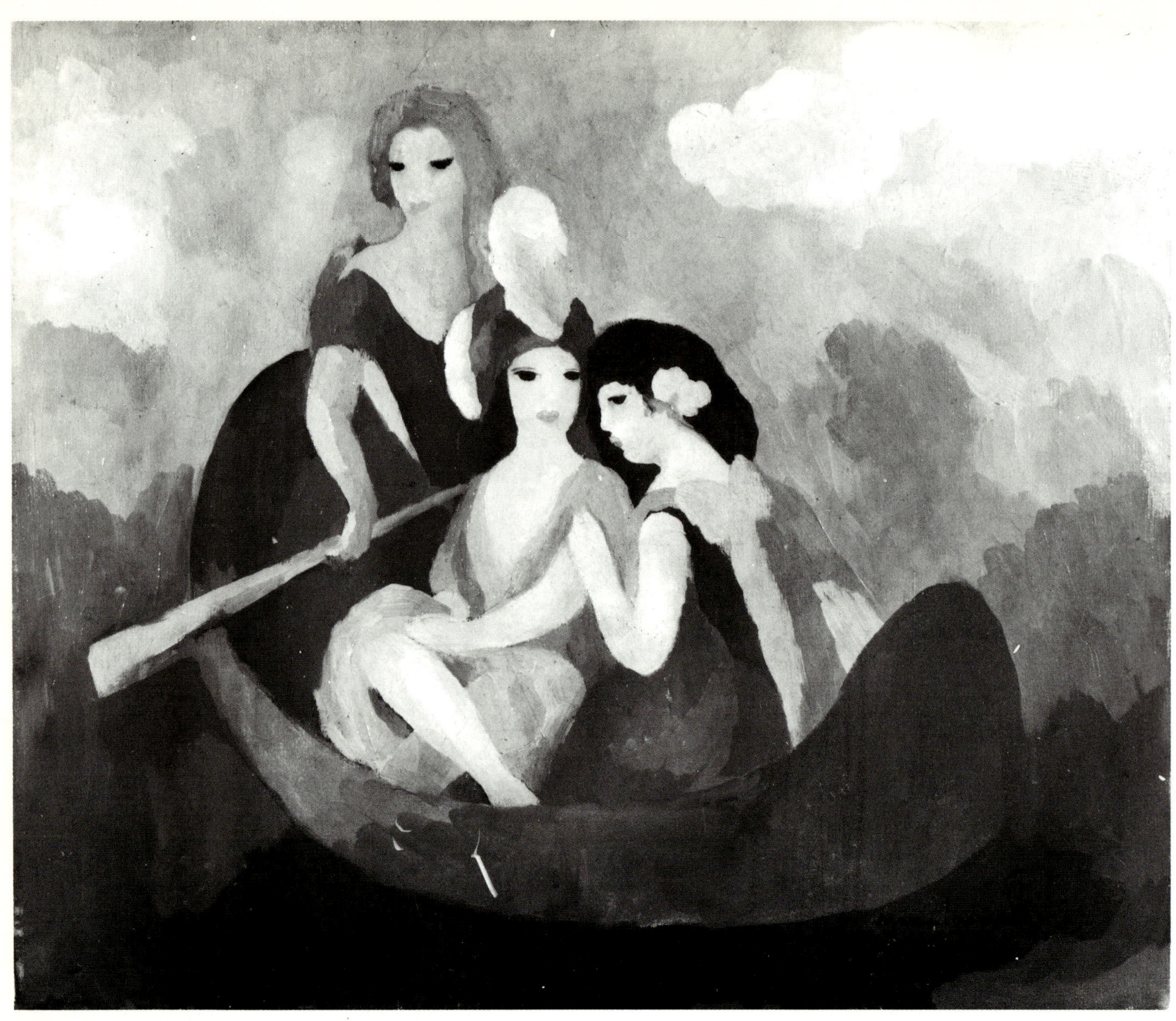

La Barque/The Boat, 1926
Oil on canvas, 45 × 55 cm. (Ex. coll. Somerset Maugham)

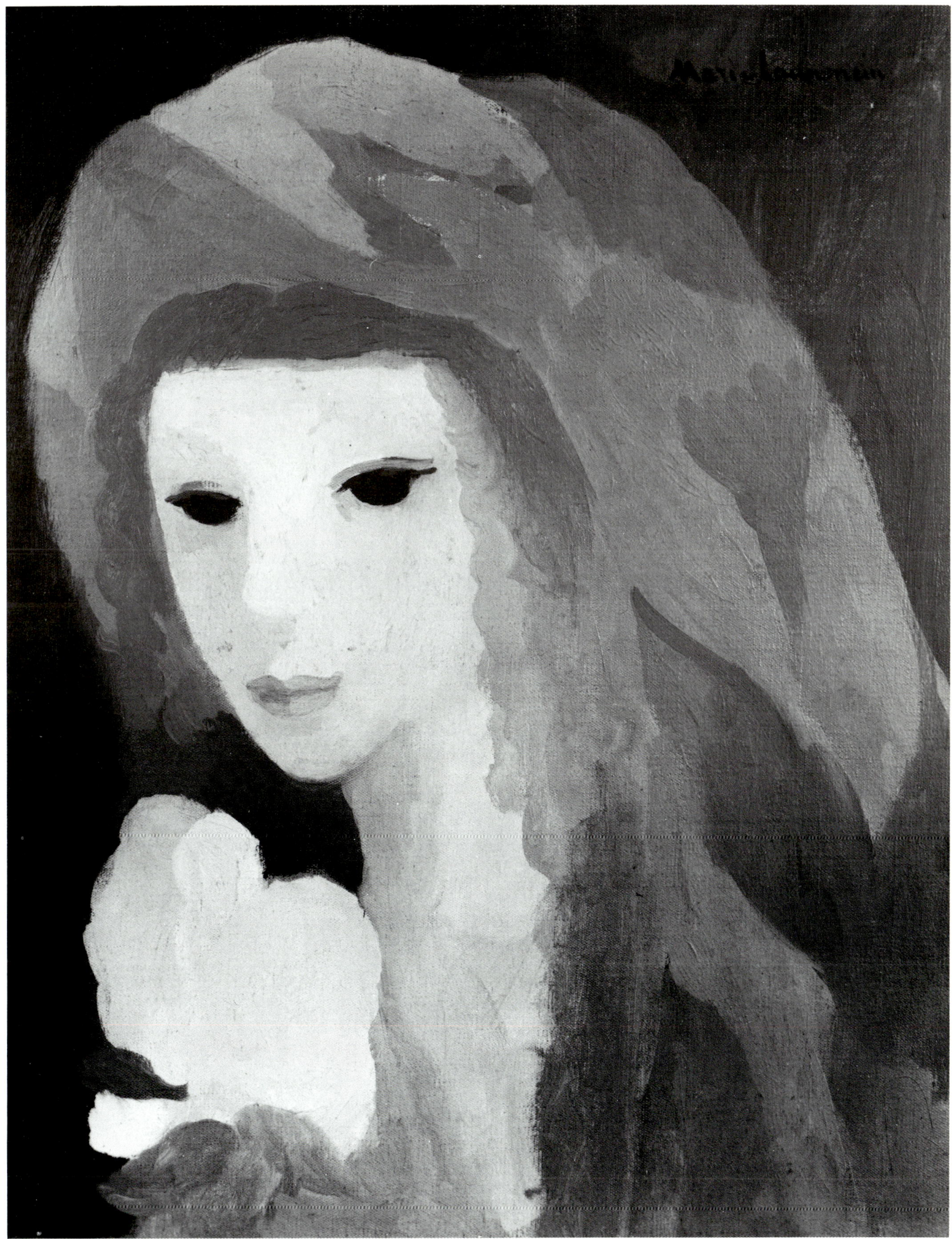

Jeune Fille au chapeau rouge et bleu/Young Girl in a Red and Blue Hat, *c.* 1927
Oil on canvas, 39.5 × 31.5 cm. (Ex. Leicester Galleries)

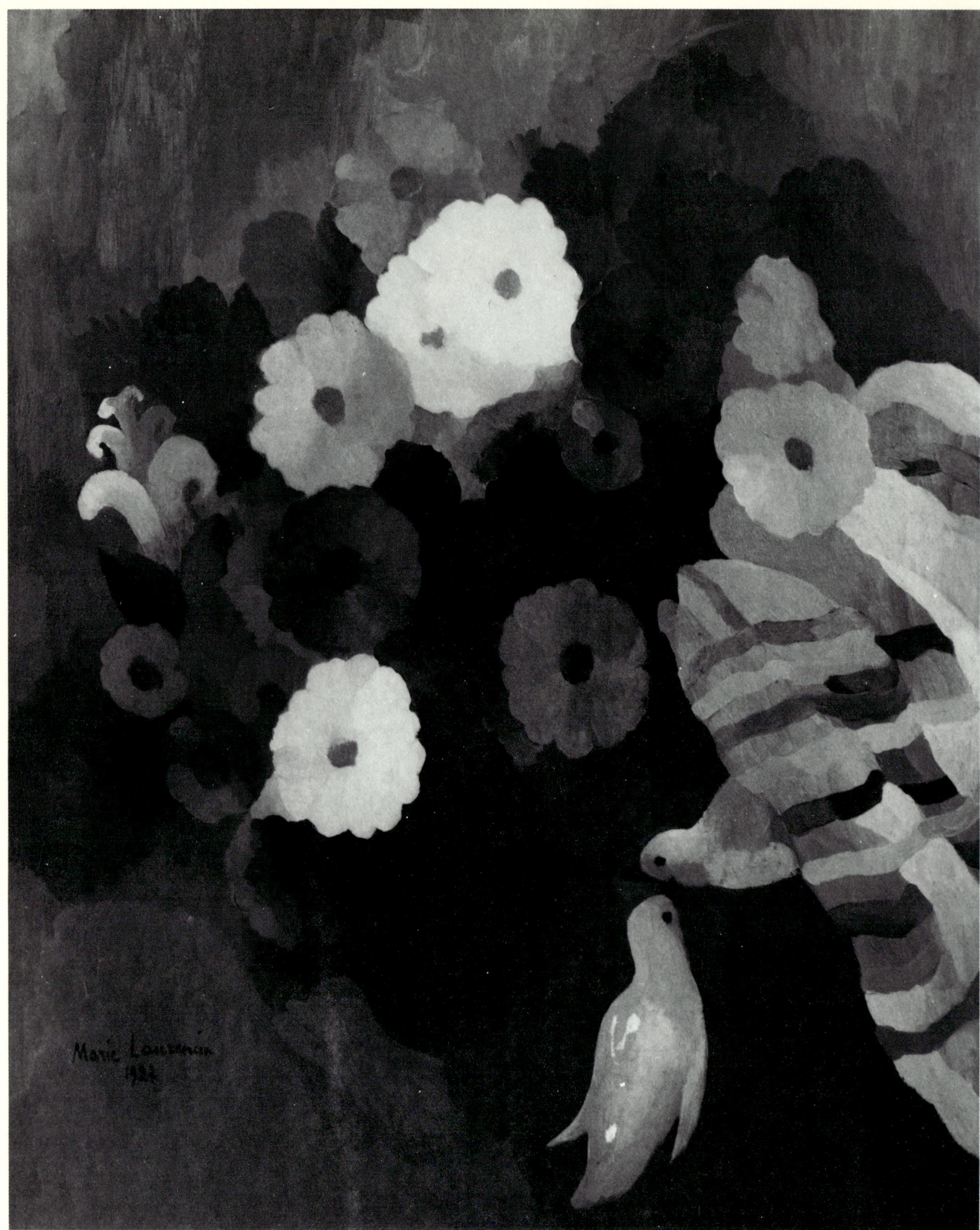

Vase de fleurs et oiseaux/Vase of Flowers and Birds, 1927
Oil on canvas, 64 × 52.5 cm.

Opposite
Jeune Femme au collier/Young Woman with a necklace, 1932
Oil on canvas, 47 × 64 cm. (Galerie Motte, Geneva)

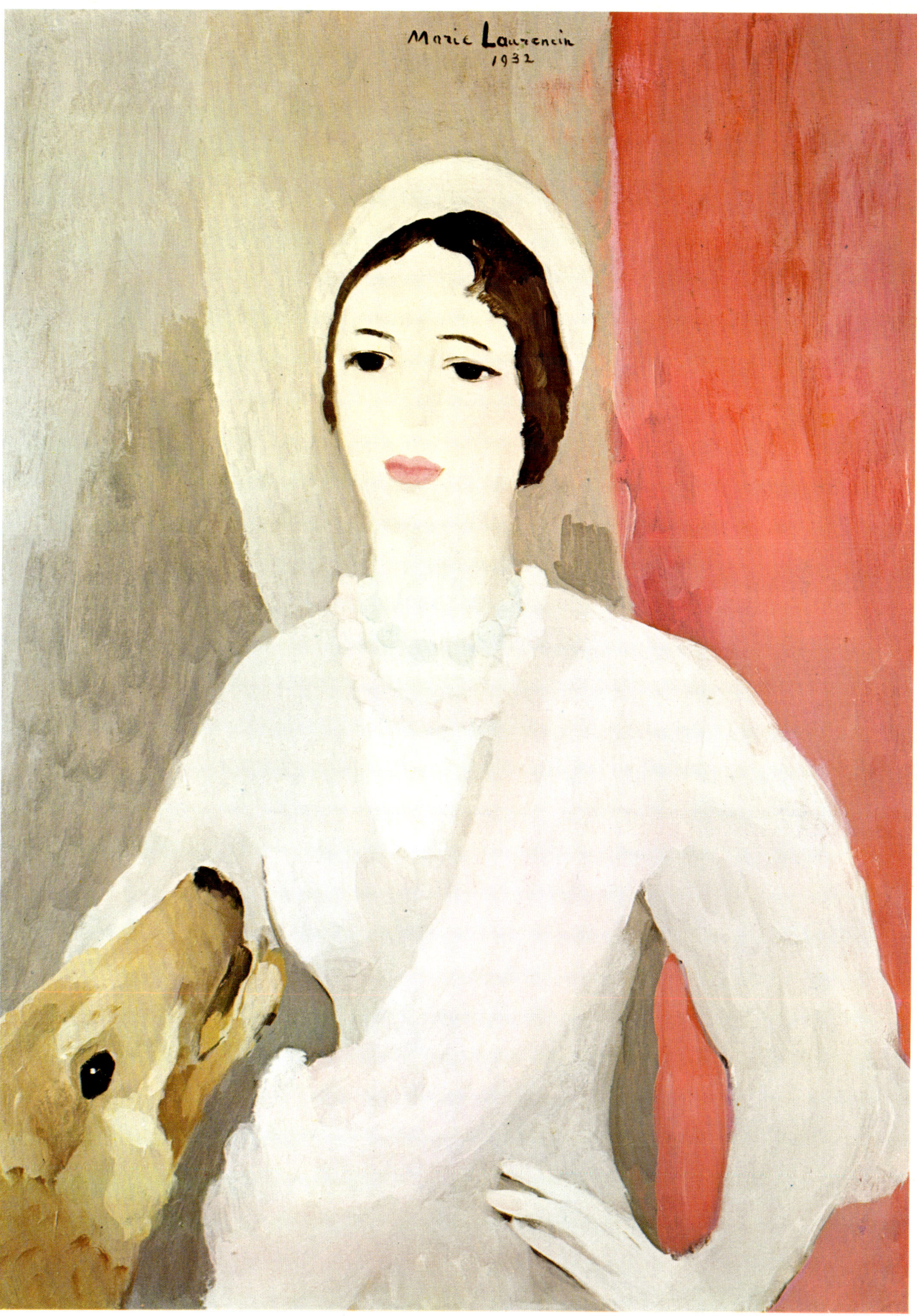
Marie Laurencin
1932

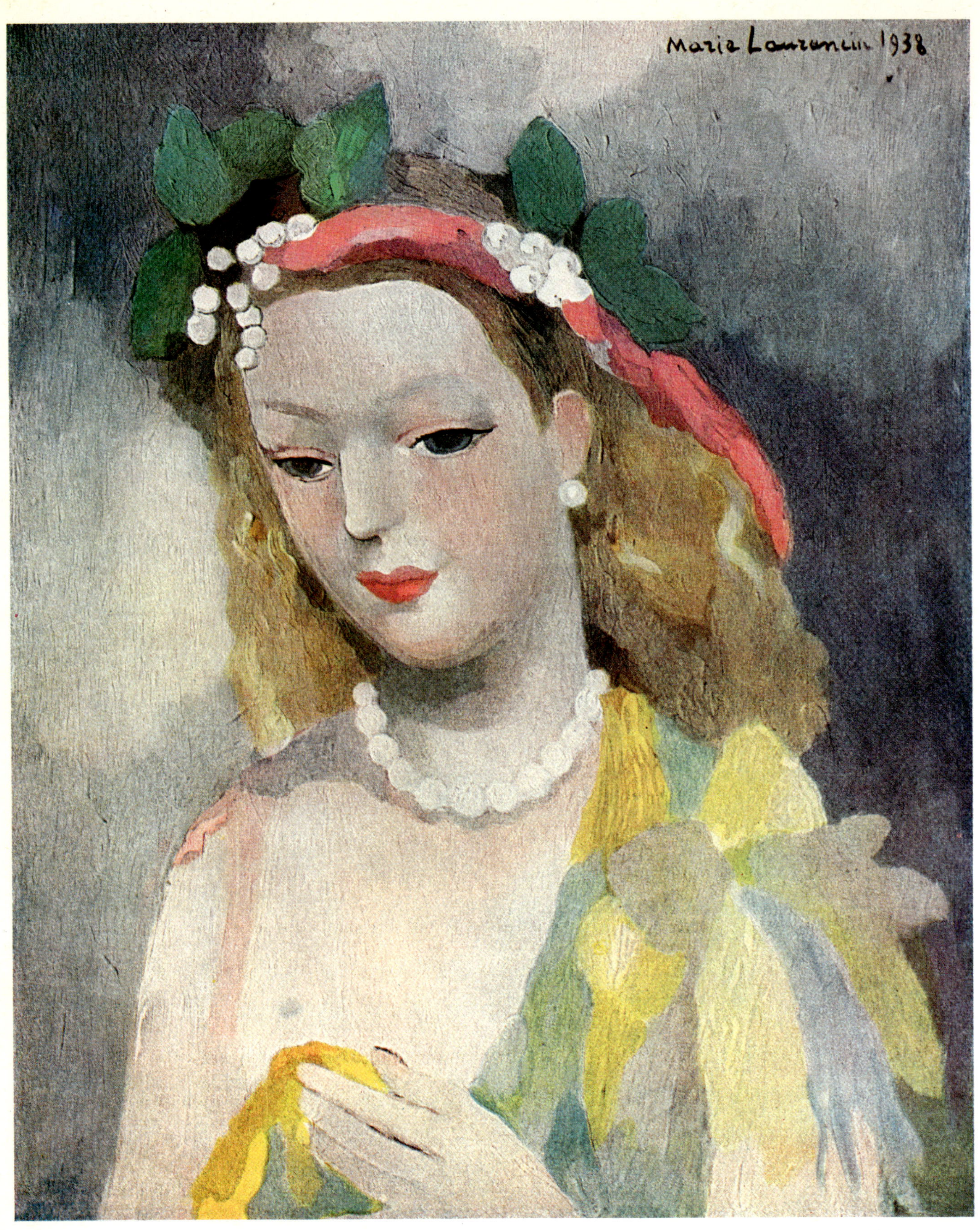
Marie Laurencin 1938

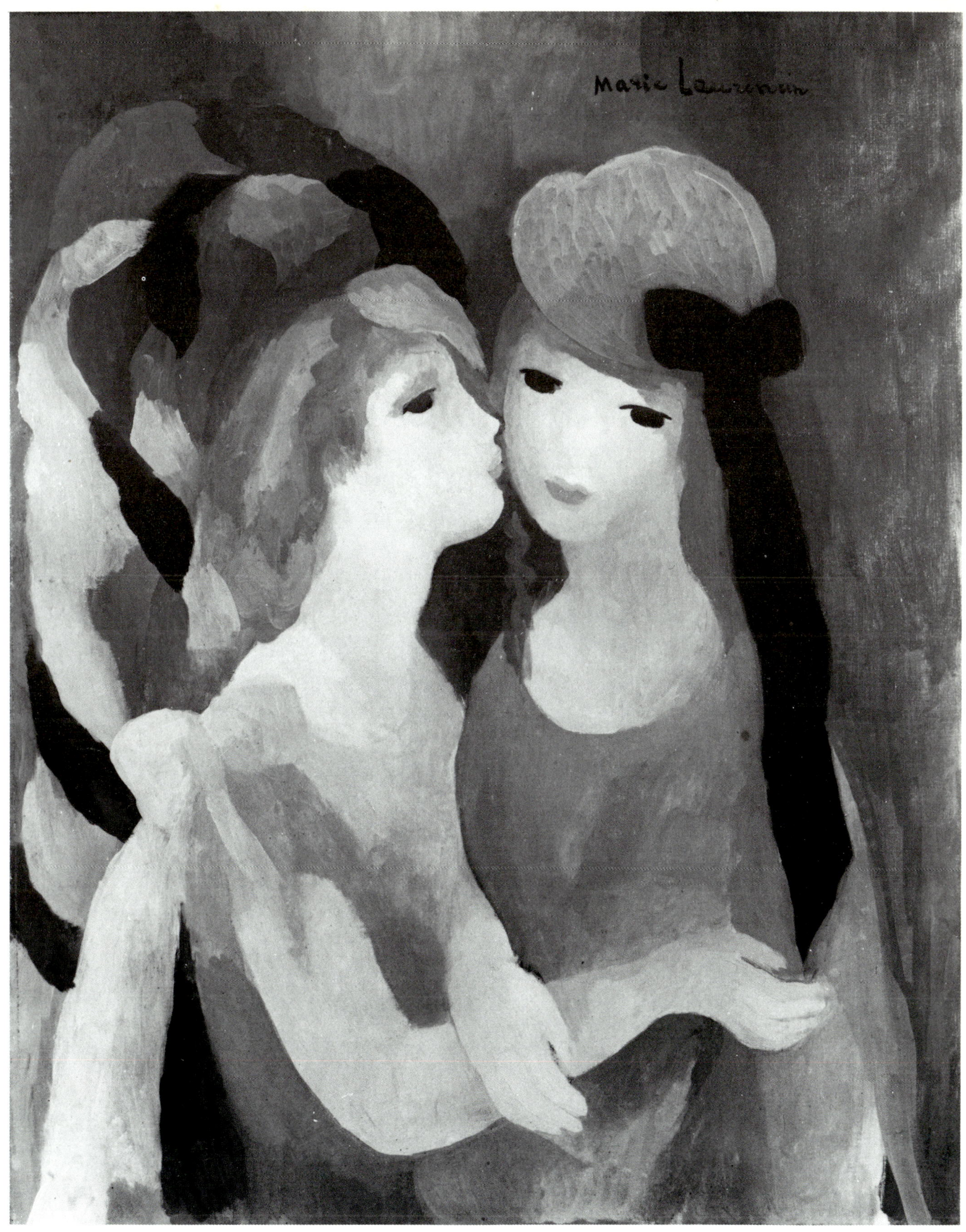

Le Baiser/The Kiss, *c.* 1927
Oil on canvas, 79 × 63 cm. (Ex. coll. Somerset Maugham)

Opposite
Julia, 1938
Oil on canvas

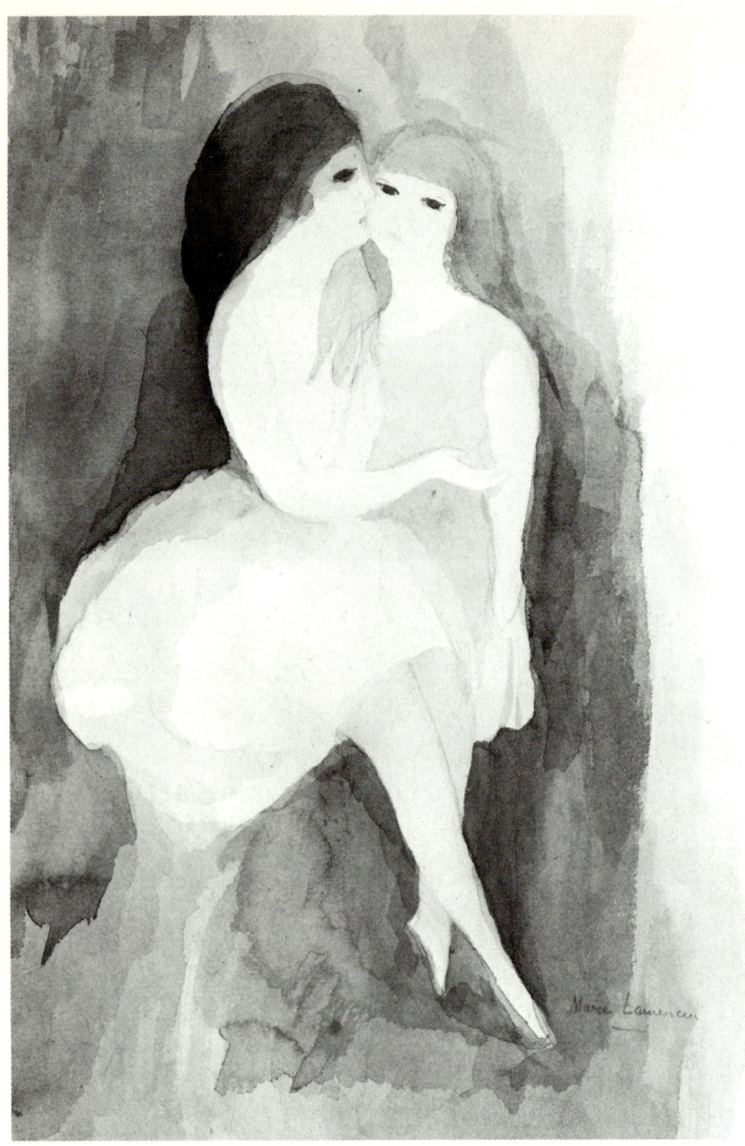

Deux amies/Two Friends, *c.* 1927
Watercolour, 31 × 21 cm.

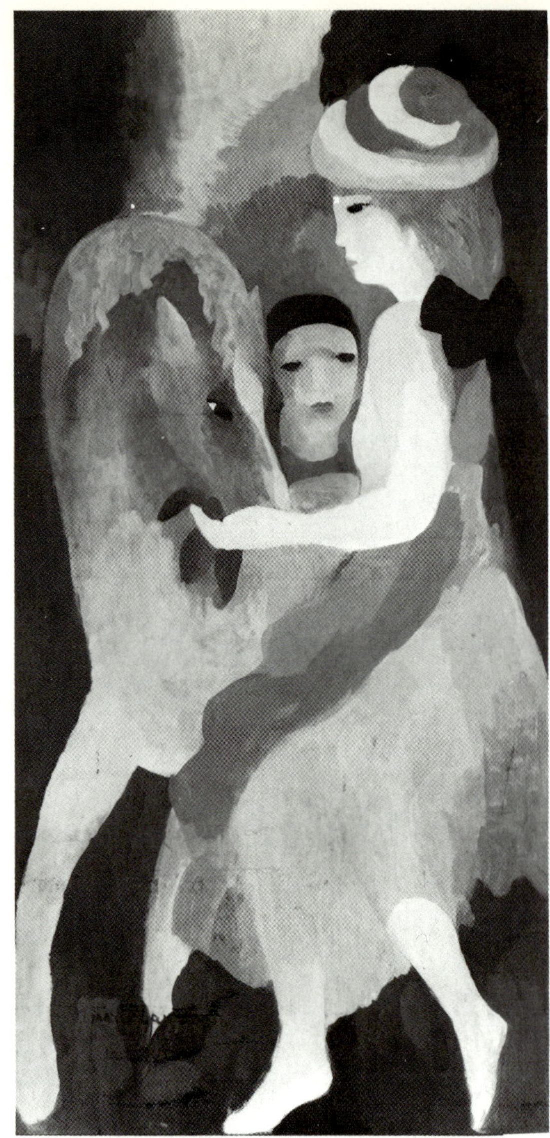

Deux filles au poney/Two Girls on a Pony, *c.* 1927
Oil on board, 102 × 52 cm.

Opposite
Jeune Fille à l'éventail/Young Girl with a Fan, 1927
Oil on canvas, 80 × 52 cm. (Ex. coll. Somerset Maugham)

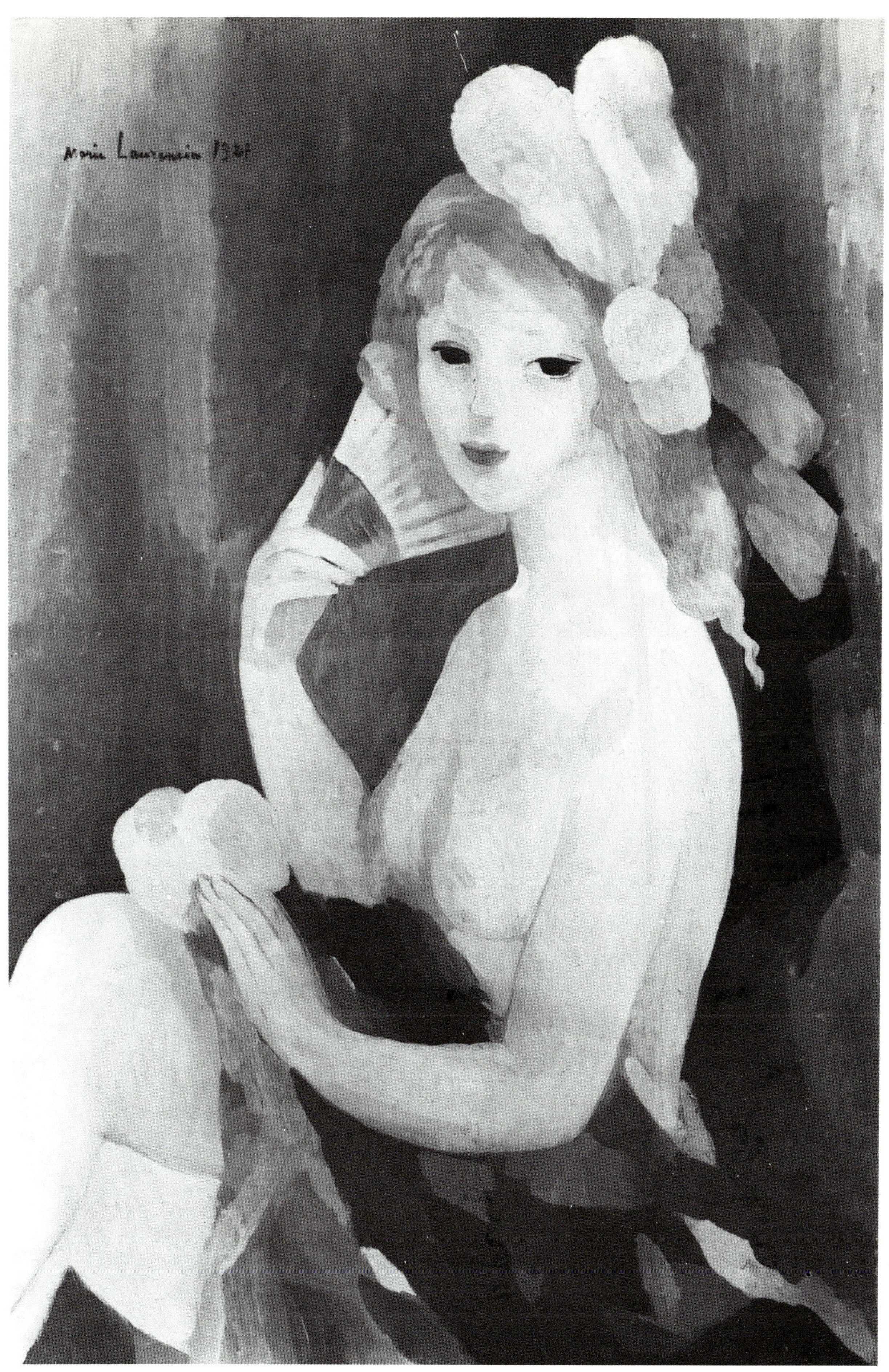

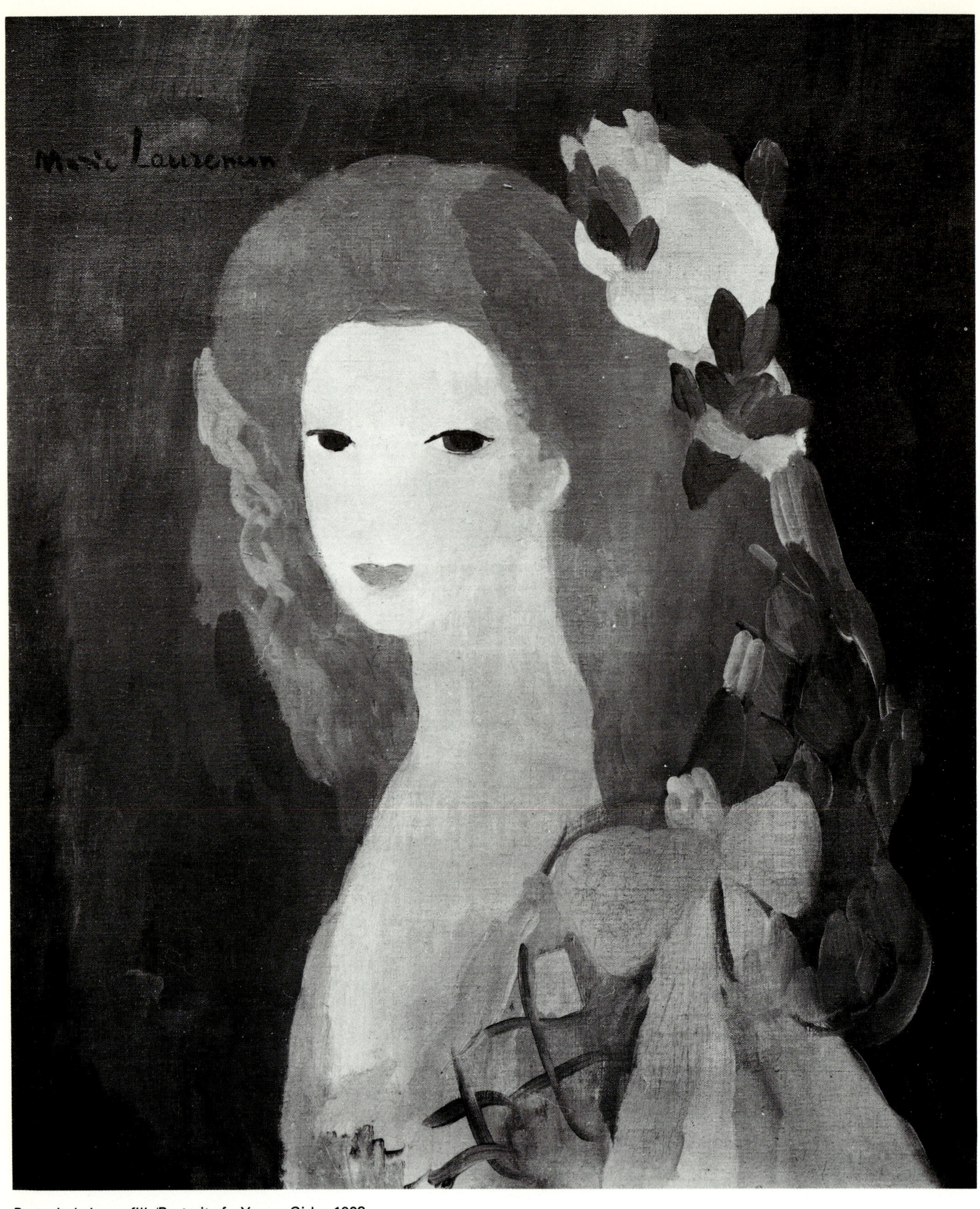

Portrait de jeune fille/Portrait of a Young Girl, *c.* 1928
Oil on canvas, 53 × 44 cm. (Christie's, London)

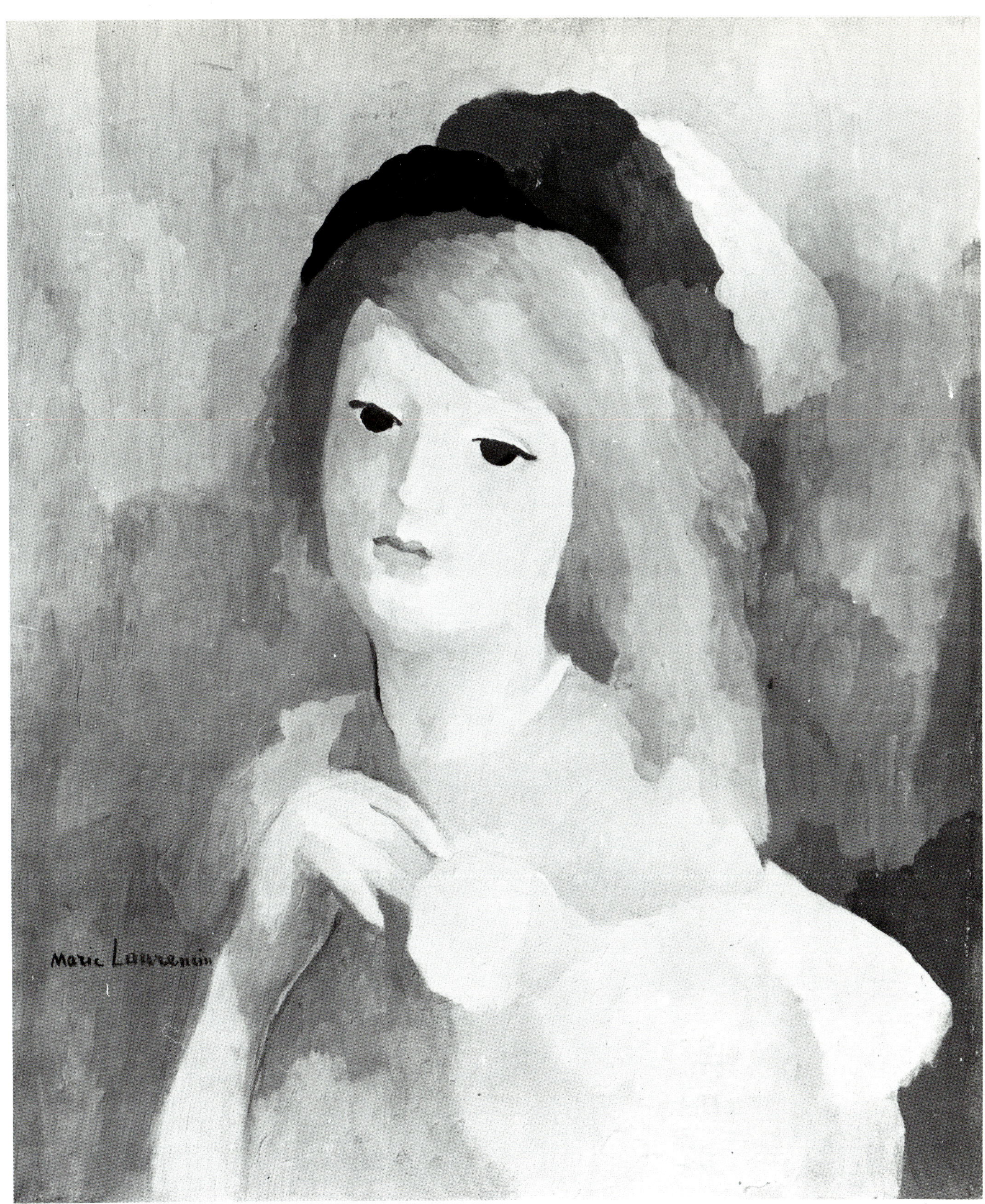

Juliette, c. 1928
Oil on canvas, 55 × 46 cm.

Charlotte Brontë, (from Les Sœurs Brontë by René Crevel) *c.* 1931
Coloured lithograph, 36 × 25 cm.

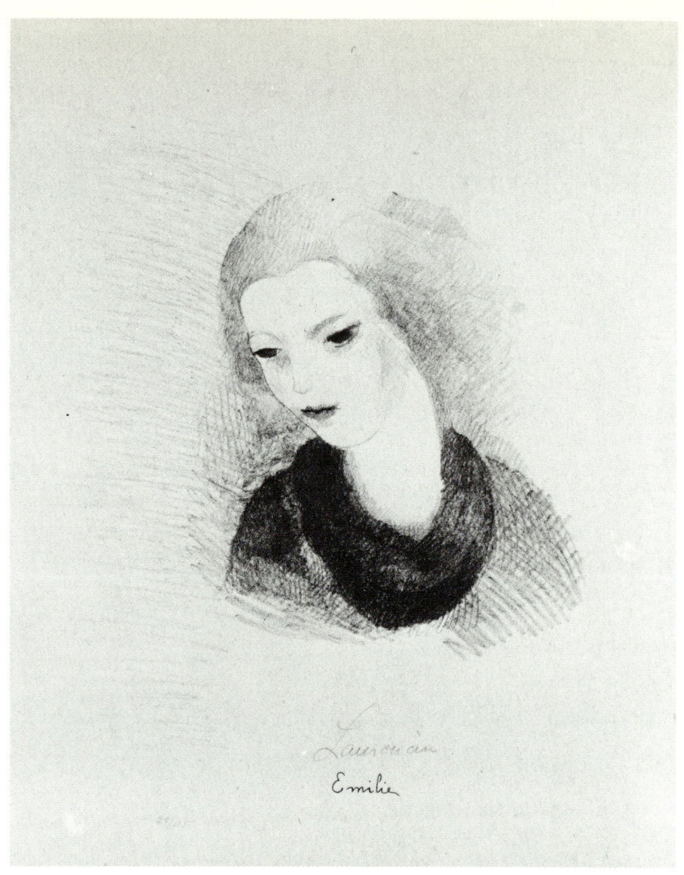

Emily Brontë, (from Les Sœurs Brontë by René Crevel) *c.* 1931
Coloured lithograph, 35.5 × 26 cm.

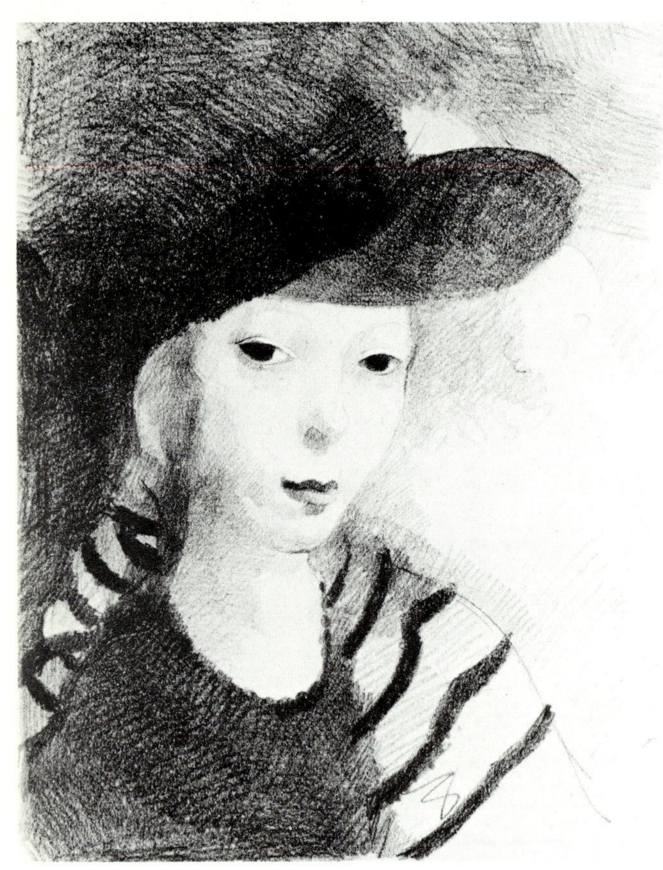

Auto-portrait/Self-portrait, *c.* 1931
Lithograph, 38 × 30.5 cm.

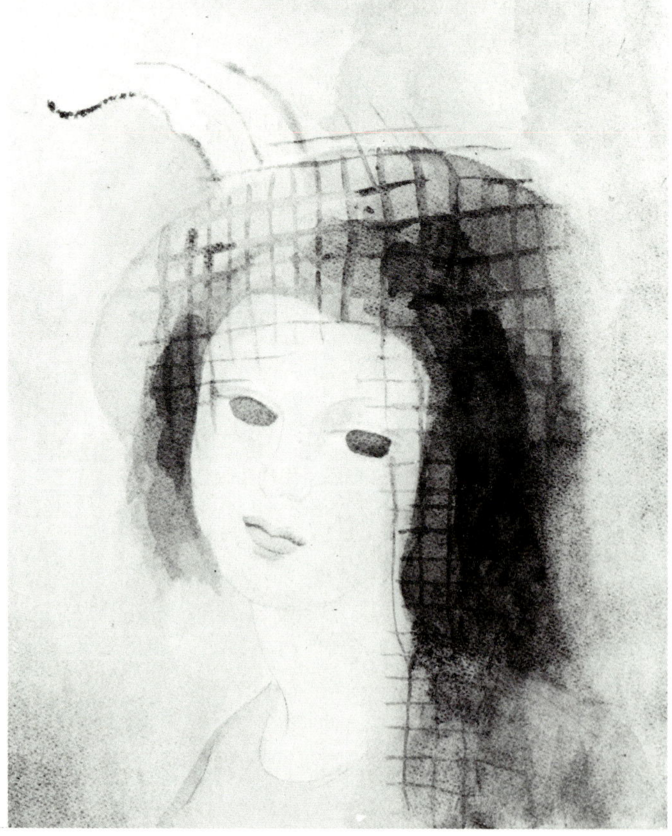

Jeune Fille/Young Girl, *c.* 1931
Watercolour, 31 × 26 cm.

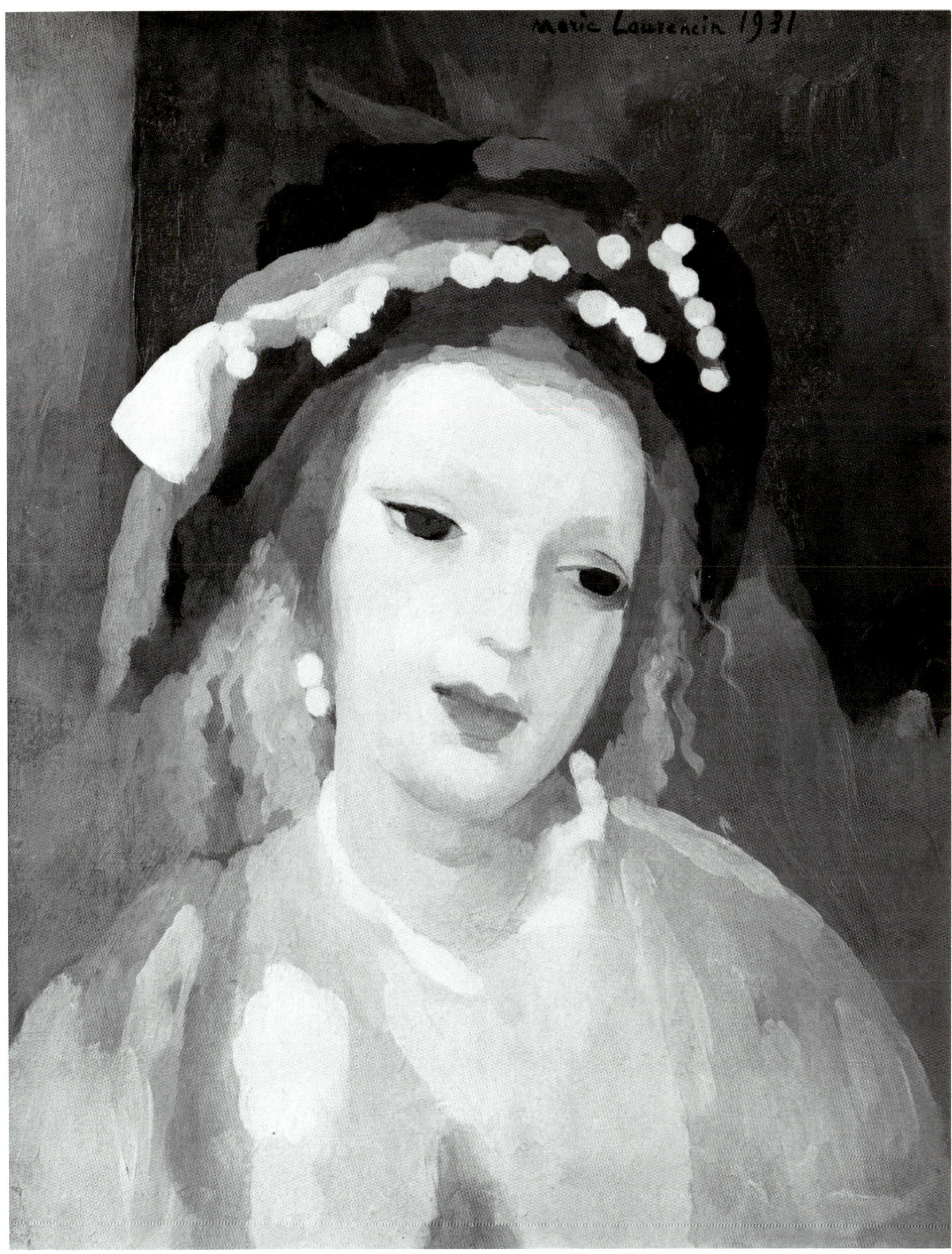

Portrait de Nicole Groult/Portrait of Nicole Groult, 1931
Oil on canvas, 41 × 33 cm.

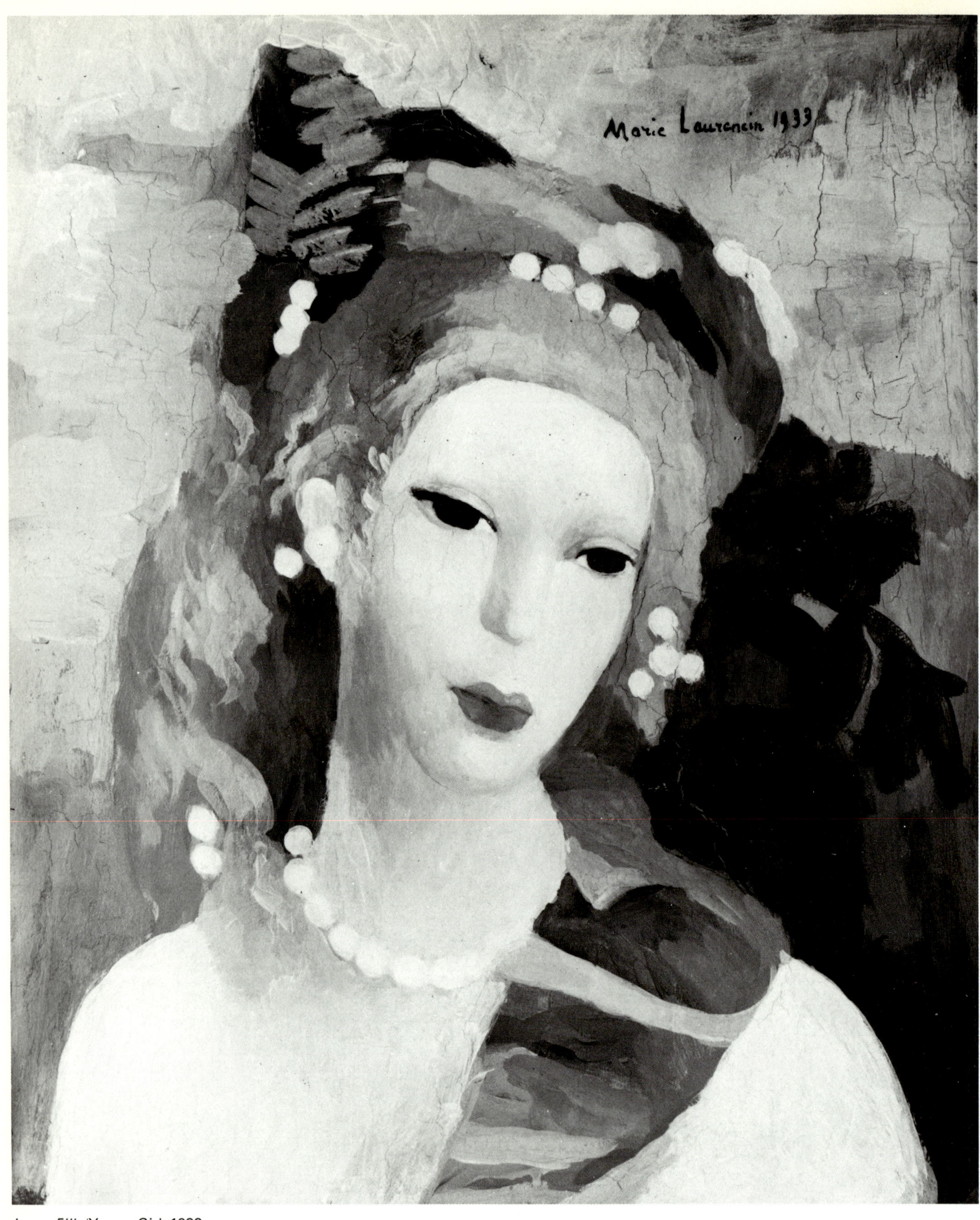

Jeune Fille/Young Girl, 1933
Oil on canvas, 44.5 × 37 cm.

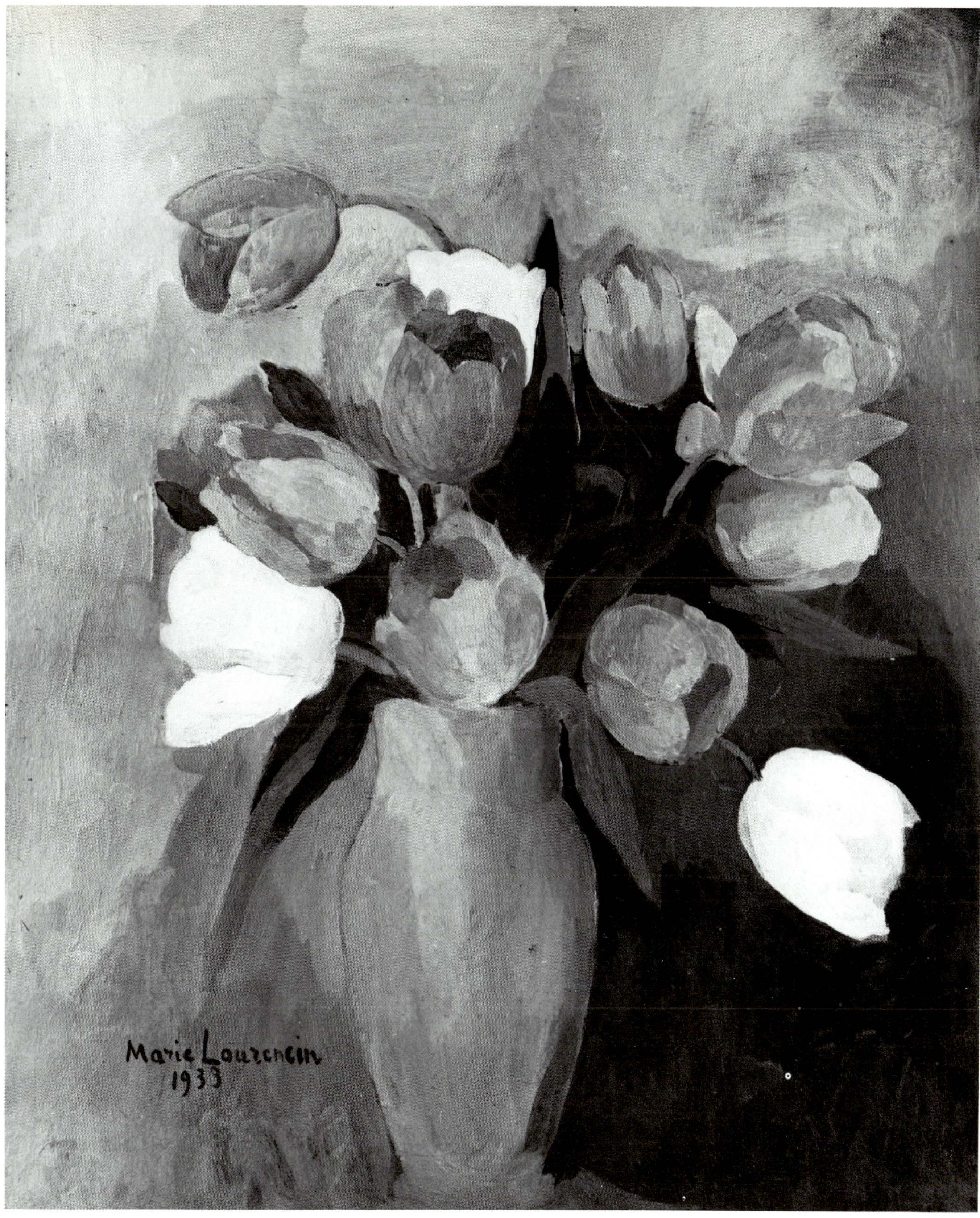

Vase de tulipes/Vase of Tulips, 1933
Oil on canvas, 59.5 × 49.5 cm.

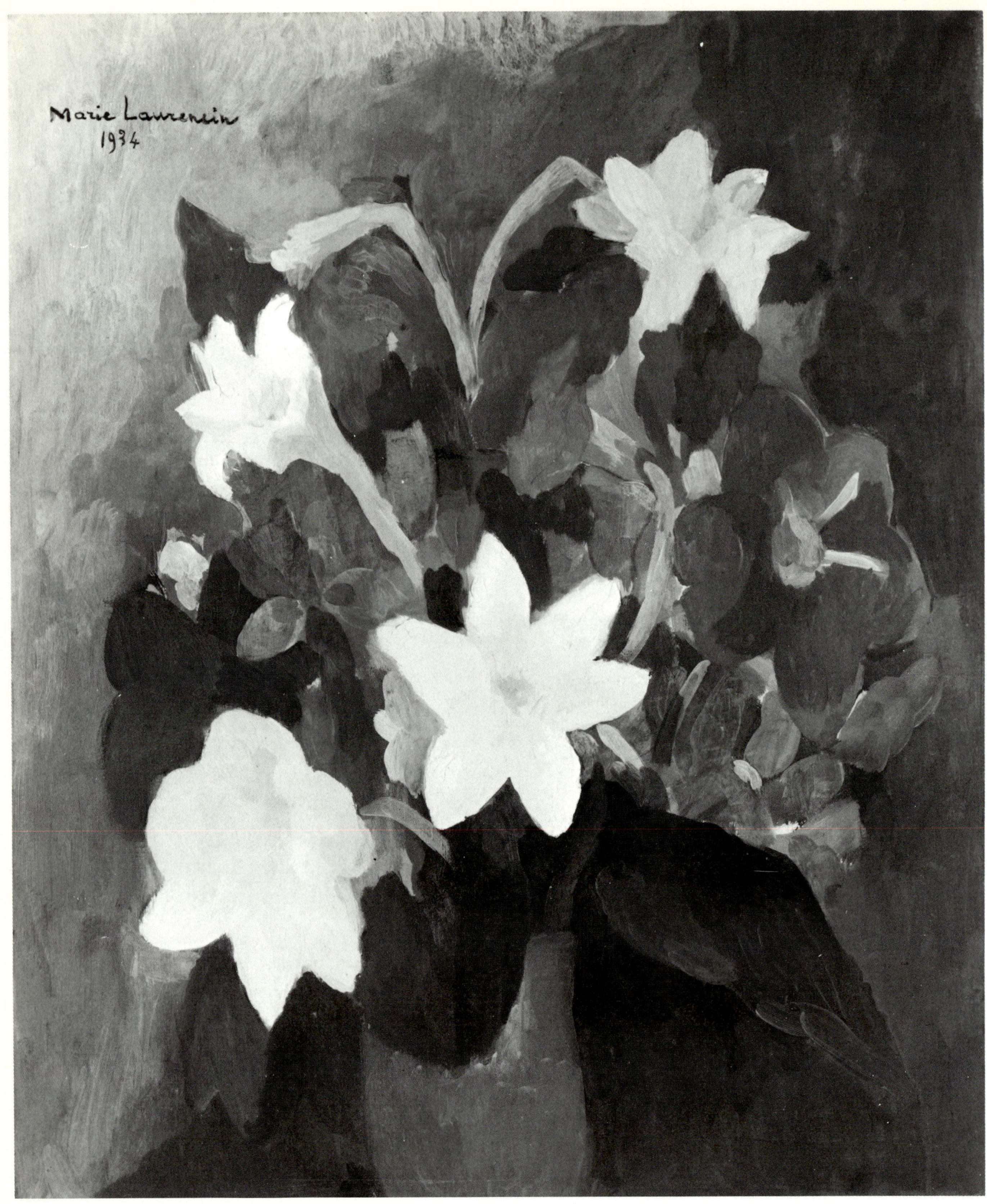

Vase de fleurs avec lis/Flower Vase with Lilies, 1934
Oil on canvas, 58.5 × 48 cm.

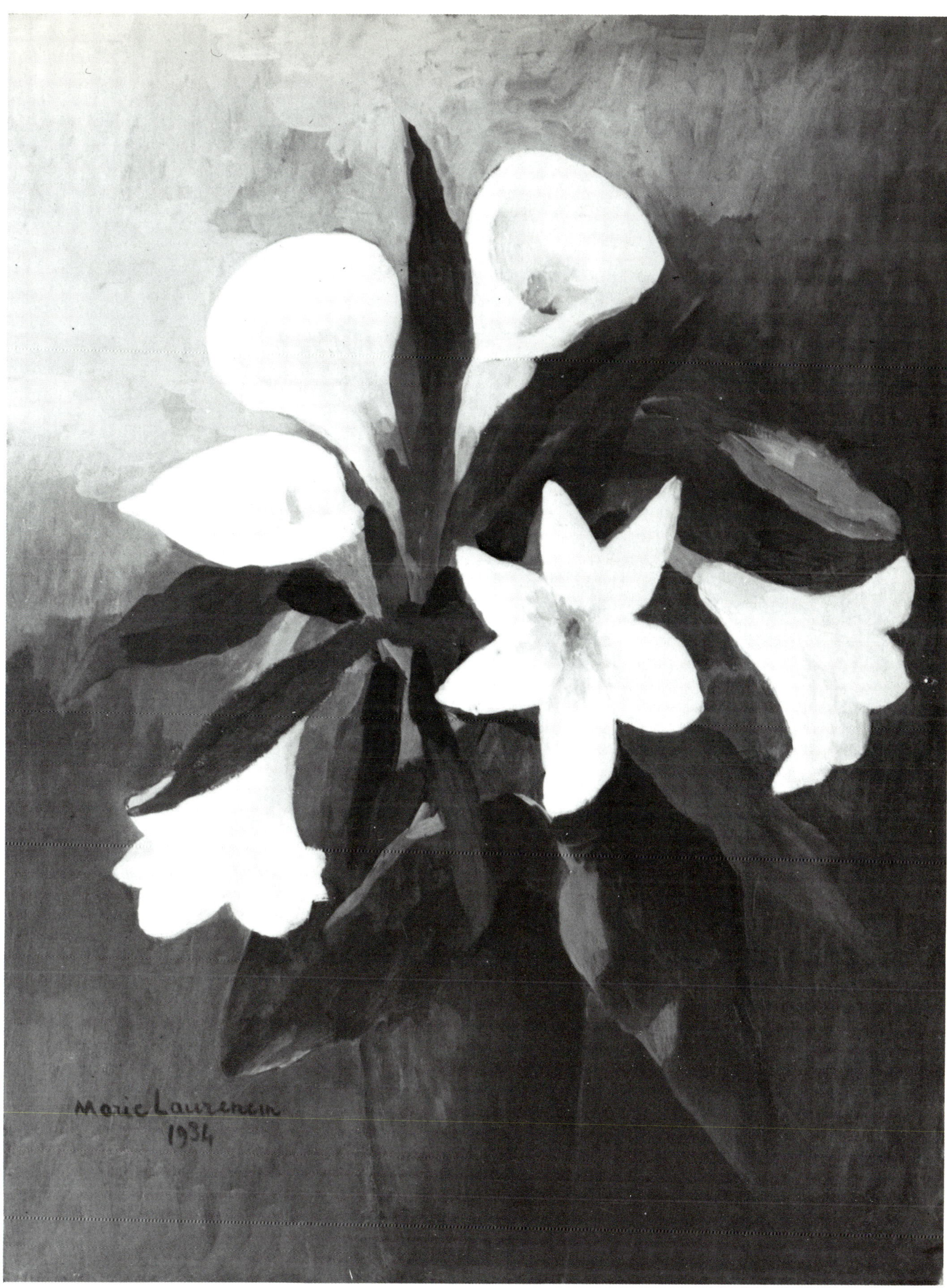

Vase de lis/Vase of Lilies, 1934
Oil on canvas, 59.5 × 49 cm. (Ex. coll. Abrahams)

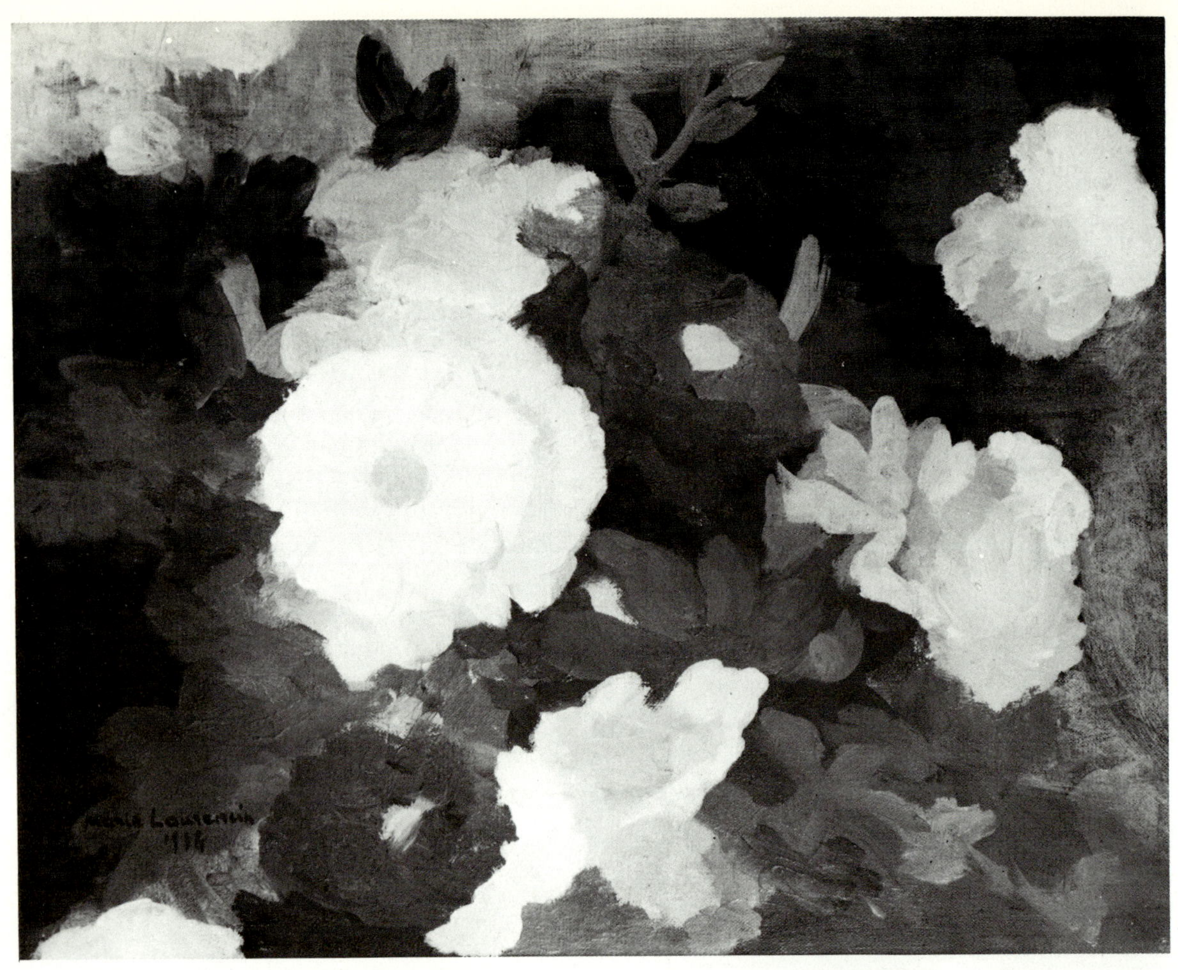
Marie Laurencin

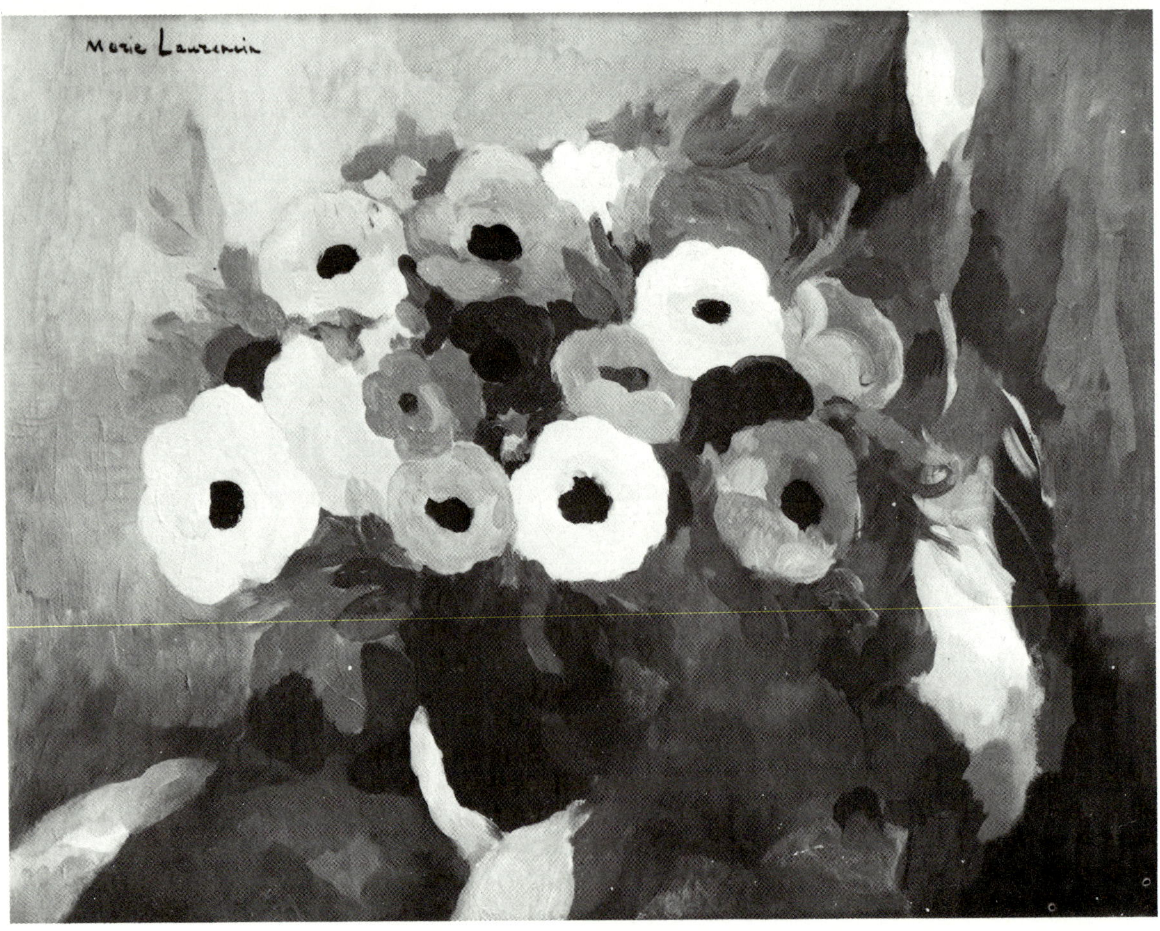
Marie Laurencin

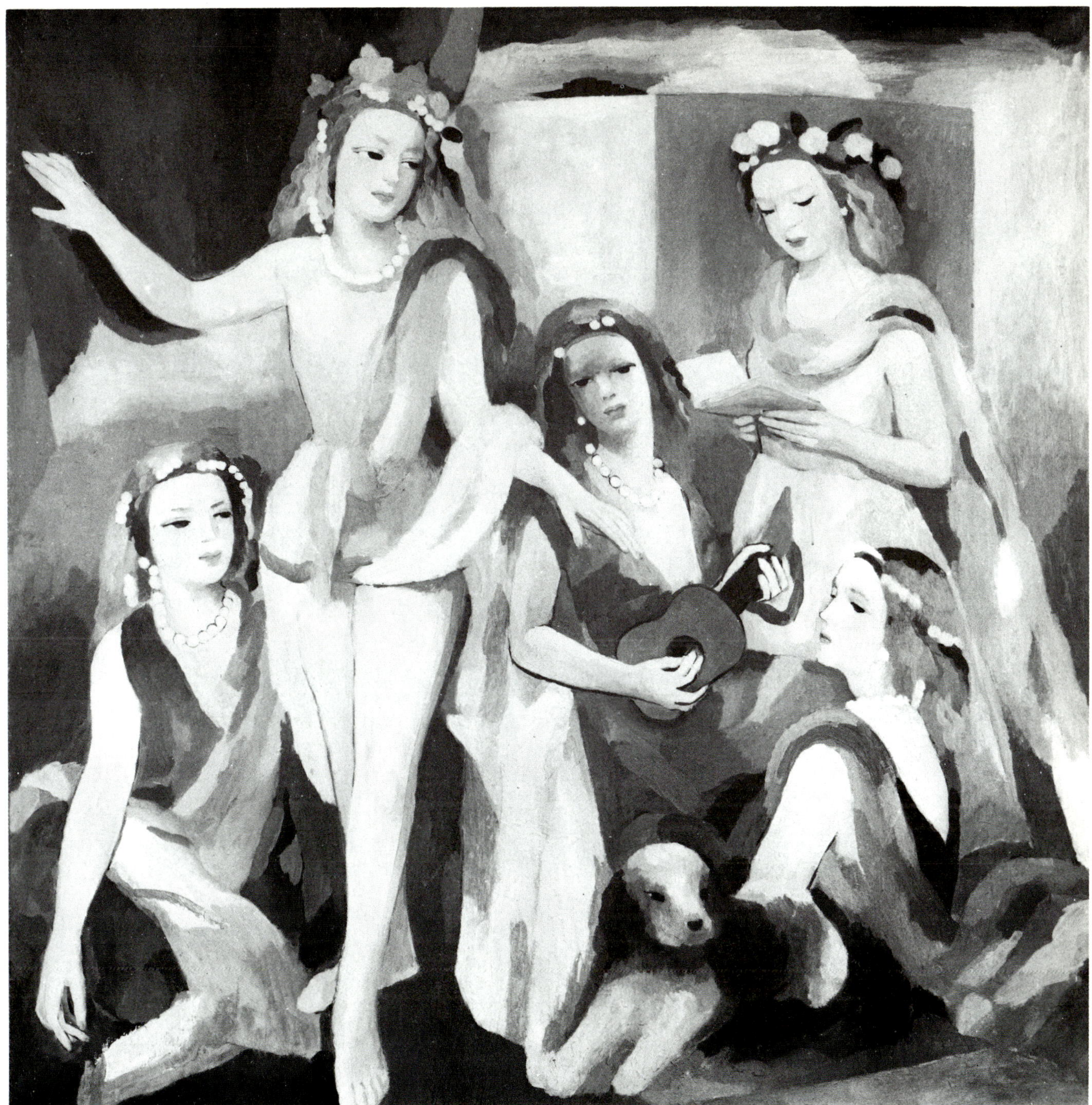

La Répétition/The Rehearsal, 1936
Oil on canvas (Musée National d'Art Moderne, Paris)

Opposite above
Bouquet de fleurs/Bouquet of Flowers, *c.* 1934
Oil on canvas

Opposite below
Bouquet de fleurs/Bouquet of Flowers, *c.* 1935
Oil on canvas, 49 × 64 cm.

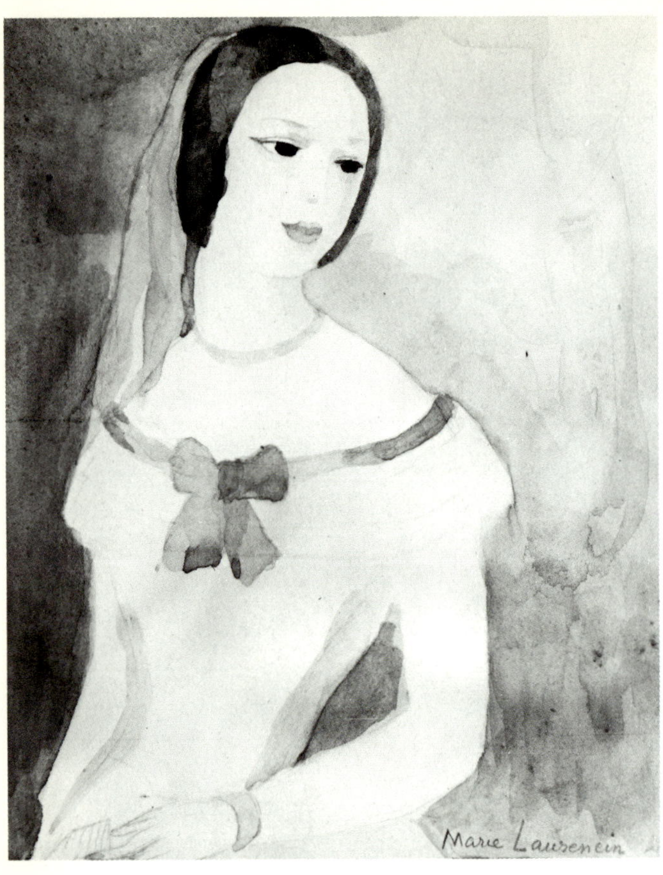

La Dame aux Camélias (for *Camille* by Alexandre Dumas), 1936
Watercolour, 20.5 × 15 cm.

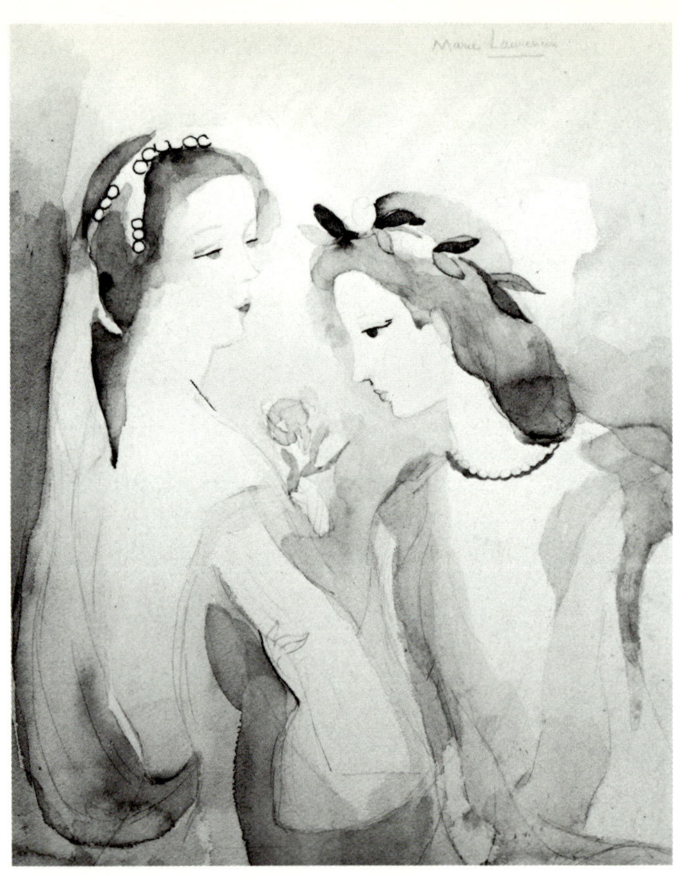

Deux jeunes filles/Two Young Girls, *c.* 1936
Watercolour, 30 × 25 cm.

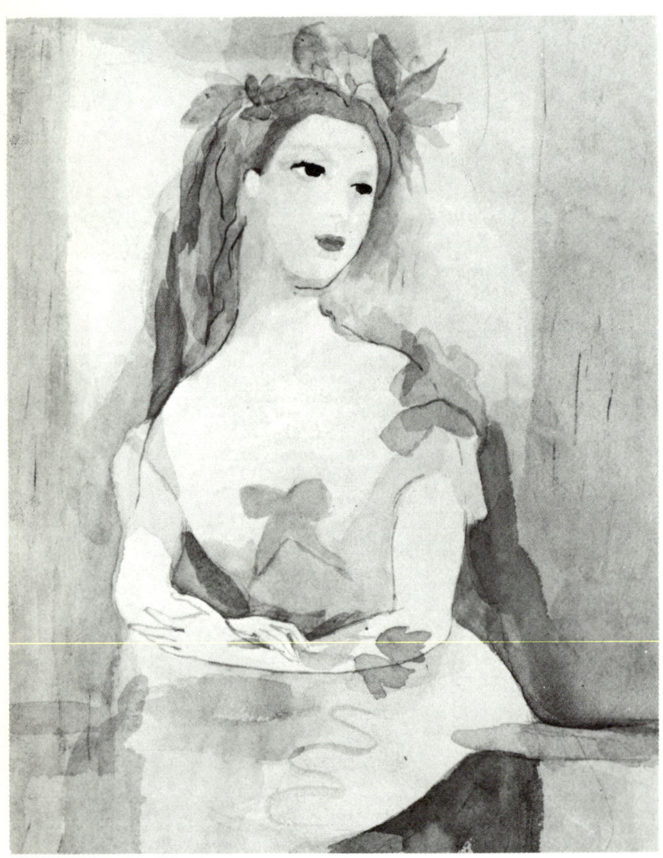

Portrait d'une jeune femme/Portrait of a Young Woman, 1936
Watercolour, 30.5 × 22 cm.

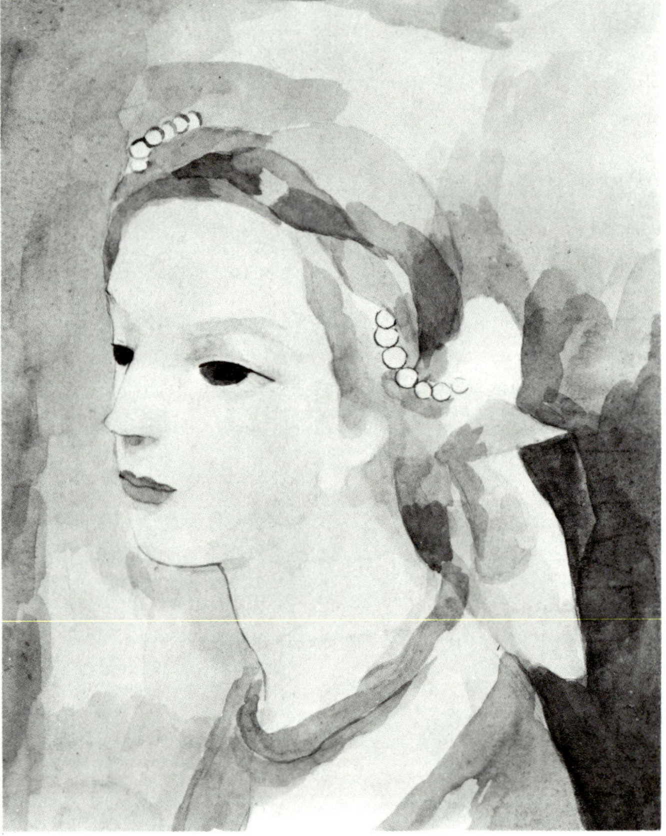

Tête de jeune fille/Head of a Young Girl, *c.* 1936
Watercolour, 32.3 × 24 cm.

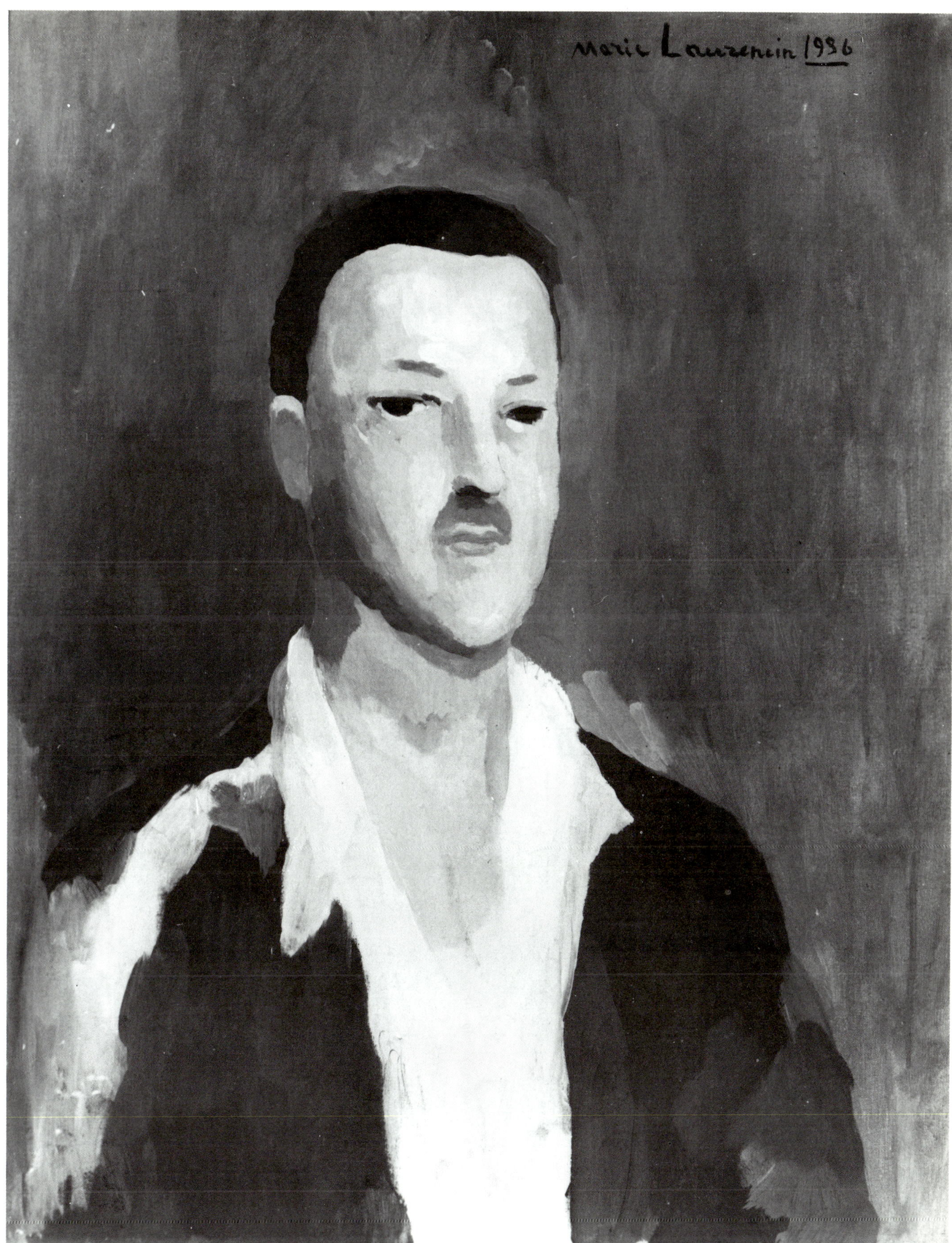

Portrait de Somerset Maugham/Portrait of Somerset Maugham, 1936
Oil on canvas, 57 × 49 cm.

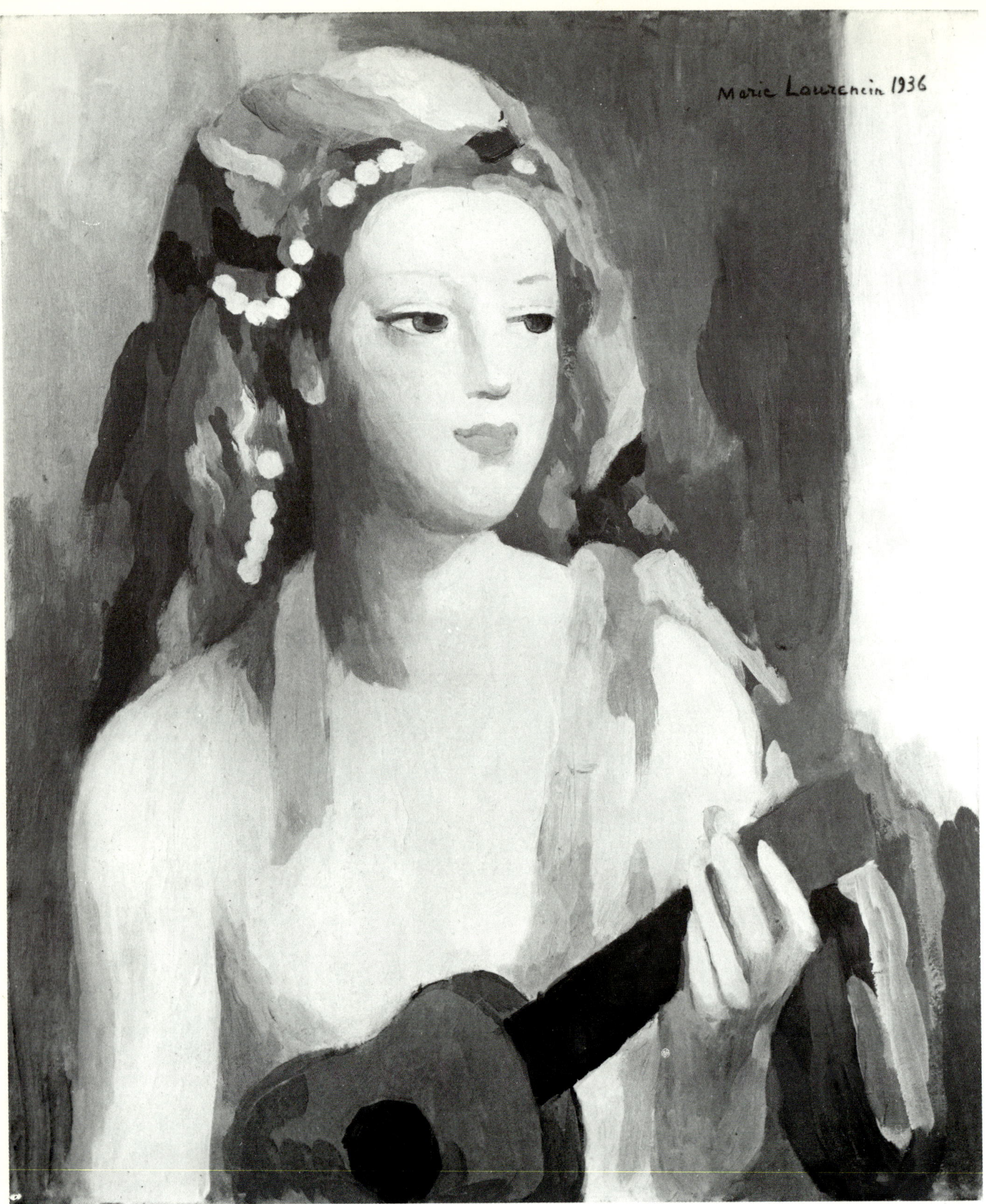

Femme à la guitare/Woman with a Guitar, 1936
Oil on canvas, 55 × 46 cm. (Ex. coll. Abrahams)

Opposite
Trois jeunes femmes aux voiles/Three Young Women with Veils, *c.* 1938
Oil on canvas, 89.5 × 71 cm.

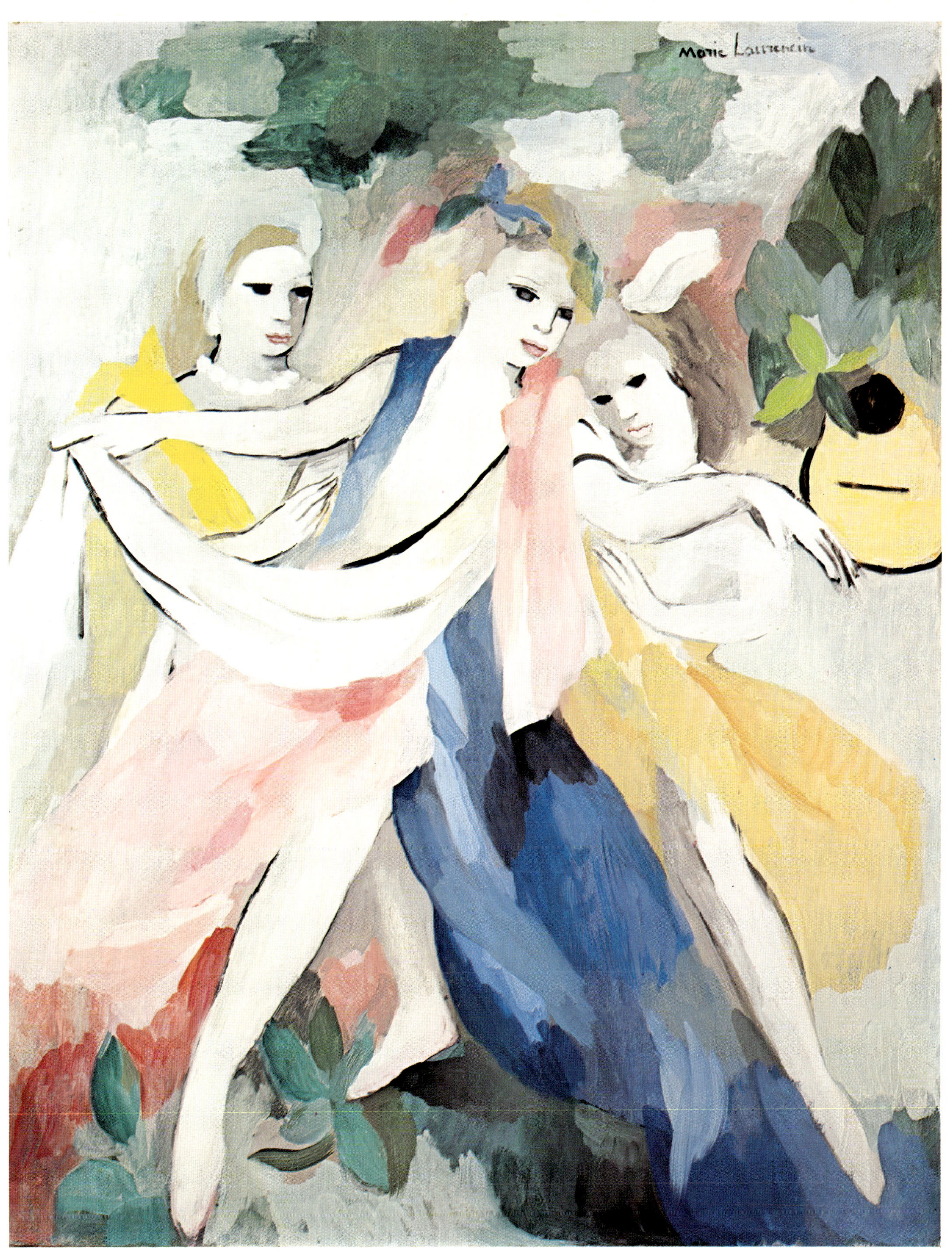
Marie Laurencin

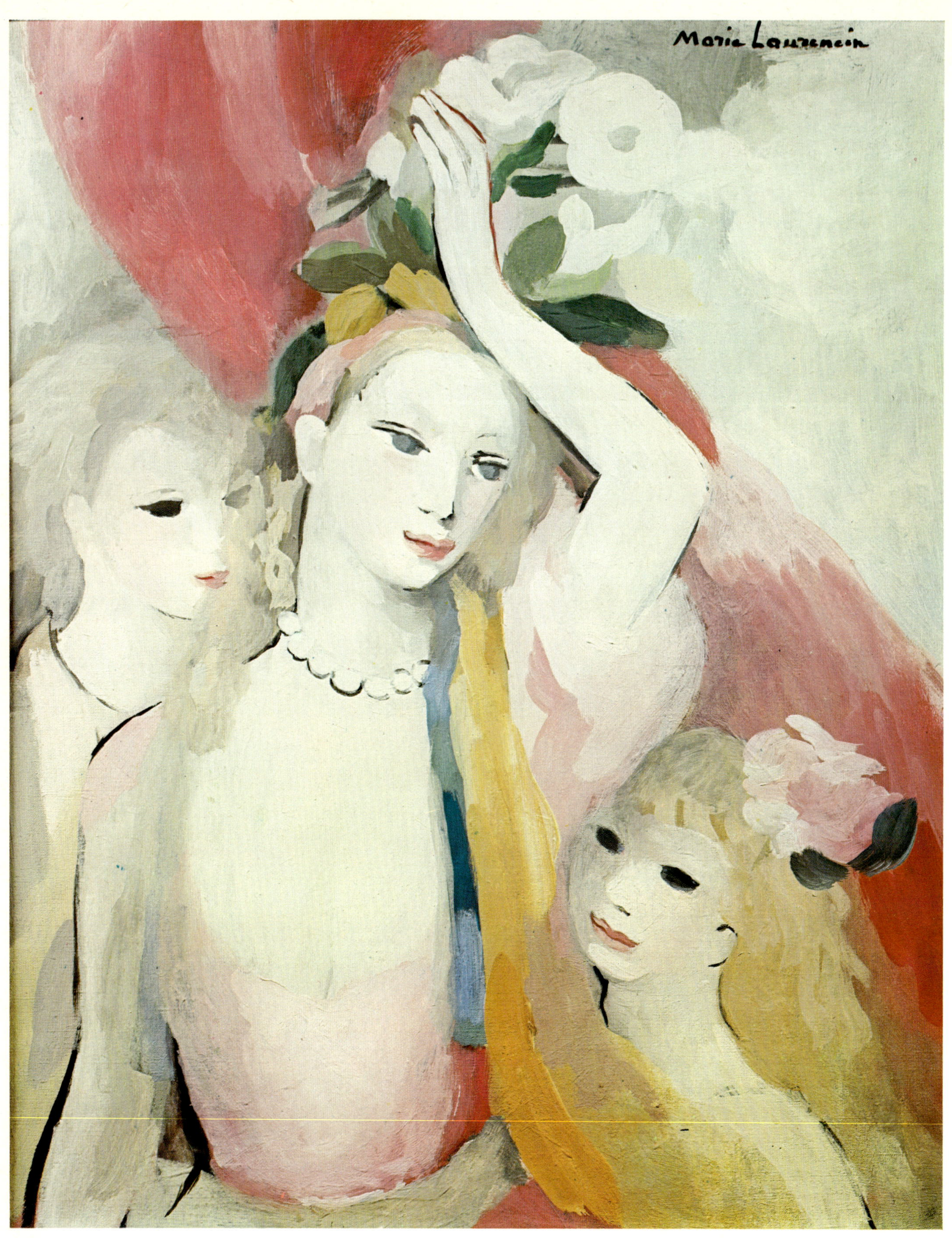
Marie Laurencin

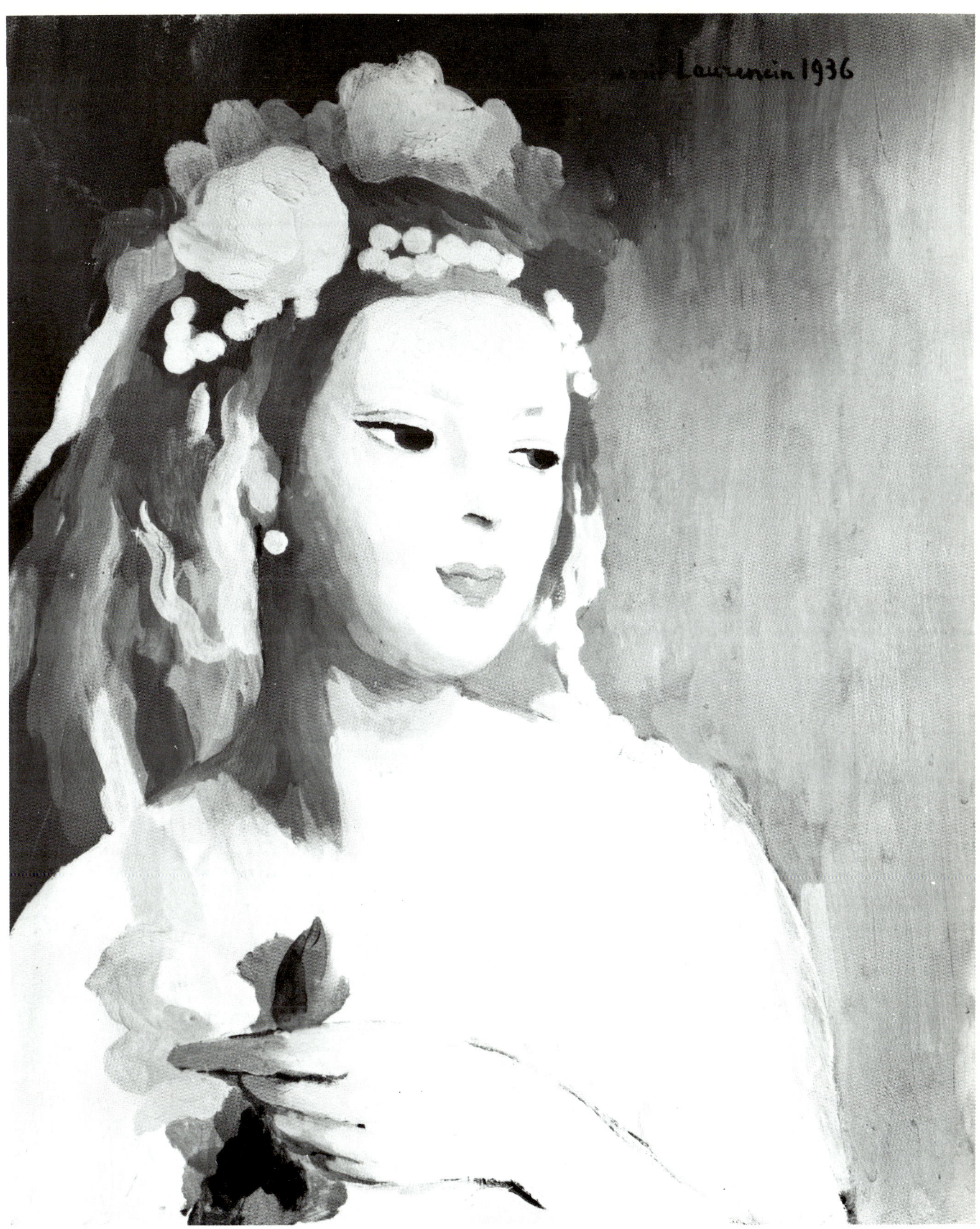

Jeune Fille tenant une rose/Young Girl holding a Rose, 1936
Oil on canvas, 55 × 46 cm.

Opposite
Trois jeunes femmes/Three Young Women, 1949
Oil on canvas, 62 × 51 cm.

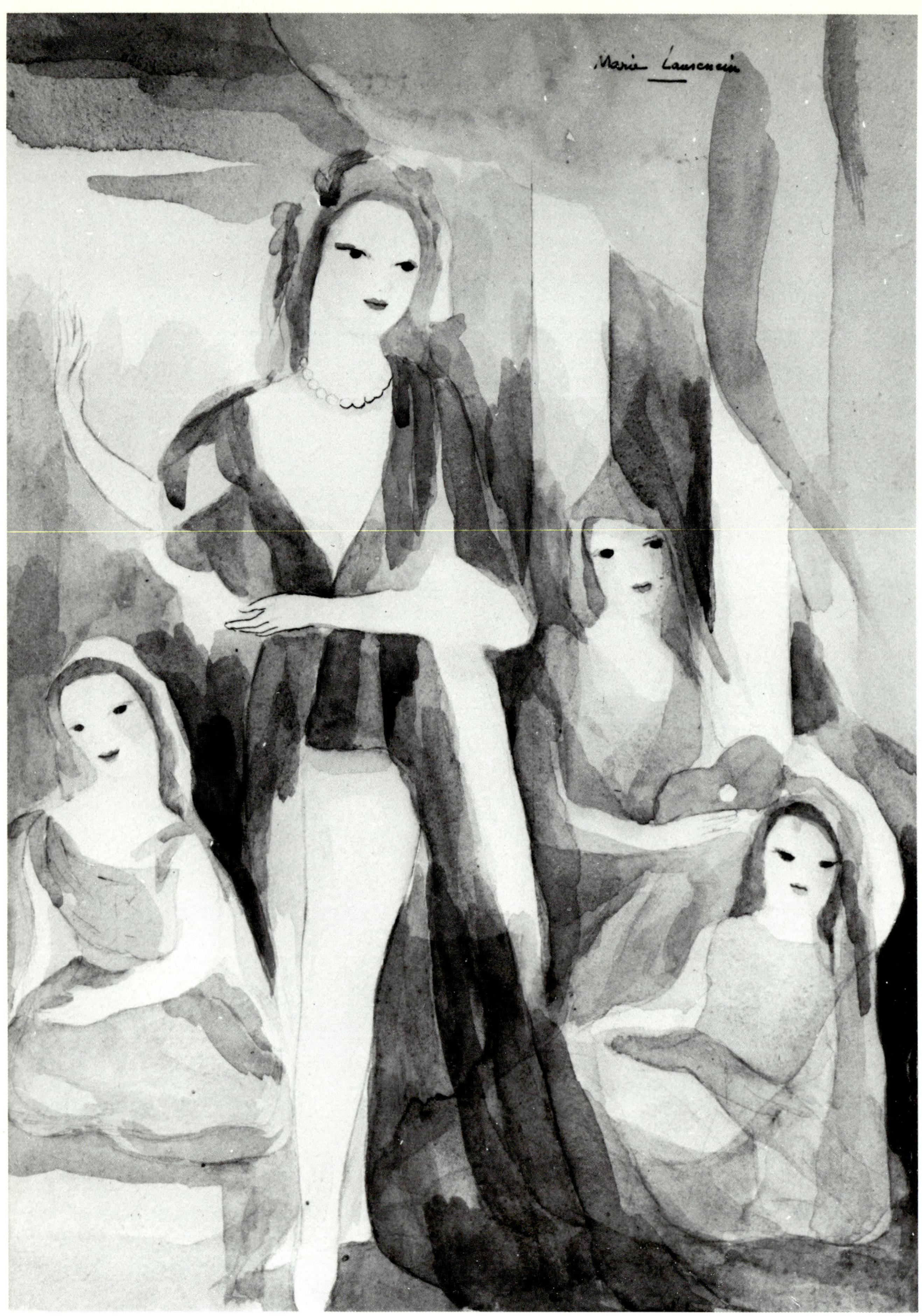

Quatre jeunes filles/Four Young Girls, *c.* 1936
Watercolour, 33 × 25.5 cm.

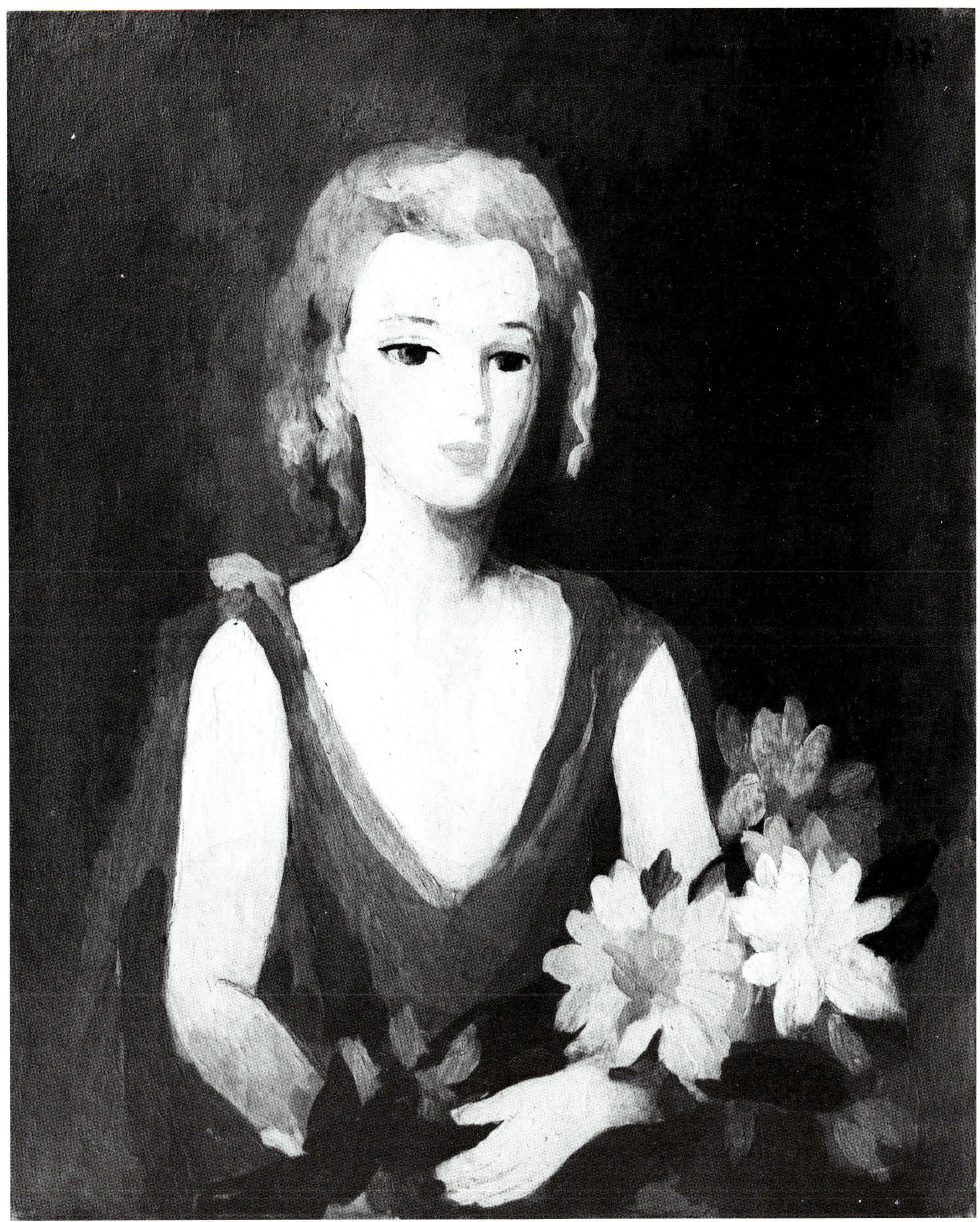

Jeune Femme au bouquet de fleurs/Young Woman with a Bouquet of Flowers (Portrait of Marion Read Barbee), 1937
Oil on canvas, 64 × 52.5 cm.

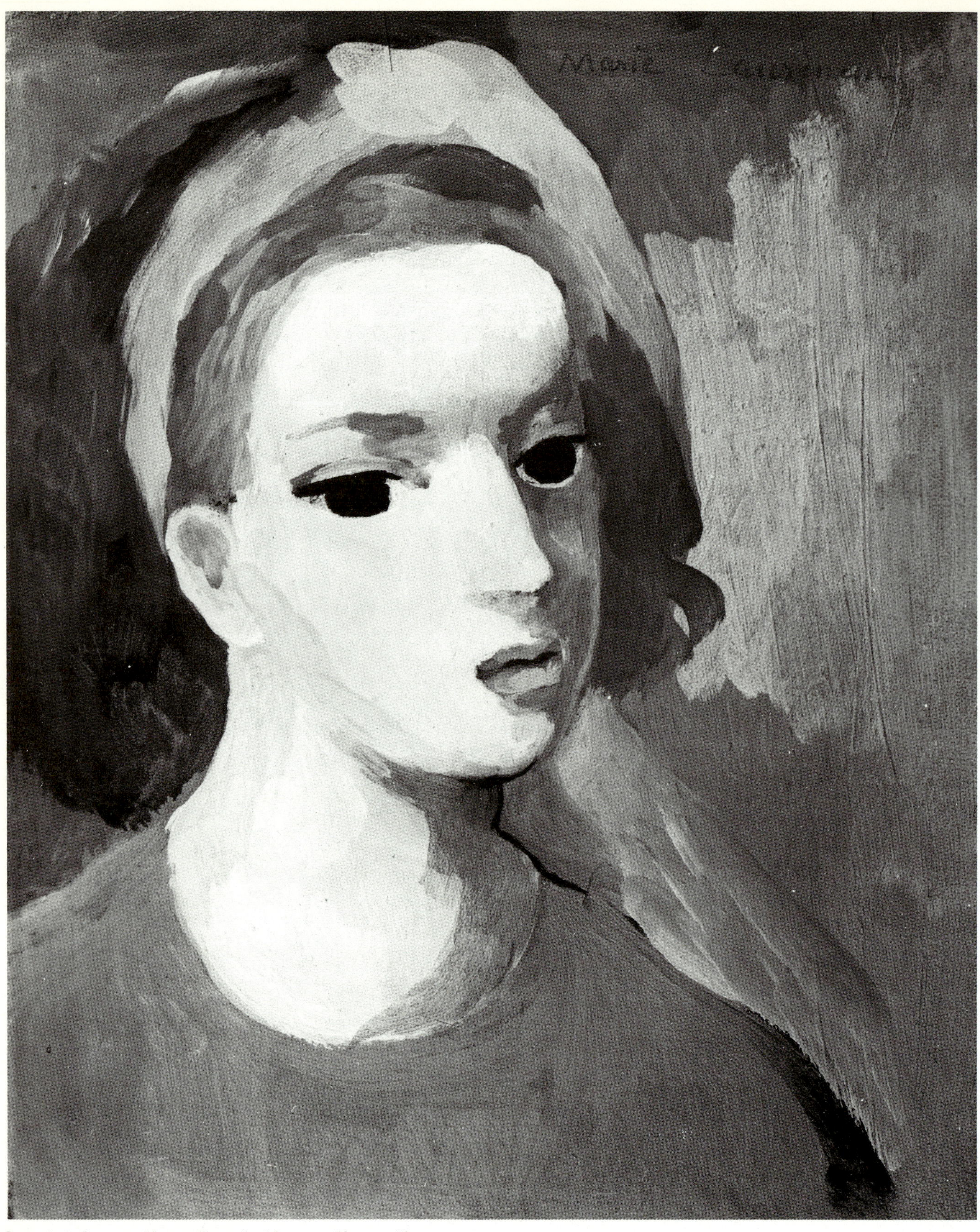

Portrait de Suzanne Moreau/Portrait of Suzanne Moreau, (Suzanne Moreau-Laurencin, adopted daughter of the artist), *c.* 1937
Oil on canvas, 27 × 22 cm.

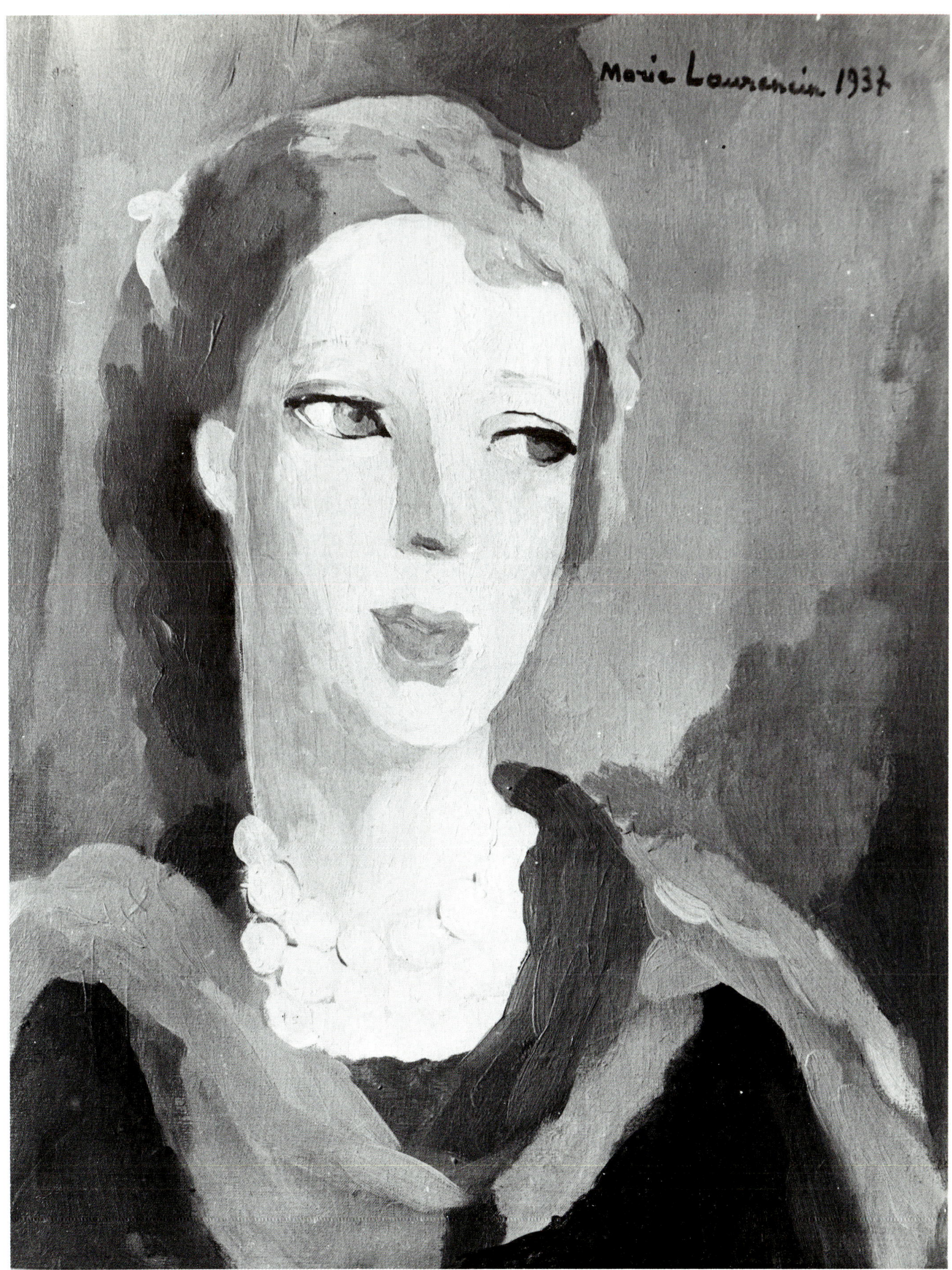

Portrait de Madge Garland/Portrait of Madge Garland, 1937
Oil on canvas (Private collection)

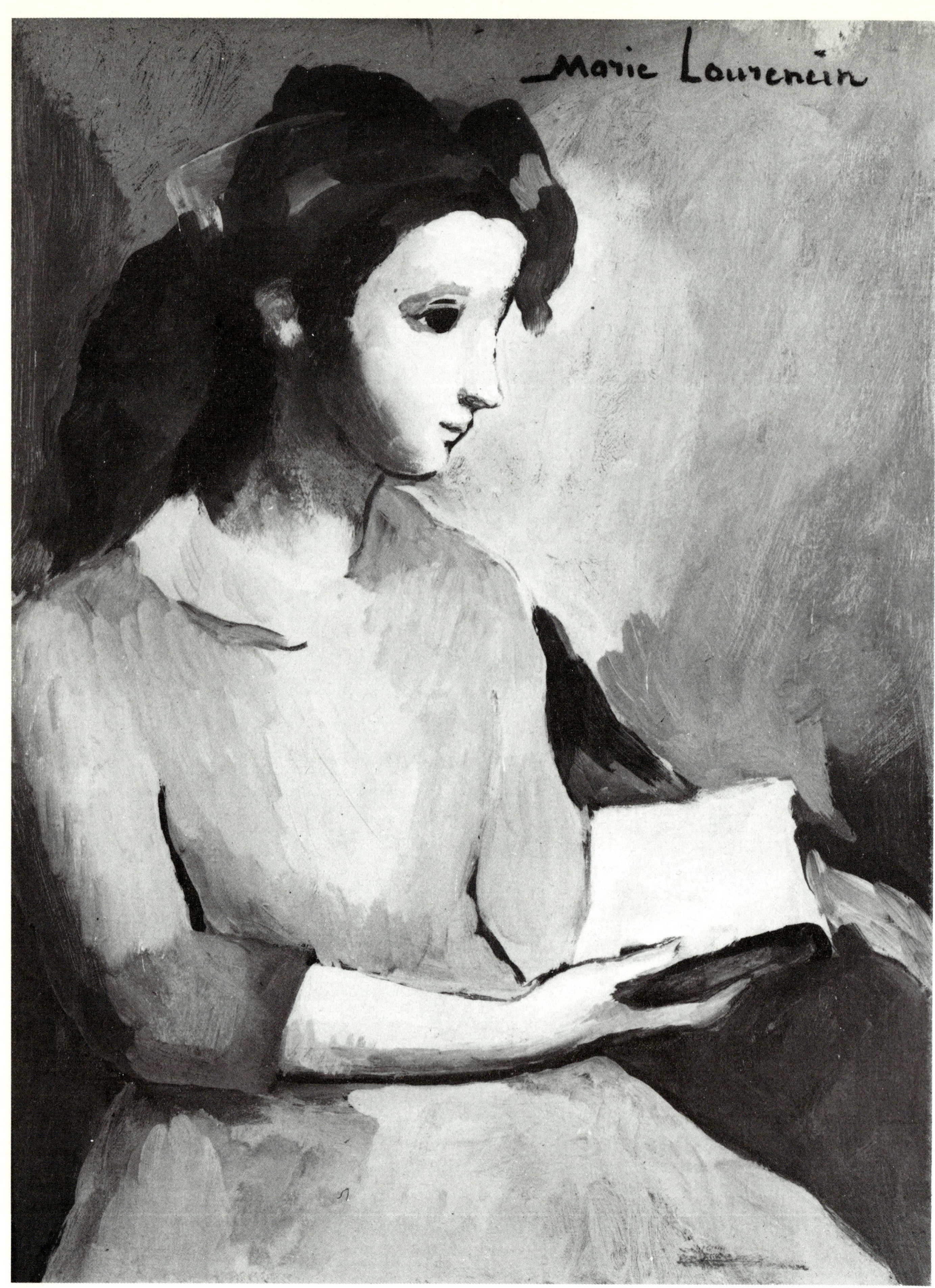

Jeune Femme lisant/Young Woman Reading, *c.* 1942
Oil on canvas, 34.5 × 27 cm.

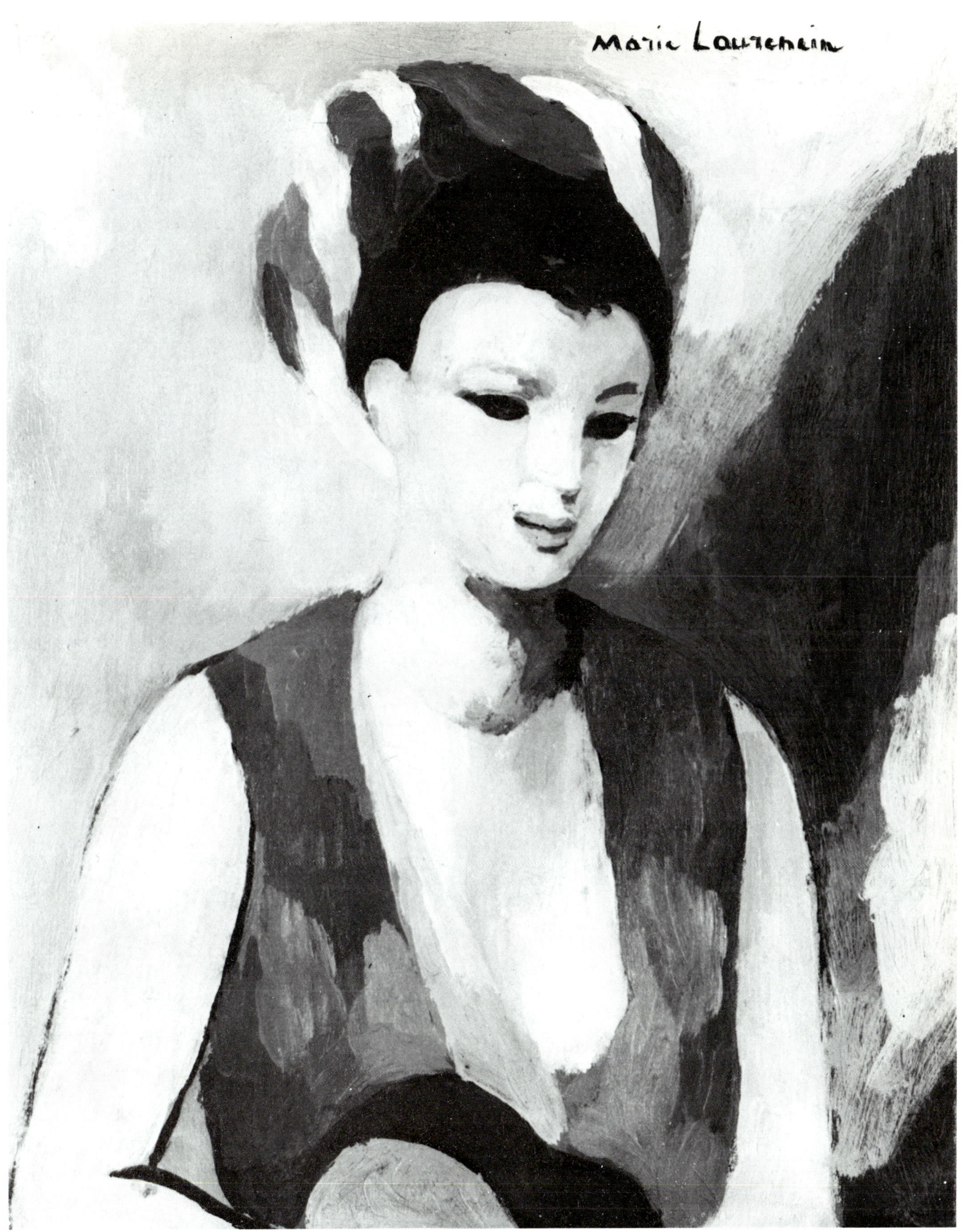

Jeune Femme au turban multicolore/Young Woman wearing a multicoloured Turban, *c.* 1941
Oil on canvas, 45 × 37.5 cm.

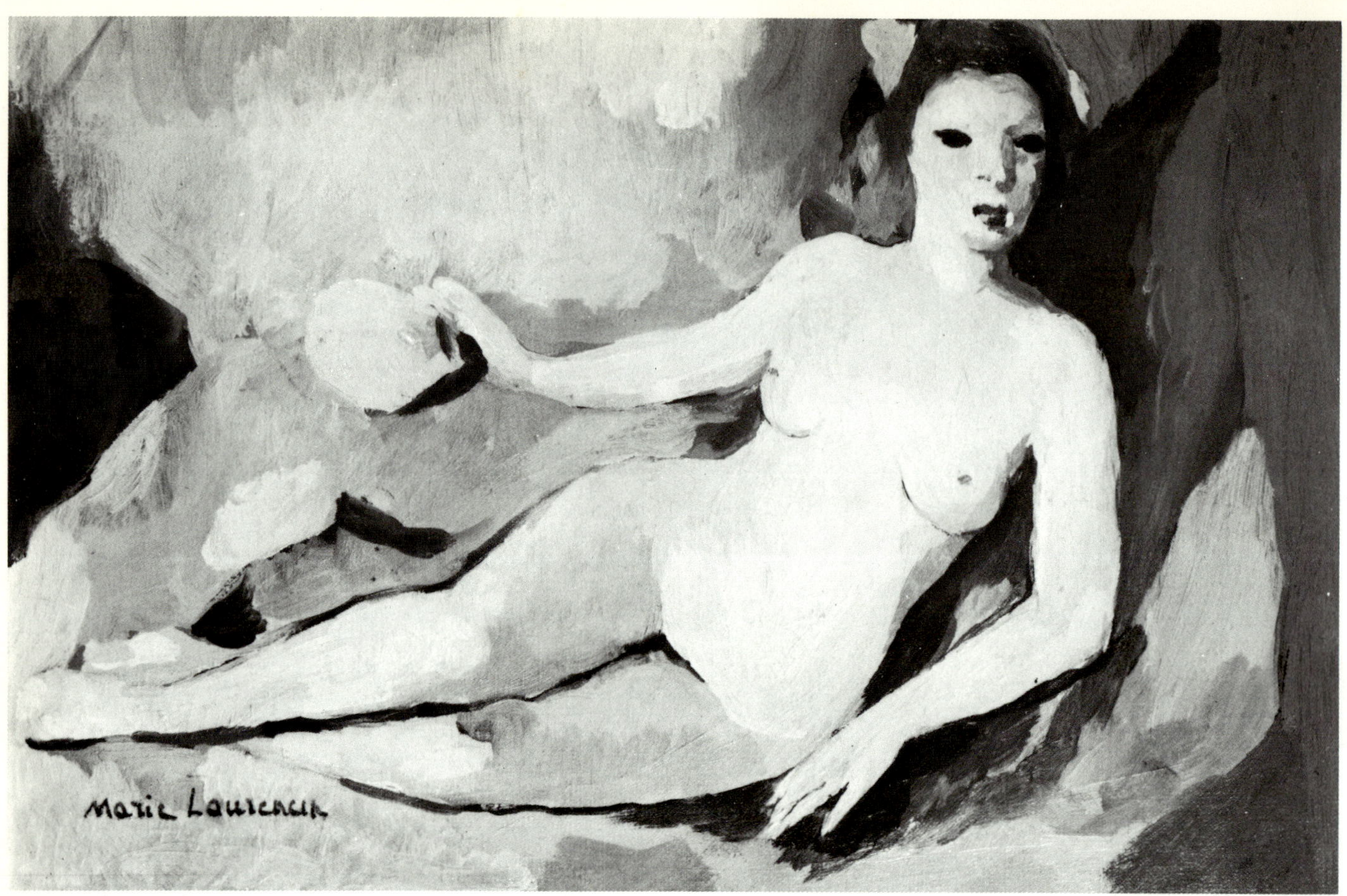

Nu allongé/Reclining Nude, 1941
Oil on canvas, 26.5 × 40.5 cm.

Opposite
Vase de tulipes/Vase of Tulips, *c.* 1932
Oil on canvas, 22 × 18 cm. (Galerie Schmit, Paris)

Page 86
Jeune Fille en bleu/Young Girl in blue, *c.* 1935
Oil on canvas (Galerie Motte, Geneva)

Page 87
Jeune Femme au collier/Young Woman with a Necklace, 1935
Oil on canvas (Private Collection)

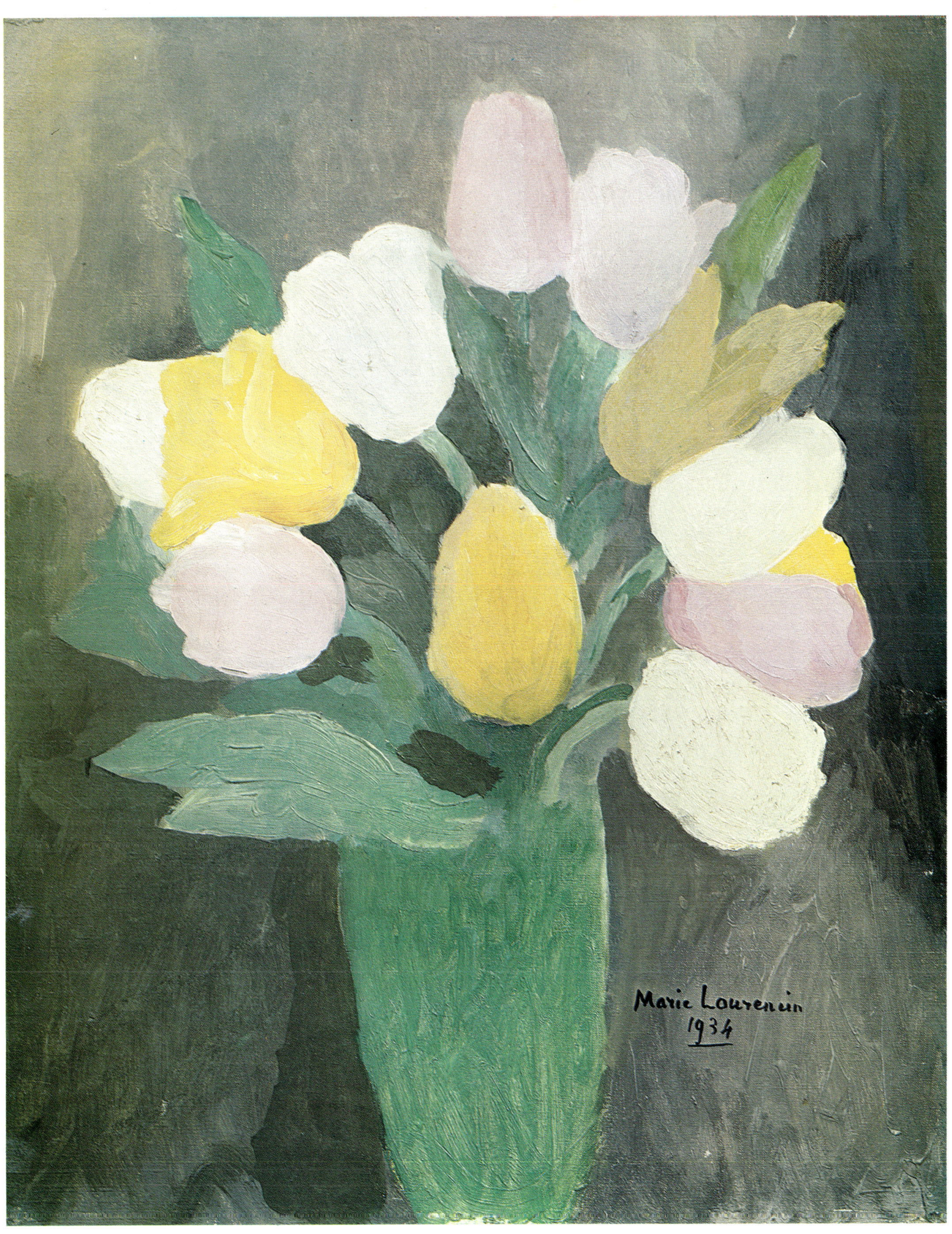
Marie Laurencin
1934

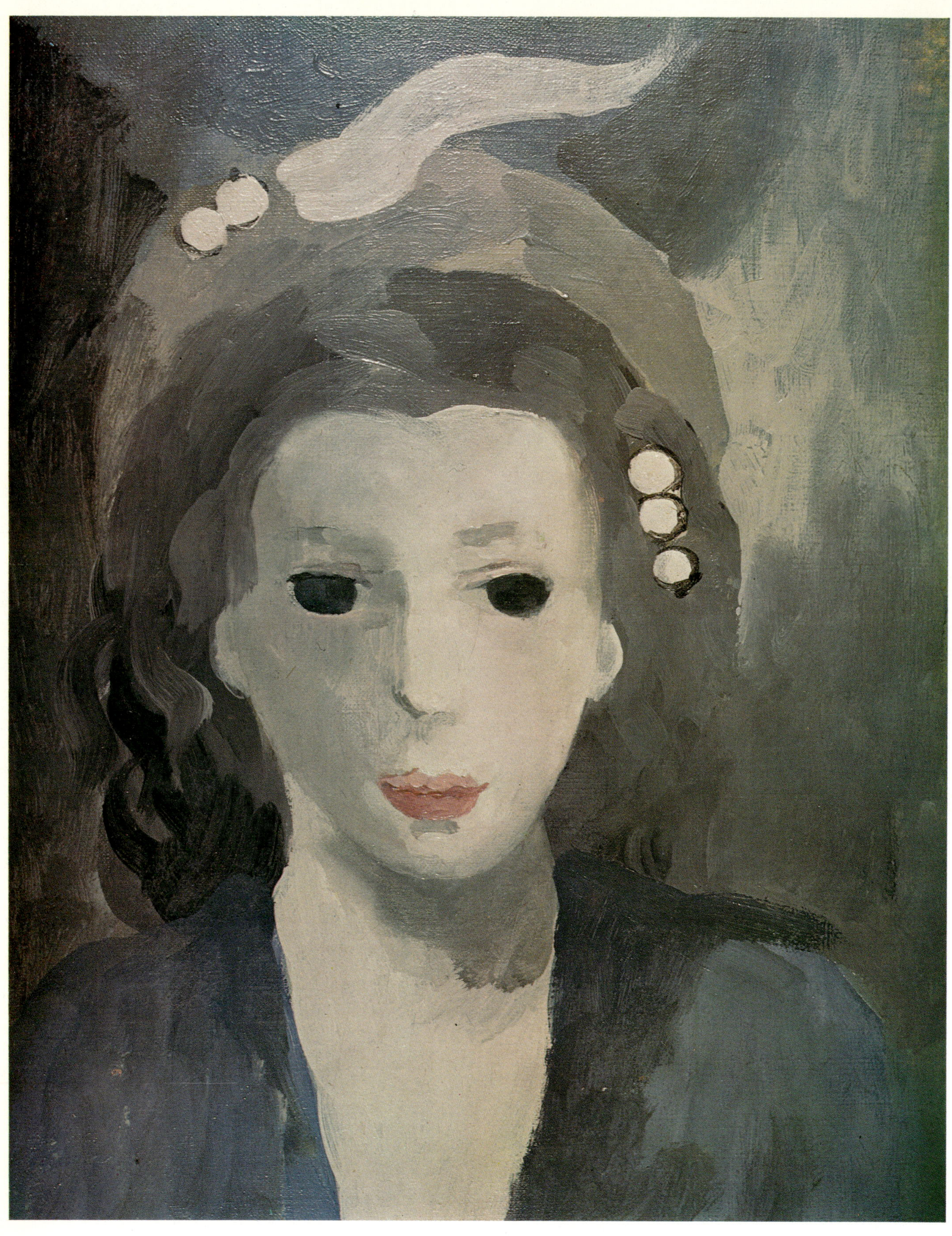

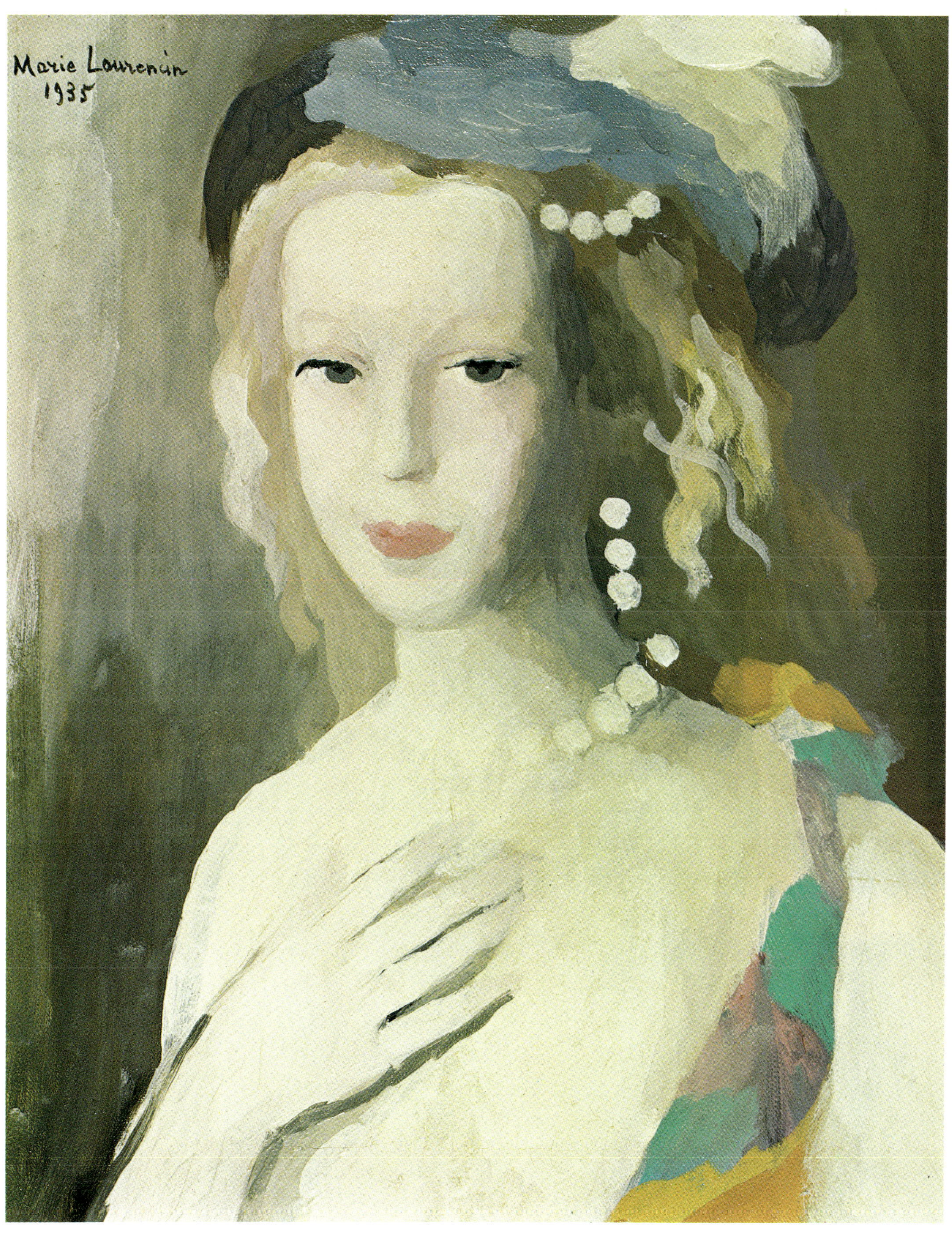
Marie Laurencin
1935

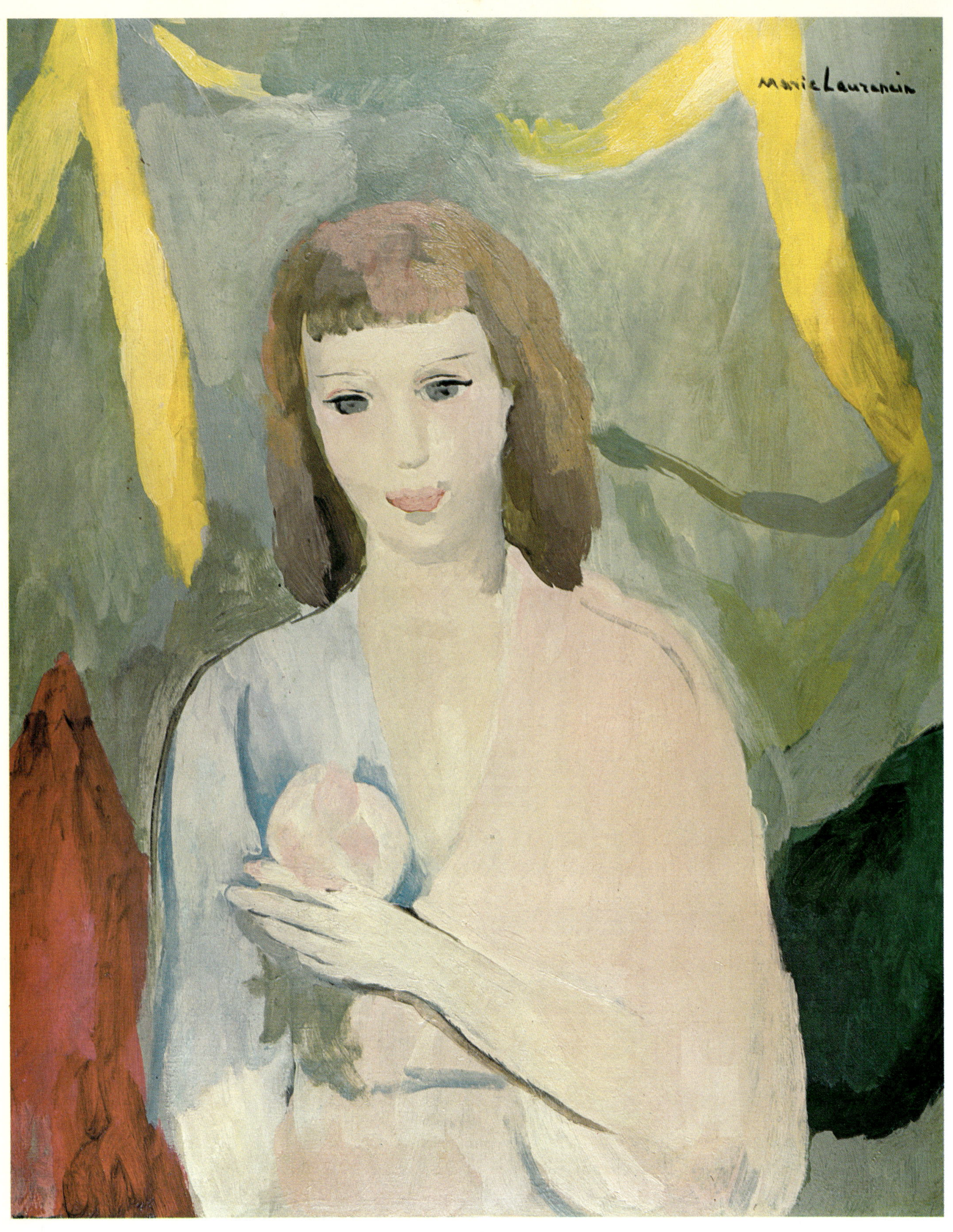
Marie Laurencin

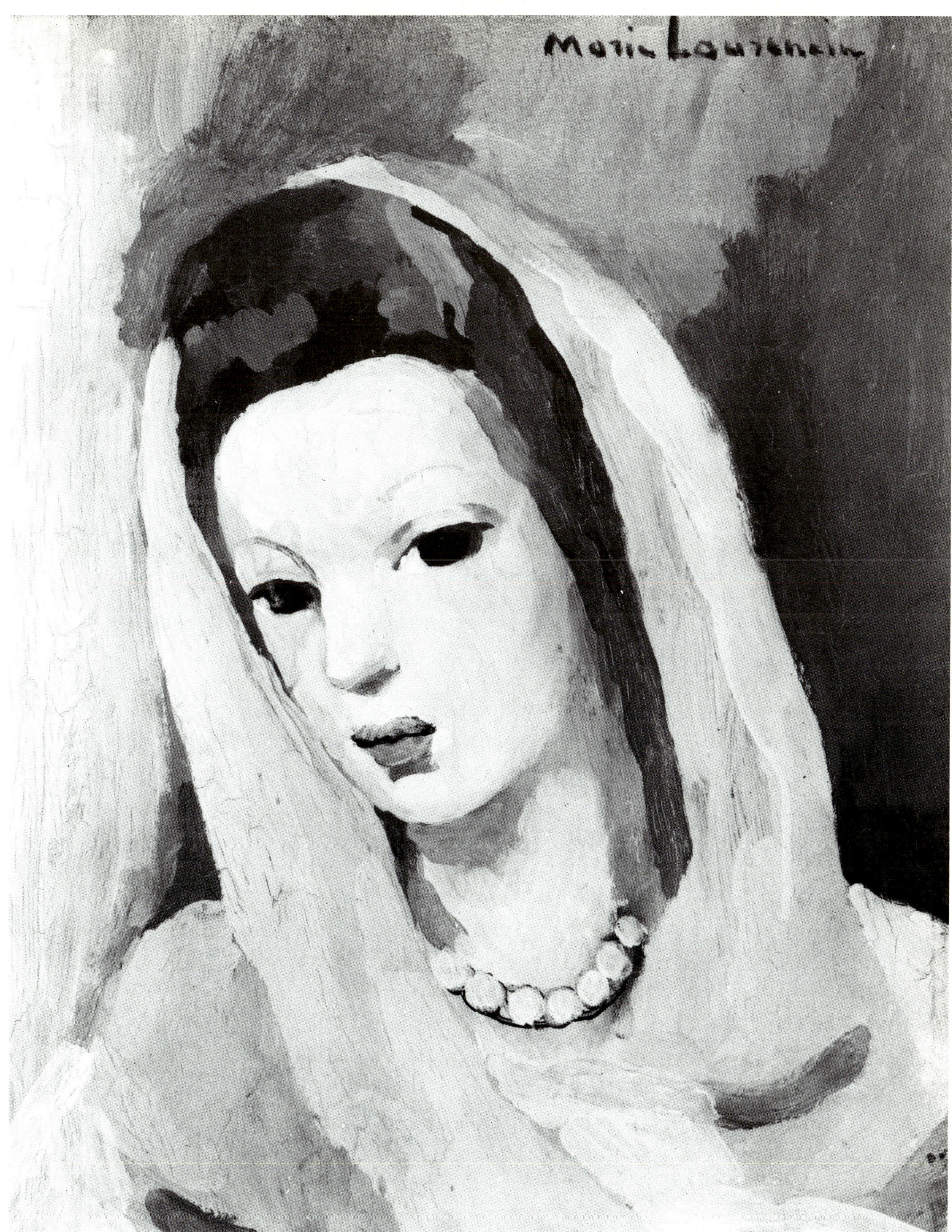

Opposite
Jeune Fille à la rose/Young Woman with a Rose, 1938
Oil on canvas, 92 × 73 cm. (Galerie Motte, Geneva)

Above
Jeune Fille au ruban jaune/Young Girl with a Yellow Ribbon, *c.* 1945
Oil on canvas, 40.5 × 32.5 cm.

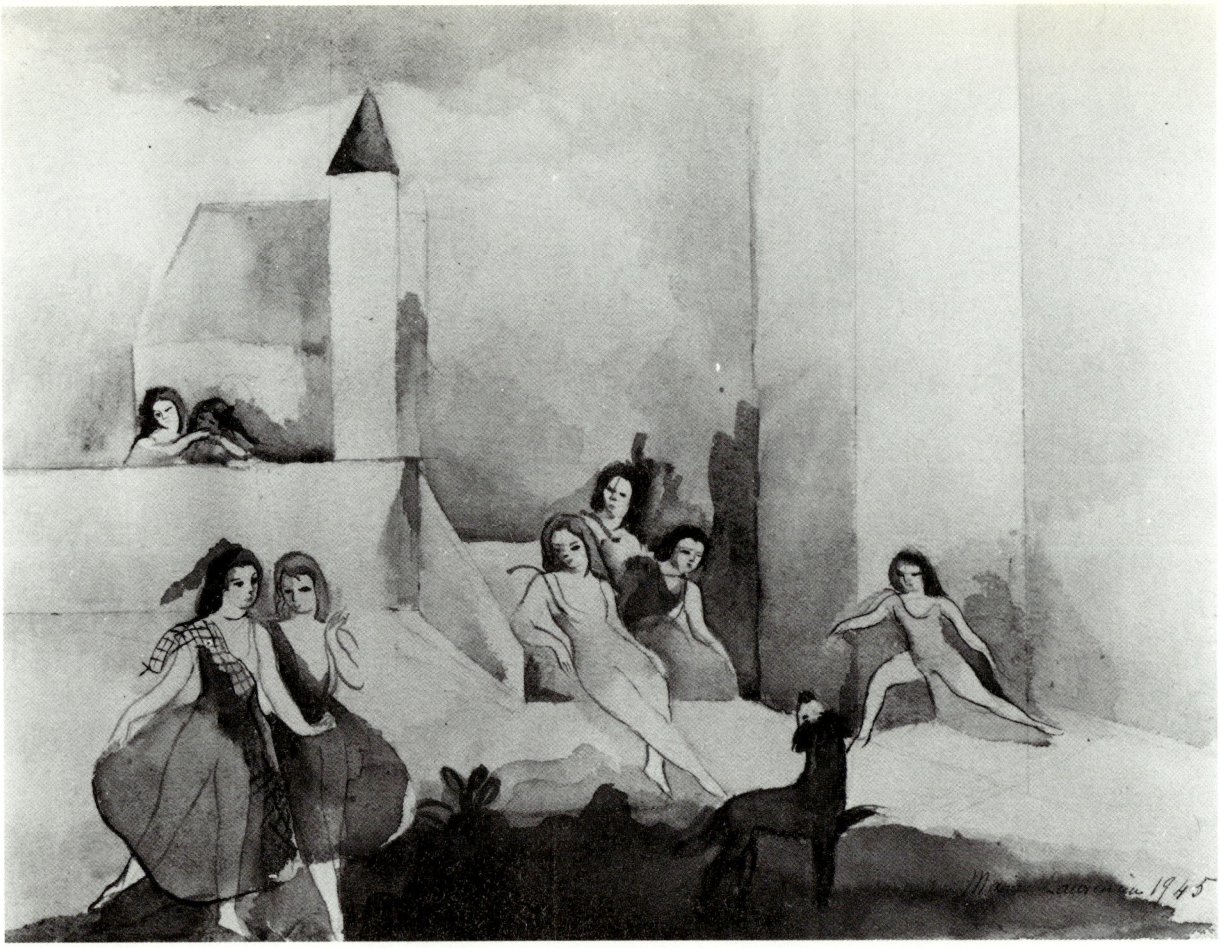

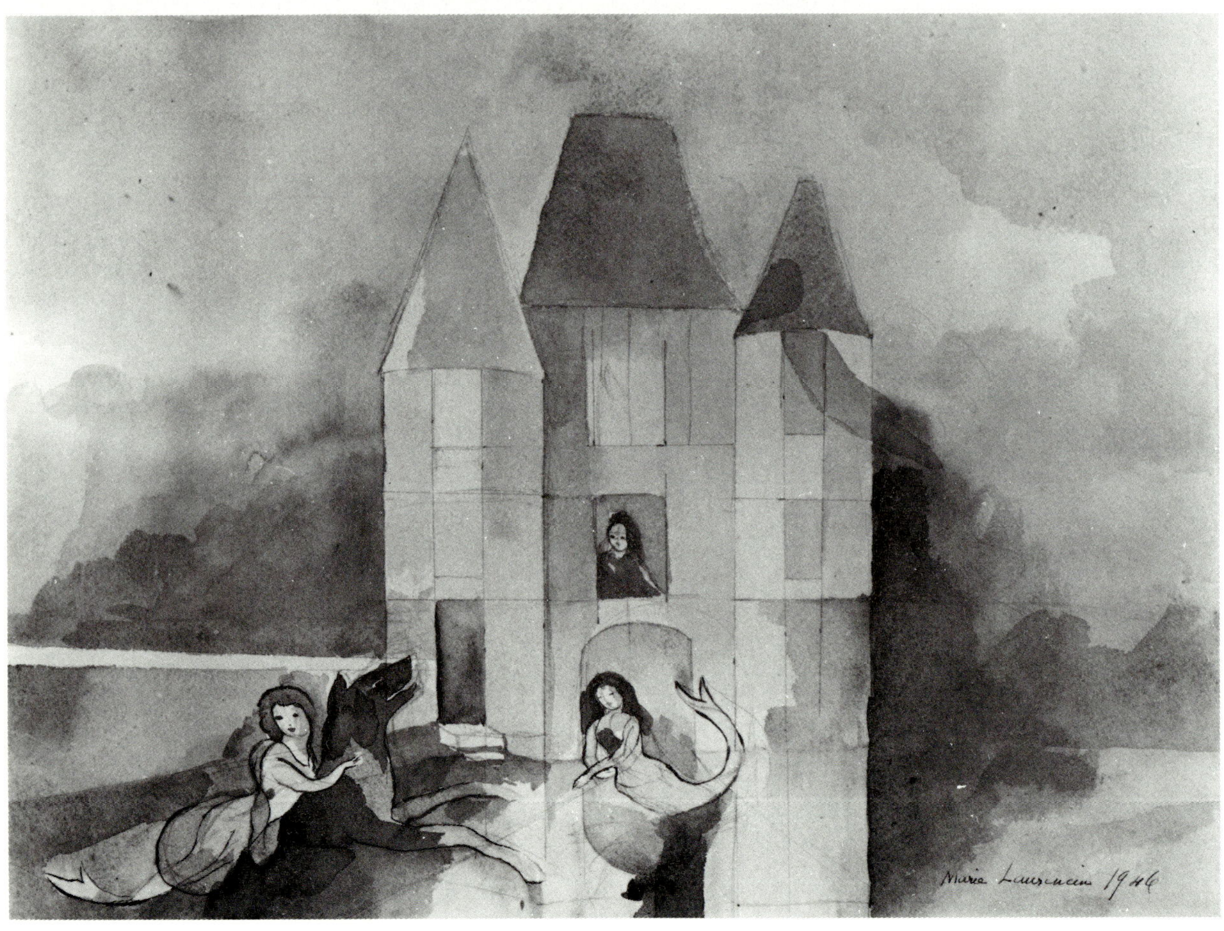
Marie Laurencin 1946

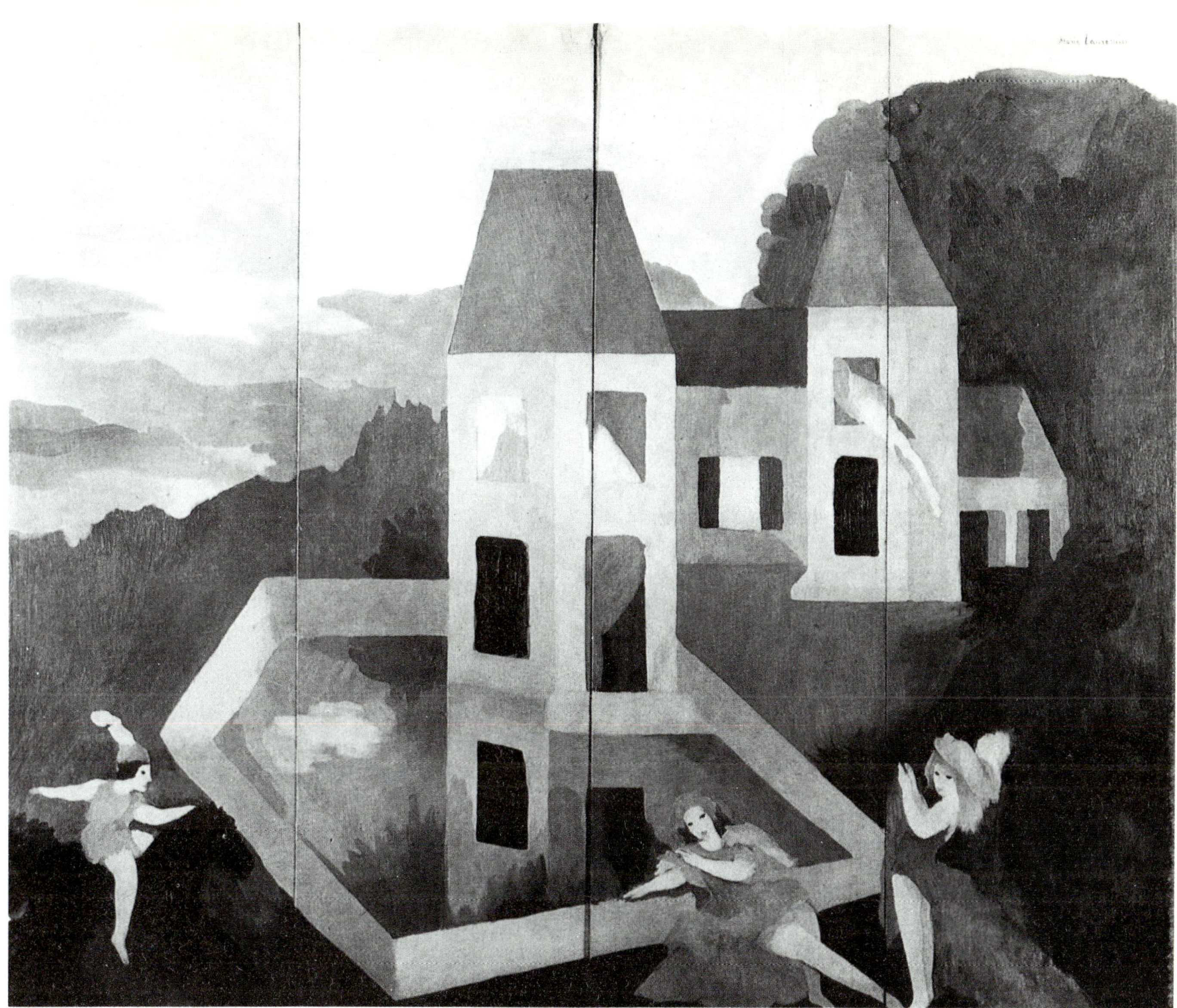

Le Château de la belle au bois dormant/The Castle of the Sleeping Beauty (for the ballet of the Marquis de Cuevas), 1947
Four-part screen, oil on canvas, 155.5 × 191 cm.

Opposite above
Nymphes et chien/Nymphs and a Dog, 1945
Watercolour, 26 × 37 cm.

Opposite below
Le Château/The Castle, 1946
Watercolour, 26 × 37 cm.

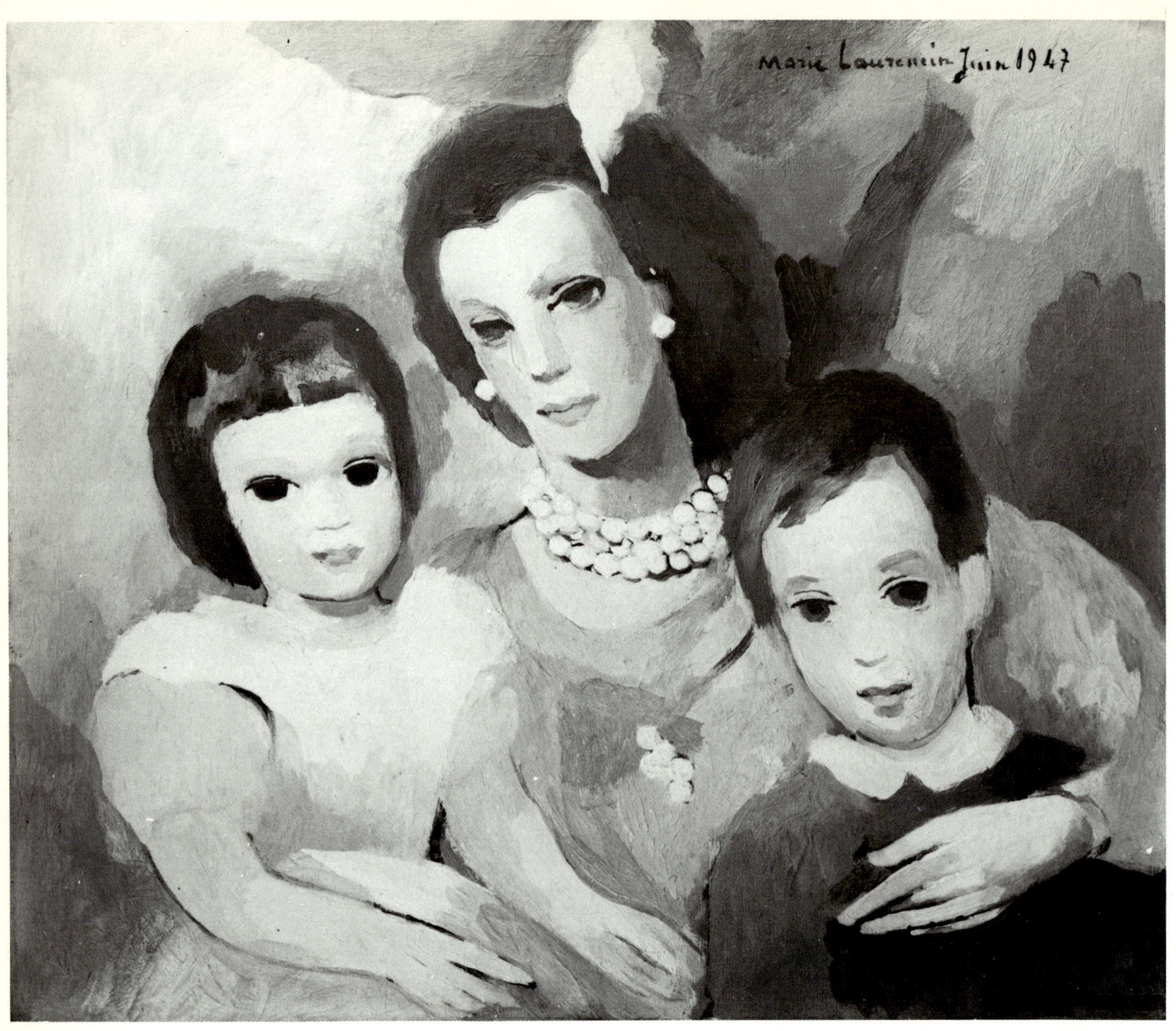

Comtesse Elisabeth Costa de Beauregard et ses enfants/Countess Elizabeth Costa de Beauregard and her Children, 1947
Oil on canvas, 46 × 56 cm.

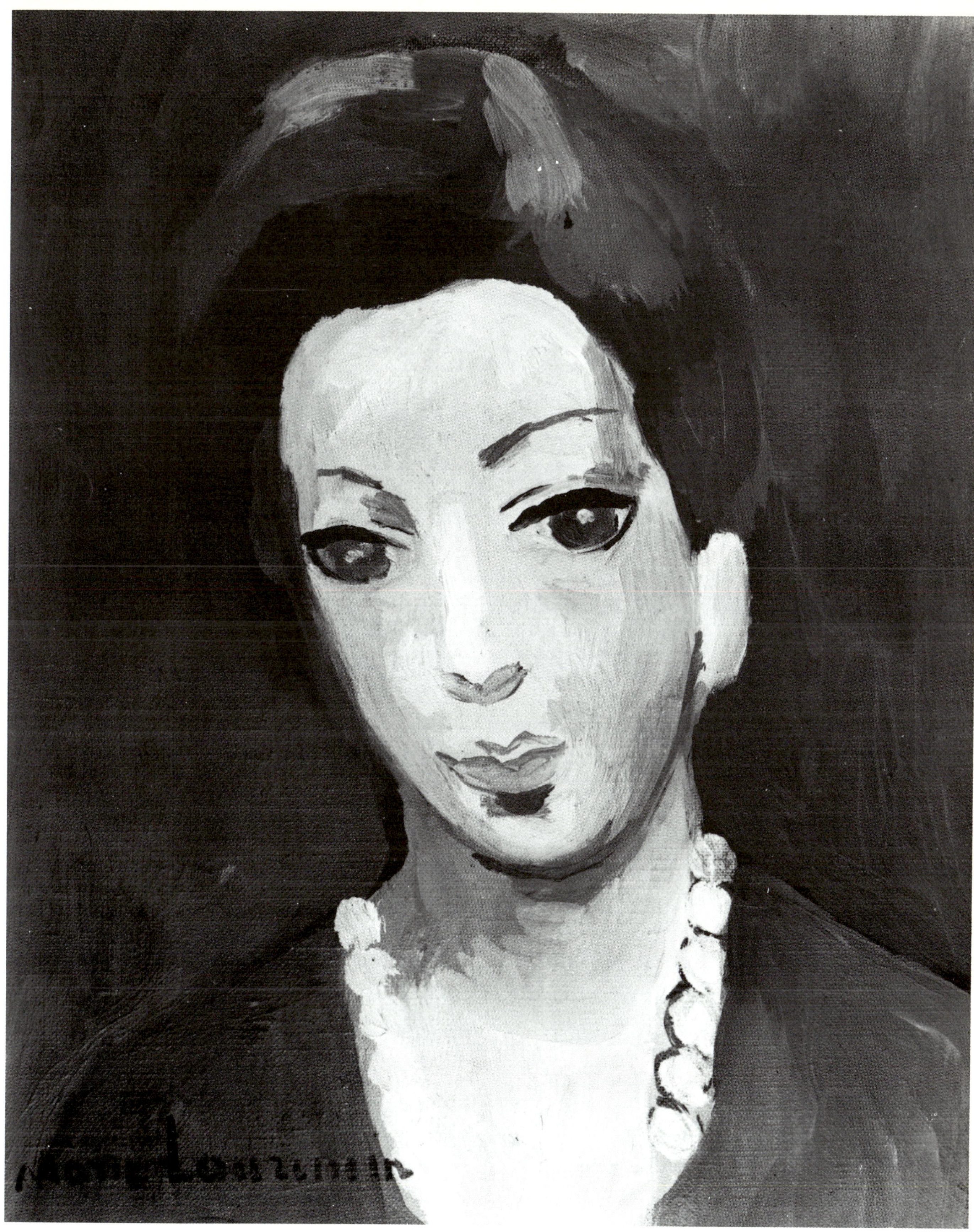

Jeune Fille/Young Girl, 1953
Oil on canvas, 25.5 × 20.5 cm.

INDEX